The Moon and the Virgin

HARPER & ROW, PUBLISHERS

NEW YORK

Cambridge
Hagerstown
Philadelphia
San Francisco

London
Mexico City
São Paulo
Sydney

1817

THE
MOON
AND THE
VIRGIN

REFLECTIONS ON THE ARCHETYPAL FEMININE

NOR HALL

Illustrations by Ellen Kennedy

COPYRIGHT ACKNOWLEDGMENTS

Grateful acknowledgment is made for permission to reprint: Excerpt from *Woman's Mysteries* by M. E. Harding. Copyright 1971 by C. J. Jung Foundation for Analytical Psychology. Excerpt from *Loba* by Diane di Prima. Published by Wingbow Press, 1978. Reprinted by permission of the author. Excerpts from "Waking," copyright 1948 by Theodore Roethke, which appeared in the book *The Collected Poems of Theodore Roethke*. Reprinted by permission of Doubleday & Company, Inc., and Faber and Faber Ltd.; lines from a poem by Guillaume Apollinaire, which appeared in *Technicians of the Sacred*, edited by Jerome Rothenberg. Copyright © 1968 by Jerome Rothenberg, and "Hymn to Phanes with Proem from the Orphic Argonautica" from *Origins: Creation Texts from the Ancient Mediterranean*, edited and translated by Charles Doria and Harris Lenowitz. Copyright © 1976 by Charles Doria and Harris Lenowitz; and "Belly Dancer" copyright © 1966 by Diane Wakoski from *Trilogy* by Diane Wakoski. Reprinted by permission of Doubleday & Company, Inc. Excerpts from *Teutonic Mythology* by Jacob Grimm, translated by James Steven Stallybrass; and "Mother Hulda" from *Household Stories* by the Grimm Brothers, translated by Lucy Crane. Reprinted by permission of Dover Publications, Inc. An excerpt from *My Mother's House* and *Sido* by Colette, translated by Una Vicenzo Troubridge and Enid McLeod. Copyright 1953 by Farrar, Straus and Young (now Farrar, Straus and Giroux, Inc.); and "Words Spoken by a Mother . . . " from *In the Trail of the Wind*, edited by

Copyright acknowledgments are continued on page 283.

Designer: Trish Parcell

Library of Congress Cataloging in Publication Data

Hall, Nor.
  The Moon and the Virgin.

  Bibliography: p.
  Includes index.
  1. Women—Psychology. I. Title.
HQ1206.H235   305.4'2   78-2138
ISBN 0-06-011703-6   85 86 87 88 89 10 9 8 7 6 5 4 3 2 1
ISBN 0-06-090793-2 pbk.   88 89 10 9 8

*Dedicated
to Deirdre,
our daughter*

Contents

List of Illustrations

Drawings by Ellen Kennedy based upon photographs or line drawings from the books noted. Full information on the books can be found in the Bibliography.

Preface

Even sleepers are workers and collaborators in what goes on in the universe.

—HERACLITUS

"This is . . . an oracle shared by Night and the Moon; it has no outlet anywhere on earth nor any single seat, but roves everywhere throughout mankind in dreams and visions."
. . . The voice was the Sibyl's, the guide said, who sang of the future as she was carried about on the face of the moon.

—PLUTARCH

The voices speaking in this book are those of dreamers, poets, soul makers, mythologists, storytellers, and others whose faith in what they know informs their work in psychology, history, religion, and the arts in such a way that they are sometimes called "insiders" or "believers." These are not the "grubby schoolboys" seeking shelter in the "hutch of reason—that dreary shed," as the poet Theodore Roethke put it, but rather those who are willing to follow an interior maze to its core to shed some light on the unknown thing that dwells there in the close darkness. Imagination is as important a tool in this work as reason.

Originally written as a series of lectures to be spoken, the chapters are more often linked by the rhythm of words and affinities of image than by the intentional development of a thesis. My hope is that the thesis, concerning the reformation of feminine values, will emerge for the reader the way insight evolves in the actual process of therapy. The book itself is in many ways an anamnesis, an act of recollection that provides the background material necessary before proceeding with an analysis (see Chapter 3). The first chapter, "The Moon and the Virgin," stands alone. Although it is intended as a tribute to the feminine, some readers who are engaged by the contemporary struggles of women will find the language problematic because of my reluctance to abandon the concepts of "feminine" and "masculine" as distinct qualities of being that draw on, yet are not bound by, the entities of woman and man. Those ideas that appear outdated are also the ones that predate us, or come first in the history of the human universe: it seems essential that we learn at least to recognize and possibly reinvest our inheritance before giving it up.

The remaining chapters, beginning with "Psyche's Search," were inspired by an article on feminine psychology written in 1934 by the Jungian analyst Toni Wolff, who described the feminine psyche as embracing four complex types[1]: Mother, Amazon, Hetaira (or companion), and Medium (or mediator). Together these types form a force field, a feminine dynamic that shapes the experience of individuals and thereby the direction of history. Dr. Wolff arrived at her conclusions regarding the nature of the feminine in her consulting room, a place that I have come to know in my own therapy practice as a *laboratory* of the soul. Such laboratories are found wherever slips of the mother tongue *(labi)*, lapses of memory and morality *(lapsuri)*, engagement in "back-bending" or reflective work *(laborare)*, and the "achievement with difficulty" *(elaboratus)*[2] converge to contribute information about what goes on in the recesses of a person. Dreams emerge from those elaborate, unconscious recesses the way fairy tales emerge from country villages and myths emerge from whole cultures.

In the course of eliciting images from these sources I have found that they do not stick to Wolff's structure, but rather that each of the four "poles" constellates a core of related images, symbols, and goddesses that seemingly belong to each type, but are nonetheless autonomous. My attempt to follow the lead of these unrestrained figures of imagination and speech accounts for the pattern of the book. There are three chapters on the Mother, one on the Amazon (Artemis), one on the Hetaira (Aphrodite), and three on the Medial feminine as sibyl, wise woman, and poet. Throughout the text I refer to myths and to fairy tales as *essential psychic facts* rather than as false stories or stories for children. (Where I have not cited a specific reference for a myth told, the reader wanting more background might refer to Carl Kerényi's *Gods of the Greeks* or to Robert Graves's *The Greek Myths*. Fairy tales in most cases are taken from the Grimm collection.) Just as dreams will often repeat themselves until their meaning is grasped, sometimes using new faces or names or times of day— but always in the attempt to circumscribe the same essential psychic fact—myths use a profusion of names and images to describe the essence of one god, goddess, or event in the history of human consciousness. Variations in surname and attributes of the deities, and of their descendants—the princesses and shepherds and seam-stresses of folk literature—occur because no single tale can tell the whole story of these creatures who represent our own psychic complexity. The individual human psyche, or soul, clothes itself in countless layers of peculiar design.

For this way of regarding the individual soul as a collective inheritance I am indebted to the work of Carl Jung and Sigmund Freud, whose differences were once described this way:

They served different gods, Freud's was sexual, Jung's mercurial —more nearly bisexual. They were imprinted by different ar-chetypes, Freud by the Father, Jung by the Son of the Mother. Freud's way was patriarchal (based on reason, logic, and the attempt to master the unconscious), whereas Jung's way was ma-triarchal (open to the irrational and imaginal, he believed in letting the unconscious live and even submitting to it). Jung's therapeutic aim was transformation and Freud's restoration—to restore the analysand to consensus reality.[3]

Although I have come to feel more aligned with Jung, my attempt to locate the feminine begins and continues where Freud left off: after tracing the evolution of paternal deities in his exposition of the Oedipus complex in *Totem and Taboo,* he says he is "at a loss to indicate the place of the great maternal deities, who perhaps everywhere precede the paternal deities."[4]

Quests for origins, of which this book is one, must begin with the Mother, with the pre-conscious matriarchal phase of human existence that resists being studied scientifically. Historically, our evidence for this layer of human community is recorded in the images of art and mythology. Individually, our experience of living within the mother realm is held in the memory—in childhood places, daydreams, sights, and fears that recall our unique past and contribute to the myth (or story) of personal origin. Jane Ellen Harrison once observed that the greatest barrier "to that *realizing* of mythology which is the first condition of its being understood is our modern habit of clear analytic thought."[5]

One of the earliest students of matriarchy, J. J. Bachofen, lawyer, historian, and social philosopher, understood the necessity of developing a method of mythoanalytic investigation in order to reach back behind the paternal façade of Roman law. He said there were two roads to knowledge, *Phantasie* and *Verstand:*

. . . the longer, slower, more arduous road of rational combination and the shorter path of the imagination, traversed with the force and swiftness of electricity. Aroused by direct contact with the ancient remains, the imagination *(Phantasie)* grasps the truth at one stroke, without intermediary links. The knowledge acquired this second way is infinitely more living and colorful than the products of the understanding *(Verstand).*[6]

Bachofen was a master of the arduous route, but felt compelled (by the nature of the material he "excavated") to choose the shorter, swifter route. Long before Crete or Troy had been unearthed by the archaeologists' picks and spades he stumbled upon "a realm of inquiry resembling a vast heap of ruins." Digging through the remains of art, classical literature, and the history of jurisprudence, he began to discern patterns emerging, symbols and myths—articulations of the souls of ancestors since forgotten. Half a century after his death he was "rediscovered" by a small circle of European artists—among them the poet Rainer Maria Rilke. They came upon Bachofen at the same time they came upon the first major publications of Freud and Jung.

Poets and dreamers weave the following chapters together precisely because of their capacity for discovery that orients us toward the archetypal material, that tends, like a mythical virgin spring, to recede as we advance. Among the more recent cultivators of *Phantasie,* teachers to whom I owe a similar debt, three stand out: Norman O. Brown, Robert Duncan, and Denise Levertov. They have given me maps for approaching realms of inquiry adjacent to their own. I work as a therapist, not a writer, but I have learned from them that being a scribe to Psyche is an essential requirement for the vocation of therapy. Like the original attendants in ancient temples of healing, who were available to the sick at the moment of awakening out of dream sleep in order to record the words of their vision, what I give to the reader is basically a transcription of what has been given to me.

I am as grateful to friends as I am to my teachers—especially to those who have shared their dreams with me; to Marly Rusoff for encouraging the expansion of the original lecture series into book form, to Jim Moore, and to Fran McCullough, my editor. Ellen Kennedy drew nuances out of stone for me; Sandra Holtkamp was an invaluable extension of my own hands. I am grateful to Miriam Meyers, Laina Giffen, Nancy Rice, and my sister Welling Hall for their readings of the manuscript.

While engaged in these reflections, I have, like the children of Night in classical myth, had my feet twisted or "turned both ways": I have gone searching for archaic roots in order to "sing about the future." That those who exist somehow outside of time and society (or on the borders of consciousness) make it possible for those of us who dwell in this present to see is a truth that I have come to understand while living with Ken Criqui. Final thanksgiving goes to him for authoring more than he knew.

Nor Hall

The Moon and the Virgin

1
The Moon and the Virgin: Signs of the Times

Bent on being an archaeologist at fifteen, I read Mary Renault's book *A Bull from the Sea*. Her weighty images of bull dancers, underground corridors at the palace of Knossos, the Minotaur and snake goddess filled my adolescent imagination and sank in deep. They remained hidden for years while I became engaged, on a conscious level, in the problems of the church and the contemporary struggle for the ordination of women. One night, ten years later, the archaic images re-emerged in a dream in which, instead of *A Bull from the Sea*, the story was called *The Moon Speaks to Me*. The moon said then:

> *Rise up, blue princess, from your plastic church steeple bed,*
> *Find a better place to lay your head:*
> *Instead of looking to the Father, Son, and Holy Ghost*
> *Look to Artemis, Aphrodite, and Gaia as guides.*

We know that when people turn blue they lack oxygen, and need breath or, literally, in-spiration. The church had become uninspiring. The breath of the father gods was cold, unfeeling, and lifeless. At the time, I understood the dream as an indicator, pointing my work toward a new source of inspiration. After a long sojourn in the realm of theological studies, the way led back, via the route of earlier fantasies, to the labyrinthine realm of the goddess, where the reigning trinity was feminine. The urge to be an archaeologist took over again—but this time I meant to study archaeology as "the excavation of the mind." Just as the archaeologist digs up artifacts, potsherds, bones, and housing foundations, the archaeologist of the mind digs up myths and stories, the foundation of human meaning.

A special tool of this science is etymology, the study of word origins, which James Joyce called "etym-smashing." One poet who wielded this tool with remarkable force called himself an "archaeologist of morning," a "digger of dreams and first things of the day." He put his concern for words into a poem called "These Days":

> *whatever you have to say, leave*
> *the roots on, let them*
> *dangle*
>
> *And the dirt*
>
>> *just to make clear*
>> *where they came from*
>> —CHARLES OLSON

My interest here is in looking at the dirt on the roots of two vital words: moon and virgin. Before our man-in-the-moon there was a virgin-in-the-moon. This sex shift from feminine to masculine is not easy to understand and any attempt to do so is complicated by the fact that there are always exceptions.[1]

In many extant "primitive" cultures, among the Eskimo for example, the sun is the sister and the moon is the brother. He is pale in comparison. And J. J. Bachofen cites a classical opinion that the moon was androgynous, "Luna and Lunus in one, feminine in relation to the sun, but masculine in relation to the earth; but its masculine nature is secondary, it is first woman, afterward man."[2] Generally, the moon is feminine and its trek across the night sky has been likened to the travels and travails of the feminine psyche. Even those who have not read the ancient hymns explored in the following pages, or the folktales from various cultures about the woman-in-the-moon, may be familiar with the way in which the cycles of the moon reveal aspects of feminine experience. Knut Hamsun had a way of teaching children to recognize the phases of the moon in his novel, *Growth of the Soil.* He said that if you can reach up and grab into the "horn" of the moon with your left hand, it is waxing or increasing, and if you can reach up with the right hand to grab into the crescent, it is waning or dying. His lesson, which can be meaningfully juxtaposed with the complex symmetry of right and left brain functions, is considerably simplified in the straightforward hand patterns of the Andaman Islanders who remember the moon's phases this way:

FIGURE 1

The new crescent is cradled in the right hand (rising in daylight, seen setting in the evening), the full moon is central, and the dying crescent is cradled in the left hand (seen rising at night). Below that, the dark moon has fallen, the time of no moon consonant with the darkness in us all, and a time which many peoples have longed to forget. Imagine the new silvery moon crescent as the virgin or the nymph, the full moon as mother pregnant with life, and the old moon as old crone or withered woman descending into the darkness of death, only to rise again. These phases variously became associated with three weird sisters, three fates, or three goddesses who, when seen together, represented the life span of women from beginning to end. Because of the spiritual promise embodied in the moon's cycle, native women in Africa pray to her, asking, "May our lives be renewed as yours is."

Women recognized their physical nature in moon cycles as well. The moon has always been associated with (if not held responsible for) the menses: the blood flow and blood rest like the tide-pull-and-flow in every woman. A woman's periodicity is measured approximately in twenty-eight-day cycles, corresponding to the lunar cycle. (Men, who have cycles too, measured not by ovulation and blood flow but by weight loss and change in the albumen content of the urine, seem to have a shorter cycle of about twenty-two days.) Certain advantage has been taken of this moon-related knowledge. In the 1960s, a doctor in physics who had been reading ancient myths and literature on sexual cycles decided to experiment with light on women whose menstrual cycles were irregular. By stimulating moonlight with a light bulb over the bed of women during the fourteenth, fifteenth, and sixteenth days of their cycles, when ovulation—the sign of fertility—is expected to occur, he found that most of the women ovulated and began to have regular cycles for the first time.[3]

There are still literal and unexplainable relationships between the lunar body and our own. These body changes are important, they are organic, "that with which one works," and inseparable from the way we move through the world. We know what the ebb and flow of psychic energy (the energy of psyche or soul) feels like. A rhythm of constant change, the waxing and waning of creativity, of love of life, of the ability to be with people, of our alertness and sexuality and health—these periodic changes of mood and being characterize the feminine principle. It is moist, cool, receptive, and then passionate and inflaming like fire. It is alternately full and available—shedding a steady radiant light— and dark and distant, untouchable. Watching the moon in the course of its monthly growth and diminishing is a way of reminding ourselves that the periodic need to be in-full-view and the opposite periodic need to be alone or withdrawn are not only natural but essential to the feminine.

I am taking care to say "the feminine" here rather than "female" or "womanly" to stress its roving home. Femininity is a mode of being human that can be lived out (and betrayed or suppressed) by both men and women. The Taoists say it this way: "He who knows the masculine but keeps to the feminine will be in the whole world's channel." We might translate this to read:

To be in the whole world's channel or to feel the rhythm of the universe, one must know the sun consciousness—the phenomenal world revealed in the bright light of reason—and yet keep to the unconscious night realm of the moon in which the spirit world is revealed in shadowy, dreamlike visions.

There was a Navajo wise man in this century who had to go about on all fours because of a congenital lameness; his people called him He-Who-Walks-Close-to-His-Shadow. Such a man would only be looked up to in a culture that valued the dark side of nature (that side that the Tao calls feminine). Isak Dinesen tells a similar story in her book *Out of Africa* about the Kikuyu people, who so valued their shadows that they were afraid to wander about at noon when the sun is directly overhead for fear they might lose them. When she asked if they weren't afraid to go out at night when all was dark, they replied that at night "all shadows lie down in the great shadow of god" and are protected.

In father culture or in patriarchal religions there is no respected place for the shadow or for the feminine, which, like the moon, has a dark side. Our Western world is rather given over to the masculine. Instead of prizing the breasts of the mother as Taoists do, we have chosen, or our ancestors chose, to publicly prize the phallus of the father: the Roman fasces or bundle of rods into which an axe head was tied, a symbol of the magistrates' power (and the word root of *fascism*) still decorates dimes in circulation. To the Hebrews it was the rod and staff that gave man comfort. The phallus or masculine creative spirit as rod and staff is represented in the shepherd's crook, king's scepter, the magician's wand, priest's crozier, all tools of the masculine commanding spirit, which is innovative, ruling, ethical, idealistic, directed, conceptual, exact, executive, historical, rational, censoring, concerned with laws and order as opposed to nature, reasonable and reliable like the regular sunrise and sunset, instead of capricious and changeable like the moon. Moonlight hardly matters anymore in a world so brilliantly lit by artificial means. Some people do not even know it is there. As in Gertrude Stein's play *Listen to Me*, "no dog barks at the moon,"

> *No dog barks at the moon.*
> *The moon shines and no dog barks*
> *No not anywhere on this earth.*
> *Because everywhere anywhere there are lights many lights and*
> *so no dog knows that the moon is there*
> *And so no dog barks at the moon now no not*
> *anywhere.*
> *And the moon makes no one crazy no not now*
> *anywhere.*
> *Because there are so many lights anywhere.*
> *That the light the moon makes is no matter.*
>
> . . . .
>
> *The sun yes the sun yes does matter*
> *But the moon the moon does not matter.*[4]

In the decade of the sixties, the attention of scientists was turned to the moon, but in a masculine manner, symbolically apparent in the name of the lunar landing expedition and its accomplishing vessel. The *Eagle* ship, under the auspices of the Apollo (or Sun) mission, landed on the moon on the very eve of her movement out of Virgo—the celestial sign of the Virgin.

One American research scientist must have felt the fiery virgin beginning to erupt somewhat that night when he conceived of a study in the "psychodynamics" of modern science. Proceeding with the knowledge that the moon had for a long time represented more than an object of scientific inquiry, and with the hypothesis that science has a hidden side, that it is not pursued only by disinterested, dispassionate, unbiased spectators, he spent three and a half years interviewing the forty-four eminent scientists who had been selected to study the moon rocks. He found that the general character of this group and the specific traits of the individuals supported an earlier Harvard study of the psychology of scientists summarized simply here in eight propositions:

1. Men are more likely to be creative scientists than women.
2. Experimental physical scientists often come from a back ground of radical Protestantism but are not themselves religious.
3. Scientists tend to avoid interpersonal contact.
4. Creative scientists are unusually hard working to the point of appearing almost obsessed with their work.
5. Scientists react emotionally to human emotions and try to avoid them.
6. Physical scientists like music and dislike poetry and art. (A student whose father was working on the moon material told me that he played Wagner loudly on the stereo until the research was done. Afterward he turned to reading James Joyce.)
7. Physical scientists are intensely masculine.
8. Physical scientists develop a strong interest in analysis of the structure of things at an early age.

His group of scientists responded neutrally to most questions designed to elicit a feeling response with the exception of the question about the moon's sex. To this question they responded with intense feeling, asserting that the sex was irrelevant, that the moon was neither masculine nor feminine. Summarizing this portion of his study, the researcher concludes that "it was man, not mankind, who in body and spirit took us to the moon, who landed on the moon, who took back some of that precious moon, and finally analyzed that moonstuff. Nowhere in all of this was the feminine principle present."[5]

The liaison between scientific attitudes and feminine modes of knowing is rarely expressed in the twentieth century. (Ecology and perhaps quantum physics might begin to close that gap.) Seventeenth-century scientists and sixteenth-century alchemists and fifteenth-century doctors of medicine such as the Swiss physician Paracelsus, who was a near contemporary of Luther, Leonardo da Vinci, Michelangelo, Copernicus, and Holbein, declared their debt to the goddess of wisdom, whom they called Sophia, daughter of light. These early surveyors of matter shared a fundamental connection to the feminine principle as it was expressed in the idea of the *lumen naturale,* the light of nature. This light, like the moon's light, was called the "lesser light" in relation to the incomparable brilliance of the sun, which was likened to God. Yet the "lesser light" of nature was essential for understanding how the material world cohered. The less revealing light showed the connections between things, it revealed the "inwardness" of God's creation. In the Kabbalistic tradition this feminine principle was called the Shekinah. She was the inwardness of God embodied in the interior rhythm of the community of the faithful. Her name means "indwelling." Like Sophia, she would have science take into account the invisible energies exchanged between subject and object, the relationship between living things.

Knowledge was thus conceived as "dwelling on matter." When Paracelsus announced his lectures in 1526, he wrote:

My proofs derive from experience and . . . not from reference to authorities. . . . It is not title and eloquence, knowledge of languages, nor the reading of many books . . . that are the requirements of a physician . . . but the deepest knowledge of things themselves and of nature's secrets and this knowledge outweighs all else.[6]

Paracelsus handled the natural world with reverence. He thought of his students as young trees and abhorred the academic practice of pruning all spontaneous growth. As a scientist, his aim was to make room for new shoots of experience. By asking nature to accommodate their inquiry, he and his students were responsible for generating the attitude of cooperation and awe before the material world that characterized the natural sciences in their inception.

Awareness of the interdependence of all things exemplified in the method of Paracelsus can perhaps be seen again in the work of contemporary physicists, who realize that the nature of the tool used to measure matter changes the nature of that which is perceived. A Minoan statue of the mother goddess from Crete embodies this message in archaic form. She stands as the original symbol of the integration of opposing hemispheres. Bearing a snake in one hand and a tool (her double-edged axe) in the other, the goddess connects the chthonian realm of matter (the Mother) and the upper world of the sky god, who calculates, measures, perceives. A. B. Cook, who has done an exhaustive study of the double-edged axe, shows that it was once considered the lightning flash of Zeus's eyes, a thunderbolt fallen to the ground.[7]

The axe came to mean many things. It is called the *labrys* and is related to *labyrinth,* the underground dwelling of the goddess. In order to pass through the labyrinth it was necessary to find the way to the center and then to make a full 360-degree turn, to turn completely around on oneself to go out the way one came in. In the ancient world this action was meaningful on what we would call a psychological level, as evident in the conjecture that it was the temple sweeper *Labys* who is credited with the maxim "Know

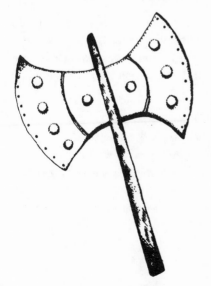

FIGURE 2

thyself."[8] Temple attendant, labyrinth, and the double-edged axe
are entwined. In another place, the axe was said to "betoken the
presence of a soul" because it was shaped like a moth or butterfly,
the Greek image of psyche or soul. Sometimes the axes are drawn
with double wavy lines as if moving in air. Because the axe is
double-edged it is thought of as bisexual, or as unifying opposites
within itself. It is also called two-faced like the moon. The blades,
which resemble horns (and which were ritually placed between
the horns of a bull sacred to the Minoan goddess), are the crescents of the new and dying moon.

The word *moon* has many meanings, multiple roots: *mensis,*
month; *menses,* blood flow; *menos,* heart, spirit; *mania,* madness,
possession (luna-cy); *manteia,* to prophesy; *menoinan,* to meditate
or wish; *menuō,* to reveal; *memini,* to remember; *mentiri,* to lie;
metis, wisdom; *metiesthai,* to have in mind or dream; *mati-h,* to
measure.[9] There are two faces here, two manifest emotional
movements: one is active, fiery eruption given to prophecy, rage,
possession, and lying (making up a story); and the other, more
measured meter given to meditation, dreams, waiting, wishing,
lingering. This moon attitude is related to memory and learning
(the outcome being moderation, wisdom, meaning).

> *Its root of white crystal stretches toward the deep.*

This is the first line of a five-thousand-year-old hymn to the
goddess at Eridu (a town in southern Sumeria), probably one of
the oldest known poems about the original tree of knowledge, the
tree that bears the moon and the Moon Mother within its
branches.

> *Its root of white crystal stretches toward the deep.*
> *Its seat is the central place of the earth;*
> *Its foliage is the couch of Zikum, the primeval mother.*
> *Into the heart of this holy house spreading its shade like a forest*
> *No man has entered;*
> *It is the house of the Mighty Mother, who passes across the sky.*[10]

This being, under whose aegis the passions erupt and dreams turn in on themselves, is the mighty Moon Mother, virgin mother Zikum, once known as Ishtar, the Babylonian goddess Mother of All called the Many-Breasted/Silver-Shining/Seed-Producing/ Green One (overseer of vegetation), Womb Opener (life-giving wild cow), White Sow Queen of the Underworld, and Queen of Heaven, like our recent (virgin) Mother Mary full of grace, who is called in Italy Mother Mary Moon of the Church.

How is it then that these moon mothers can be called virgins? The word *virgin* means "belonging-to-no-man."[11] Recall the line from the Hymn of Eridu: "Into the heart of this holy house . . . no man has entered." *Virgin* means one-in-herself; not maiden inviolate, but maiden alone, in-herself. To be virginal does not mean to be chaste, but rather to be true to nature and instinct. In Ishtar's realm, wild animals roam free. (*Virgo intacta* is not a state particularly pleasing to the great virgin goddesses.) The virgin forest is not barren or unfertilized but rather a place that is especially fruitful and has multiplied because it has taken life into itself and transformed it, giving birth naturally and taking dead things back to be recycled. It is virgin because it is unexploited, not in man's control.

The virgin acts according to her own nature; she may give herself to many lovers but, like the moon, she can never be possessed. She is not the counterpart to a male deity (unless it be her divine son), but is rather a goddess in her own right. She is the goddess of childbirth and the womb opener, the goddess of fertility, but not of wedlock. Children born out of wedlock are called virgin-born.

Ishtar is depicted in an ancient ivory wall panel as seated in a window frame; she is called here Kilili Mushriti or "kilili who leans out"—the typical pose of the prostitute, the all-accepting one. She (like Mary Magdalene in Christian tradition) is the protectress of prostitutes. Ishtar says: "A prostitute compassionate am I." She symbolizes the creative submission to the demands of instinct, to the chaos of nature. The prostitute and the virgin are

both archetypes or archaic images of the free woman, as opposed
to domesticated woman, the wife and helpmeet, whose life goal
is union with the male. The ideal of the married woman faithful
to the father of her children and to the *domus,* the heart of the
household, is threatened mightily whenever the "Ishtar energy"
begins to erupt. (In a girl's life this often happens when she first
falls in love. A girl who has no intention of marrying or being a
wife isn't considered grown up by the patriarchate and will sometimes—just at the point of recognizing her own virgin nature—
be called a "whore" by her personal father.) There are goddesses
who sanction domesticity, but Ishtar does not. In fact she con-
demned her husband Dumuzi to be taken to hell in her place. She
chose a life of wandering instead. When Ishtar is imagined to be
the wandering moon, Dumuzi is an onion bulb buried beneath
earth with lawless green shoots that reach skyward to capture her
diminishing radiance as she wanes. (Most plants were thought to
grow in the wax and wither in the wane.) A poet captures Ishtar's
double reflection in the green growing things of earth and in the
images of queenly women:

> *So:*
> *praise the green thing*
> *in the hand*
> *in the eye*
> *in the*
> *Earth!*
> *Perfect.*
> *And: the queenly women of our youth,*
> *Middle age, old age, and the grand princesses*
> *Of death*
> *if any such be*
> *it clearly behooves us to praise*
> *Most highly.*
> *Here, then:*
> *Hear!*

I begin
with

Jenny.

. . .

Moon in Virgo.
—TOM MC GRATH, *"Letter to an Imaginary Friend"*

Ishtar is made present in songs of praise. When she is absent she has descended into the Land of No Return. Then there is no singing and no sex:

> *The bull does not spring upon the cow, the*
> *ass does not bow over the jenny—*
> *The man no more bows over the woman*
> *in the street,*
> *The man lies in his own chamber*
> *The maiden lies on her side.* [12]

When Ishtar returns she turns the female toward the male, the male and female toward each other again. Denise Levertov sings this "Song for Ishtar," in her mudmother animal aspect:

> *The moon is a sow*
> *and grunts in my throat*
> *Her great shining shines through me*
> *so the mud of my hollow gleams*
> *and breaks in silver bubbles*
>
> *She is a sow*
> *and I a pig and a poet*
>
> *When she opens her white*
> *lips to devour me I bite back*
> *and laughter rocks the moon*
>
> *In the black of desire*
> *we rock and grunt, grunt and*
> *shine*

That is the *lumen naturale,* silver bubbles in the mud, or sparks of stars against the dark night sky. Excavators of Troy found the figure of a pig dotted with stars, evidently representing the sky-woman as sow: her who nightly devours her star-children. Elsewhere, the stars are called the golden girdle of Ishtar, which she removes before making the descent into the underworld. Those luminous, far-seeing eyes cannot go with her on the road through the Land of the Dead: "the dark road from which there is no way back, is bereft of light . . . dust is the fare of those who enter and clay their food." When Ishtar descends (in the time of the dark moon or when winter approaches and barrenness falls over the land), she approaches the gatekeeper of the underworld, saying: "O gatekeeper, open thy gate, Open thy gate that I might enter! If thou openest not the gate so that I cannot enter, I will smash the door, I will shatter the bolt, I will smash the doorpost, I will move the doors, I will raise up the dead, eating the living so that the dead will outnumber the living."[13]

A certain balance of life and death in the world (and of depression and animation in our psyches) is overseen by Ishtar if she, or the principle of transformation she represents, is given due attention. Ishtar is of a twofold or two-faced nature, both waterer of green shoots of life and piglike destroyer. Paying attention to her means admitting paradoxes of intention and action. It means learning a kind of rhythm method: measuring one's movements according to emotions and feelings, activating a relationship with nature and other beings that is like the blood bond of pregnancy, a bond that is broken in its own time when the moment of creative fruition has come. It means listening to inner voices or going to the oracle of one's own dreams when blinded by the too constant light of day. In his account of an initiate's visit to the Delphic Oracle, Plutarch describes the voice there as that of the sibyl singing of the future as she was carried about on the face of the moon. The voice of the oracle has no single outlet but "roves everywhere in dreams and visions." Thoughts inspired by Ishtar are not logical or academic but intuitive and intoxicating; once conceived they grow of themselves if the period of gestation is allowed. To the ancient Sumerians and Babylonians she was the giver of dreams, omens, revelations, and understandings of things that are hidden. In her words:

> *Ishtar speaks:*
> *to give omens do I arise*
> *do I arise in perfectness.* [14]

Part of this proposed rhythm method is watching for signs, looking for the right approach to intersections: there is probably some crisis, choice point—or life crux—when someone approaches an intersection in a dream. Several possible paths cut across each other as they do at the intersection where Oedipus met his father, or where Dorothy, in *The Wizard of Oz,* stopped to ask directions of the scarecrow.

By striving for exact information, one loses the capacity to live with the wax and wane of doubts and certainties. Things become one-sided and unbalanced. In placing too much emphasis upon achievement and production, in the excessive valuation of logical conclusions, in placing inordinate emphasis on youth and beauty, in pushing the environment for an ever-increasing energy yield, we set ourselves up for an invasion of the opposite side: cultural destruction, poverty, madness, death, ugliness, famine, and the depletion of natural resources. In other words, by denying the shadow side we incur it. Or, by repressing the feminine, one encourages a violent emergence. Freud must have known this when he called the feminine (which is unconscious) "enemy to civilization."

The word "civilization" is related to "being civil" or "polite" and therefore to "police." It is the police world that is most threatened by the feminine because the feminine (as incarnate in Ishtar) does not live according to the rules of worldly authorities. As Ishtar leaves the upperworld to go down to the nether regions she becomes increasingly dark and unreachable. She sheds her shining jewelry and brilliant garments as she approaches the core. By the time she reaches the gatekeeper's door she is naked and enraged: her perseverance is expressed in the *Tao Te Ching*'s description of the feminine principle:

> *It is named the dark animal goddess*
> *And the doorway of the dark animal goddess*
> *Is called the root of Heaven and Earth.*
>
> *Like an endless thread she is as if persevering*
> *and accomplish[ing] effortlessly.*

Her ineluctable thread and the thread of the chapter then is that the feminine moon spirit is at the doors of our underworlds (telling the gatekeeper to let her pass). She requires something of women, of men, and of our culture.

In women she is asking for reverence, that we see ourselves "with a dry eye"[15]—capable of the turn from tenderness to the mad devouring of our own creations. She asks us to learn the dance "in which the dancer contradicts the waste and easy gesture"—to know our own "true hips"—of what swaying and standing firm our bodies are capable. To know our natures, to be "self-housed" or self-contained, giving over to the love of children and of women friends and men when our instinct demands it. She asks us to carry our dark sides with us as surely as the moon does—to see that we carry death on our backs and the green brightness of morning out front.

In men she is asking to be recognized, that there be a listening to "the data giving depth of your own tissue" (Charles Olson), that a dark place for secrets be opened to the new rain of Ishtar. A Sanskrit poem warns a man that impatience is deadly: "In all he does, whether good or bad, a wise man should consider the effect. Deeds done too quickly ripen into thorns that pierce the heart til death." She asks that men admit her beneficent and terrible presence in the wax and wane of relationships. As the amorous mother she pulls a man too much toward her; he needs to know how to stand up to her, how to reject the pull of instinct which renders him incapable of loving later. The virgin goddess asks then to be recognized as a sister and lover, as a part of the not-yet-known self that commands attention in depressions and outbursts of anger. "Whatever one has within oneself but does not live, grows against one." If she is ignored, if her ardor is not returned, she sends the Bull of Heaven after you (as Ishtar did to the hero, Gilgamesh), thus destroying your animal nature and uprooting the seat of desires, making the love of companions impossible. And she asks that men be aware of the axial moments in their own creativity: conception, incubation, and pains of labor, that these feminine mysteries be felt as deeply as the confidence that the phenomenal world can be understood and managed.

She stands at the door of our culture, transforming before our eyes, a sign in process, a moving revelation—like the sign the poet H. D. saw in a burnt-out London after the war: a half-charred apple tree bursting into bloom. A sign or "a new sensation is not granted to everyone," she says, "not to everyone, everywhere, but to us here a new sensation." By "us," she intends the "straggling company of brush and quill who are driven together to praise and care for what is left of creation."

The goddess demands that we admit our willful ignorance of evil—that we open our eyes to the *lumen naturale* that shines in poetry and dreams. She asks that we value the irrational, the instinctual, the uncommon sources of knowledge.

The goddess has come to the door periodically. One clear announcement of her coming was uttered by Peter in the New Testament account of Pentecost:

> *On that day*
> *the Spirit will be poured out on all flesh*
> *and your sons and your daughters shall prophesy.*
> *Your young men shall see visions,*
> *Your old men dream dreams.*
> *I will pour out my spirit . . .*

And I will show wonders in the heaven above
and signs on the earth beneath,
blood and fire and vapor of smoke.
The sun shall be turned to darkness
and the moon into blood . . .
before that great and manifest day.

The thing that was manifested or "at hand" that day was the fiery, bloody eruption of the moon spirit given to prophecy, possession, and blazing tongues. The ecstasy was irrational, and explained away as drunkenness by onlookers. But anyone with eyes to see and ears to hear could tell that something extraordinary was happening; something was happening between people—they all spoke their different mother tongues but understood each other for the first time as if they were speaking one language.

The goddess who "accomplishes effortlessly" will express herself. If she is given space (as in the expectation and waiting that preceded Pentecost) she will come into consciousness and culture positively: healing divisions, generating warmth and insight. But if she is not welcomed (or worse, is devalued and kept outside the outer walls) she will break the doors down and come in to individual or cultural consciousness in a negative, devouring (literally "shit-eating"), stone-cold way. An ancient inscription describes her thus:

> *Three-headed, nocturnal, excrement-eating virgin,*
> *holder of the keys (maiden) of the underworld,*
> *Gorgon-eyed, terrible dark one.*[16]

But it is "the foul (foetid) earth that quickly receives the white sparks" and it is the goddess as well as god who is found in the dung: *Deus absconditas in stercore.* Consequently it is not as important to look at our modes of growth and development as it is to consider how we rot. (Sappho said, "If you are squeamish do not prod the rubble on the beach.") The decomposition of matter precedes any reordering. The point is that, if we have the courage

to face into the dark, we may witness the slow epiphany or showing forth of the feminine.

One of the quite useful and typically humble suggestions that
Freud once made in answer to his own questions about the nature
of the feminine was, "look to poetry, to your own experience, and
lastly to our science [meaning psychology], but we in the last
category do not know much yet."[17] Turning to poetry for the final
image we hear the Sufi angel Madonna Intelligenza crying out
that her epiphany has been nearly overlooked:

Dearly Beloved!
I have called you so often and you have not heard me.
I have shown myself to you so often and you have not seen me.
I have made myself fragrance so often, and you have not smelled
me. . .

Why?[18]

Before my visible Form you flee into the invisible . . .
But truly my hearth and swelling are in the Invisible. . . .

Look well! for. . .
and I am new moon, Image in the heart.[19]

2
Psyche's Search

We need them.
Brands that flare to show us
the dark we are in,
to keep us moving in it.
—DENISE LEVERTOV, *"An Interim"*

In the old story, Psyche, the maiden, was urged by her bitterly jealous sisters to light an oil lamp at night to look upon the body of her lover, whom she had never seen. What she had known in the dark was lovely to her, but her sisters planted a gnawing seed of doubt when they suggested that it was not a youthful god in her bridal bed but a horrible, monstrous snake. A fatal drop from her curious, sputtering lamp sent Eros, the beautiful boy god, soaring heavenward out of sight and embrace of the girl. In a flash she had seen and lost and then began her exhaustive, nearly endless search for reunion. Psyche ventured out of the unlit realm of not knowing, an unconscious, all-embracing place, where fascination holds sway. Step by step she moved through that dark of loss. By error and by trial she came eventually face to face with her other half. She made the journey from earth to heaven, where, finally welcomed by Aphrodite, she was reunited with Eros and gave birth to the child Bliss.[1] Psyche divinized is consciousness raised. Her journey is the feminine journey from blind instinctual attraction to a knowing, individuated love.

When I say that Psyche came face to face with her other half I mean that she had lost herself and found it again. Her "other half" turns out to be not only a mate who vanishes during the nine months of a wearisome pregnant search, but also the half of self that is seen as if in a mirror, an opposite but equal reflection. Eros was her own blind, soaring spirit, a psychological element called *animus* in women, a masculine "breath" that inhabits the body of a woman and comes and goes, with a capacity to both cripple and inspire. A man's "other half" is called his *anima*, his soul image ("the new moon in his heart") or *psyche*. In one of the lighter of his thousand ways of speaking of the psyche, Jung conjures up the Greek sense of butterfly: the quick-moving creature, changeful of hue, reeling drunkenly from flower to flower, living on honey and love.[2] Psyche's journey is "heavier" or more burdened than that of the butterfly. Perhaps she moves more like the soul in its cocoon stage. (Her reeling is from task to task; the first was to sort a welter of seeds: barley, millet, poppyseed, peas, lentils, beans. A *welter* is a great disordered upheaval of things, a confusion. *Welter* also means to go downstream with the flow—rolling, reeling, surging, or to go with a heavy rolling gait like a young wife. To be a wife is to be overwhelmed, capsized for a while. Wife/wave/weave—a weaving walk, heavy with the burden of creating a new life.[3])

The gradual and unexpected transformation of a sheltered chrysalis into a free winged creature represents a form of the search for soul that begins with being shielded or veiled to the outside world. Psyche put on a wedding veil. Dreamers pull shrouds over themselves, wrap pink flowers in thick dark cloaks, or crawl into caves. The story of Psyche and Eros is such a story within the cloak of another story. It occupies more than half of the story of *The Transformation of Lucius* or *The Golden Ass*, written by Apuleius in the second century A.D. Lucius is changed into an "ever-rutting" ass while engaged in an erotic aside on his way to being initiated into the priesthood of the goddess Isis.[4] In his ass form he encounters a band of robbers who have abducted a maiden on her wedding day. They withdraw into a cave together, where an old woman working on behalf of the robbers tells the tale of Psyche and Eros in an effort to quiet the mournful girl. In this context Psyche's search becomes the search of Lucius's soul for wholeness and bliss. But for the maiden the period of pre-nuptial isolation in the cave is the first stage of her initiation into the greater feminine mysteries of erotic *(eros)* and spiritual love. A cover of darkness, separation, and confusion (the "welter" of seeds) are necessary prerequisites for the eventual rebirth of a lost and wandering soul.

Like the butterfly or moth after which she is named, Psyche is drawn from darkness to light. Her journey begins in the darkness of first love, when she is compelled by fear and ignorance (per-sonified in her sisters) to shed some light on a situation she had never questioned. Her sisters were wrong about the monstrous nature of Psyche's lover in one sense. In another sense they were right because she was held captive by Eros's "monstrous" insis-tence that she never truly see him. Learning to see began with an act of disobedience, like Eve's disobedience in another paradisia-cal situation. Eve was prompted by a snake; Psyche was prompted by the virulence of the suggestion that there was a snake in her bed. Distrust, jealousy, hatred, fear—the violent eruption of these emotions can open a space for the psyche's understanding of itself. Invariably these negative feelings bring about separation on many levels: families are torn apart, lovers separate, individu-als feel divided within—describing parts of themselves as being "split off." By attending to the self in isolation, rather than re-pressing its demands or seeking distractions, the process of dis-covery is furthered.

A woman once told me she dreamed the sentence "The moon contains the seeds of the process." Like Psyche in that original stunned moment caught holding the lamp by which she betrayed her lover, this woman could not control the oil leaping in her heart—or the flickers of consciousness that would burn her lover.

Her dream words about the moon indicated the need for patience now that her companion and her composure were gone. Her next steps required discrimination. According to Hindu belief, the moon is the overseer of germination and is called Cup-of-Offerings. It is a chalice filled with semen—a cup holding a confusion of seed. The disoriented psyche's first impossible task is to sort through this confusion. By "the process," she meant partly the arduous journey toward relationship again, and partly the process of therapy, the recovery of self. The moon contained the secret because of its periodic nature: this woman who despaired over the loss of love and the incapacity to work knew that the wax and wane were a sign to live by. Therapy is a method of cultivation, of planting according to the moon. A therapist is one who tends the seeds where they fall. A psychotherapist ("in Psyche's cult"[5]) is an attendant to psyche, one who helps in the search for lost parts of the self, one who helps to stretch a restricted imagination, the opposite of a "shrink."

Therapy understood as Psyche's attendance has ancient roots in the ritual practices of incubation and initiation. Incubation or "sleeping-in" in the temple of a healing god or goddess was undertaken by suppliants in need of a restorative dream or vision. Initiation rites, which enabled the passage of a person from one life stage to another, often included this first step of incubation in order to ensure the kind of isolation and self-containment that makes one receptive to the unconscious. Connections between these rites and modern psychotherapy have been made by psychoanalysts, who have seen the symbols of an ancient initiatory process emerge repeatedly in their patients' dreams and fantasies.[6] Because religion rarely performs the initiating function in any contemporary society, Psyche's search for meaning and completion is generally undertaken by individuals in the private space of the therapeutic encounter. That this process occurs at all anymore, without the aid of collective rites and ritual, can best be explained by the existence of archetypes—life energies and forms that structure psychic growth. Jung described archetypes this way:

From the unconscious there emanate determining influences which, independently of tradition, guarantee in every single individual a similarity and even a sameness of experience, and also of the way it is represented imaginatively. One of the main proofs of this is the almost universal parallelism between mytho-logical motifs, which on account of their quality as primordial images, I have called archetypes.[7]

An archetype is a primordial pattern or deep "imprint" on the human psyche. Freud called this component of one's unconscious life the "archaic memory." Charles Olson, in the context of a poem addressing the same dimension of experience, said: "Instead of 'archetypal,' read 'organic'—that with which one works." Images and symbols—like Psyche's lamp, the crescent moon, a cave—are visible archetypes. (I want to work with these in this chapter, which is itself a welter, a phenomenology of the soul's conundrum and a search for resolution, and I hope that my readers can let the images reverberate or work in them without trying too quickly to sort out and move on.)

The archetype of rebirth is initiation. Initiation is an active entry into darkness. It means to "enter into" an experience of psychic significance with one's eyes closed, mouth shut, wearing a veil—a kind of veiling that paradoxically permits seeing. Covering the eyes for a time to the external world permits an inward focusing that tends to draw one's attention "down" and sometimes "backward." There is evident in dreams an internal terrain of the modern psyche that corresponds to the actual experience of initiates in ancient rites. Dreams of falling down into a hole, "going under," looking back, sliding from a narrow space into an opening are all ways of beginning the search for what is missing. One of Psyche's first unsuccessful attempts to deal with her misery was to throw herself into a river. In a symbolically related tale, Alice in Wonderland falls down a dark hole that "seemed to be a very deep well," to find herself in a place creatured with fabulous men, women, and animals. Wonderland is characterized by a dreamlike suspension of time and alteration of space that is reminiscent of the most ancient rites of initiation. One such trans-formative hole in history is found at the oracular site of Zeus-Trophonios. According to the Greek historian Pausanias, who consulted this oracle himself, an initiate approached the incuba-tion cave by descending through a small chamber to a place where there was an opening in the ground. To get into the cave "he lies down on the ground . . . thrusts his feet into the opening and pushes forward himself, trying to get his knees inside the hole. The rest of his body is at once dragged in . . . just as a great and swift river would catch a man in its swirl and draw him under."[8]

Before entering the sacred cave the initiate, or incubant, had to first go through baths of purification and a ritual anointing. Then, at the place where two springs met, he drank of the waters of Lethe and Mnemosyne, forgetfulness and memory. Drinking of the stream of Lethe meant one could forget the past (and the daylight world) for this while, and drinking of the stream of Mnemosyne meant one would not forget what was about to hap-pen. In psychotherapy these streams are called *amnesia* and *anamnesis*. [9]

Amnesia is an essential sacrifice of the self, a deep sleep or complete death to an old way of life. And anamnesis is recalling your entire story, a narrative of experience, telling the tale of "passing through the double rocks of the sea" as through the birth canal into daylight. The beginning of life is entry into the cave. From the infant perspective it is the lowering into the pelvic cave of the mother. In Porphyry's *Cave of the Nymphs,* the spirit children call their mother's vagina the "rock hole." When they intend to be born they say, "I am going into a rock hole."[10] Like the mountain cave the children disappear into following the Pied Piper of Hamelin, the rock hole is the womb of the mother, great bulk body, place of eruptive creation, place of origins.

Going into the oracular cave of Zeus-Trophonios meant going into the hallowed birth cave of the god. Here the infant god was fed and attended by giant bees, whose nourishing honey was considered divine amniotic fluid.[11] Mead, the honey drink of the immortals, flowed from that cave annually in commemoration of the birth. We know from other stories, such as the miraculous birth of St. Ambrose with a swarm of bees around his infant mouth, that the bee attendance portends the gift of honeyed speech, a golden tongue, a promise of nourishing words. In keeping with the bee metaphor, the initiate was called an *incubant,* from *incubare* or "to dwell in a hive." A set of ancient instructions says that the first temple was, like a hive, constructed of bees' wax and birds' feathers: "Bring feathers, ye birds, and wax, ye bees." The temple attendants were priestesses called *melissae,* or "bee maidens." Men followed bee leads to find sources of wild honey hidden in divine caves. Once four honey robbers approached Zeus's cave intending to take a portion of the god's natural treasure. Zeus would have killed them for the outrage, but because his cave had been decreed a sanctuary, he only changed them into birds.

The story of the honey thieves is important because it shows the necessity of making a right approach to the cave of rebirth. Only one person ever died consulting the god at Trophonios and he went into the cave hoping to find gold and silver rather than self-knowledge. Approaching the task of anamnesis is like this— one must not consult the oracle of one's own memory until the proper ritual prescriptions have been carried out (bathing, cleansing, divesting oneself of the outer layer, the *persona* or mask by which the world recognizes us) and then the desire to descend into the incubation chamber must be prompted by an authentic searching rather than mere curiosity. Entering the cave with inappropriate intentions robs one of the psychic energy necessary to effect a healing transformation. (Rather than emerging richer with the gold of the gods, the robbers emerged poorer, having been transformed into birds who would never again walk the familiar earth.)

After bathing and drinking, initiates at Trophonios lowered themselves into the dark hole to be swept away for three days of visionary solitude. Then they were drawn out, in a rather dazed condition, by *therapeutes* or attendants, who would place them on the throne of Mnemosyne to make possible the freeing of tongues thickened by fear and sleep. (Mnemosyne is memory, the mother of the muses. She is not the kind of history-class memory that strings dates on a line with facts but the kind of re-membering or putting together again the body of our outward and inward journeyings. It is the kind of memory that calls up dreams, myths, and stories—the kind of memory that gives birth to the arts. An initiate's groping is toward Mnemosyne in order to find a new bearing in the world.) The attending therapists, who sat the initiate on the lap of memory, functioned as midwives for the psyche. They brought the initiate back to life "by asking of him all that he has seen and learned. Then when they have heard it they put him in charge of his friends . . . for he is still in the grip of fear and unaware of himself and those around him. But later on his wits will return to him unimpaired, and in particular he will recover the power of laughter."[12]

The *therapeutes* recorded what they heard. Many of these ancient "case studies" were carved in stone. Words of one incubant were put to song.[13] Paying attention to words was the primary task of these attendants. (Attention is the tool of more than one calling: Denise Levertov says it is the poet's task "to dwell in that ecstasy of attention to words." This of course was Freud's insight—that the healing of the psyche could be accomplished by paying attention to the spoken word.)

From eyes shut to eyes opened, mouth closed to mouth open, every night we go through this journey, and yet what happens between the going under and coming up is so little valued. To start each day on the throne of Mnemosyne would be to remember your dreams:

> *Memory is a kind*
> *of accomplishment*
> *a sort of renewal*
> *even*
> *an initiation.*
> —WILLIAM CARLOS WILLIAMS, *Paterson*

Memory makes initiation—and individuation, the modern parallel—possible. It is essential for psychic growth to throw oneself
into the flow of unconscious life, not to forget, not to diminish,
not to demean or degrade as "mere" fantasy one's adventures in
the other world.[14] When the initiate returns to this world—and
to his or her senses—it becomes important to share the experience with others who are capable of understanding.

This urge to express what was seen and heard beneath the
surface of ordinary reality requires a "language of the soul" and
is one of the ways mythology comes into being. Putting the events
of the extraordinary experience together in a meaningful way
makes a *muthos,* a myth—not a made-up story but literally a
"mouthing," a telling of primary experience using the first words
of coming to consciousness. (One of the first cries signifying
awareness in newborn children everywhere is the sound mmm,
mem, mum, mu, me. James Joyce affectionately called Memory
"Mememormee." Language evolves from the experience of
being held by our actual and archetypal mothers: myth is the
original mother tongue.)

A young woman in the first stage of the search had an illustra-
tive snatch of a dream in which she "with great effort and turbu-
lence all around, managed to jam the word into a tube to incubate." She was tired of old words in the mouth. Her facility with
"the word"—*logos,* or rational thought—was great but she was
ready to sink that function into a tube or cave where, as Rilke said,
"the word unspoken might ripen still." Because of the common
condition called by the Chinese the "mad-mind," which consists
of wandering aimlessly about in thoughts of oneself, she needed
to concentrate, to focus in on the birth of feeling. (An example
of Psyche needing Eros.) Her need to give energy to the incubating word meant to me that mythopoetic speaking is essential to
the work of therapy, not only because of Freud's injunction to
look to the poets for knowledge of the feminine psyche, but also
because those who fashion myths and poetry know about waiting

for fresh words to come out of a brooding silence. The language we await is feminine. It is not pure *logos*, but *muthos-logos*, or mythological. It is an evocative language—like the tongues of fire at Pentecost—that evokes the soul or calls psyche forth from the cave as it speaks.[15] (For my client this meant she needed to stop analytical work for a while, to go into herself and be silent. Later, she would emerge ready to work on a feeling level for the first time.)

In Levertov's "Song for Ishtar" quoted in Chapter 1, the poet swallows the mother tongue—her myth is grunted around the moon caught in her throat. Part of ourselves has never forgotten certain elements of the primordial language of myths. Literature records these connections, between the moon and the transforming mountain goddess, for example. Mount Sinai, the mountain remembered in connection with the laws of Moses, was first the mountain of Ishtar, daughter of the moon god Sinn.[16] Sinai was the Mount of the Moon long before Moses received the tablets of the ten commandments there. Hebrew tradition holds twin concepts of law that reflect (probably not intentionally) these layers of Sinai's history. They are called the Halakah and Aggadah. Halakah (reminiscent of Moses) is the law of traditional, social, ritualized behavior to be explicitly observed. The Aggadah (reminiscent of the moon deities) actually translates "legend" and includes the realm of imagination, myths, and dreaming. One is the law of outward observance, codified and finite. The other is like a law of inner movement, fluid and impossible to codify. Aggadah is this unconscious force, free streaming and untrammeled by the outward-looking law.[17] Both of these antithetical laws of human nature and the tension they create are essential for life—but it is in the irrepressible law of the legend that the feminine lives most deeply and makes its home.

Recalling fantasies is as important as recalling facts in the recollecting work of anamnesis, whether it is an individual or cultural attempt to tell the unbroken story of emergence into consciousness. The search for psychic origins and this "backward"-looking study of the feminine thus rely on one's willingness to find meaning in myths, symbols, dreams, and poetry—all appropriate source materials for expressing hidden nature. When the right image is struck it buoys our enthusiasm, raising the sleeping head of the "god within," literally *en theos*. If enthusiasm for the search ° is lacking one remains in the dark—not necessarily unhappily so (Psyche lived in luxury and with complacence in her dark kingdom for a while). However, the kingdom of the complacent psyche is essentially pre-creative. Psyche and Eros are united in love, but nothing comes of it (no child, no actual creation) until their original unity is split. Myths repeat this truth in diverse images of creation.

Before the world began there was a perfect sphere, or a formless void, or a coconut, or an egg, or a god with an erection. Eventually, the sphere split into halves, male and female. The formless void conceived of form. Varimate-takara, a South Sea goddess, came and divided the coconut into seven layers, out of which came all the living creatures of the world. The egg hatched. The god Atum masturbated and from his semen rose Heaven and Earth. Before the division there was unity. All things of earth and sky have their origin in an androgynous figure capable of autonomous creation. One thing splits into two. The complications of this image of creation are manifold. Is the inherent twofoldness of the original being something we try to outgrow, something we yearn for, something we strive to become? In what sense are we made in the image of such a creator? Speculating on the sexual paradox, Virginia Woolf in *A Room of One's Own* elaborates on a description of a scene on the street below her window:

. . . the sight of the two people getting into the taxi and the satisfaction it gave me made me also ask whether there are two sexes in the mind corresponding to the two sexes in the body, and whether they also require to be united in order to get complete satisfaction and happiness. And I went on amateurishly to sketch a plan of the soul so that in each of us two powers preside, one male, one female; and in the man's brain, the man predominates over the woman, and in the woman's brain, the woman predominates over the man. The normal and comfortable state of being is that when the two live in harmony together, spiritually cooperating. If one is a man, still the woman part of the brain must have effect; and a woman also must have intercourse with the man in her. Coleridge perhaps meant this when he said that a great mind is androgynous. It is when this fusion takes place that the mind is fully fertilised and uses all its faculties. Perhaps a mind that is purely masculine cannot create, any more than a mind that is purely feminine, I thought. But it would be well to test what one meant by man-womanly, and conversely by woman-manly, by pausing and looking at a book or two.[18]

Virginia Woolf raises the possibility of androgyny within a person. A mystical Eastern theologian goes further to imagine it between persons:

The union of the sexes is four membered rather than two membered: it always means the complex union of the male element of the one with the female element of the other, and of the female element of the first with the male element of the second. The mystical life of the androgyne is realized not in one bisexual being but rather in the quadripartite union of two beings.[19]

Freud speculated on the union of the sexes, saying: "There are four members present in every act of intercourse." He meant the woman's father and the man's mother were there too. Jung called the androgynous elements *animus* and *anima*. In Taoist tradition they are yang and yin (see page 69), or the dragon and the mare. It is difficult to saddle the mare without awakening the dragon (as it is to measure the particle without disturbing the wave), but it is occasionally necessary, when the system is unbalanced, to concentrate on one side of the matter. The story of Psyche does this for us by circling around the core of the feminine problem of losing and finding the self. It shows what happens when the "two are rent asunder"—from the woman's point of view. (Her husband is locked away in a room in heaven, observing, until the end of the story, when his wound is finally healed enough for him to move actively toward Psyche.) The original union of opposites had to fall apart in order for a conscious and differentiated union to occur on a higher level; this typically happens to married couples. But the more important, and universal, message of the story is that the pattern of splitting and reunion is an internal one that engages the psyche of every person who searches for meaning. A clarifying and creative androgyny is thus a goal of Psyche's search.

How this quest to re-create oneself goes forward can be seen in the lives of countless women who are seeking their own particular economy (meaning the management of one's own dwelling). Women wander, in themselves or in the world, to locate the places where they feel at home. One can see this boundless wandering now in women (and in men) who live in materially sufficient cultures. Those who have found ways to meet the basic needs of physical comfort, intellectual stimulation, and companionship feel a greater need underriding these accomplishments for discovering what is at the core of the experience of self. Is there a feminine fundus or fulcrum—an inner, archetypal point of stability, balance, and leverage? Women who were once the fundamental guardians and converters of elemental energy (tending hearthfires, drawing well water, bearing and feeding children) now need to know if there is an inner source out of which all of this basic transforming energy radiates.

Reference points for psychic life are harder to see than the old family hearth and the village well (referents for social life). One of the people who worked on locating potential reference points for the feminine psyche in Western culture was Toni Wolff, a close colleague and companion of Jung in Zürich in the 1930s. She developed a fourfold structure for analyzing archetypal components of the feminine principle.[20]

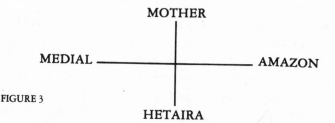

FIGURE 3

The mother pole opposes the hetaira, which is companion (concubine) to men. Wolff describes this axis as "personally related." The pole stretching from the medial (one who mediates the unknown) to the amazon (one who goes off alone) is impersonal in comparison. Every woman (and the feminine face of every man) lives primarily at one end of this structure. Usually, one has access to another one or two of the "arms," but making contact with the opposite pole is extremely difficult. If a woman experiences herself primarily as a mother, she might have access to the medial aspect of herself, but the amazon nature would be barely present and the hetaira personality probably repressed. To make the representation more complex—and more real—each pole has both positive and negative aspects (the other face of the nurturing mother is the devouring mother; there is a hetaira that is inspirational and another who leads to death, and so on).

Although I have already mentioned states of feminine being that do not coincide precisely with one pole or another, wife and virgin, for example—and Psyche, who circumambulates them all —I will use Wolff's poles in the coming chapters as if the structure were a divining rod, passing over fields of the feminine to find places of archetypal convergence. One of the things to hold on to in this exploration is the difference between a *stereotype* and an *archetype*. A stereotype is a stricture where an archetype is an enabler. (A stereotype is literally a printer's mold cast in metal.) When someone calls a woman a "man eater" they are generally stereotyping her, putting her in an immovable position without recognizing the archetypal form of the man-eating mother that is asleep, or astir, in all women. Wherever the archetypal nature of words and images has been intentionally recharged by referring to roots of meaning there is a correspondingly greater freedom to explore the parameters of feminine identity.

Toni Wolff describes the process of psychotherapy as a withdrawal into an alchemical vessel where a woman is healed by coming in closer to her unconscious nature. She enters into it (as Yeats said of himself in another context) "looking for the face I had before the world was born." Psyche's final labor is related to this sense of psychotherapy. She is required to go down to hell to ask the Goddess of the Underworld for a vial of her precious beauty ointment. Although she was forbidden to look at it, Psyche opens the flask on her way back and falls into an inadvertent slumber. This is her *incubatio,* the sleep that precedes the final transformation.

Many women undertake this modern form of ritual withdrawal into the unknown self because they feel they are not beautiful. (As always, the essence of beauty is hidden. In Psyche's case it is born out of the descent to face death.) Wolff noted in 1934 that women were brought to the task of self-reflection by archetypal disorientation resulting from centuries of adapting to a predominantly patriarchal world. The world at large, not just woman, is "caught in a sort of hell," estranged from femininity, and waiting for a boon from the goddess.

A poet asks this last and leading question:

How shall he who is not happy, who has been so made unclear,
who is no longer privileged to be at ease, who, in this brush,
stands reluctant, imageless, unpleasured, caught in a sort of
hell, how shall he convert this underbrush, how turn this unbidden
place
how trace and arch again
the necessary goddess?

        —CHARLES OLSON, *"In Cold Hell, in Thicket"*

A magnificent Egyptian over-arching sky goddess once curved protectively like the upper half of an eggshell over man and all creation. The darkness was illumined with her star teats and her loins sent forth a rain of energy and life. When the goddesses above are gone, who can one look up to? Who will teach us to read those "scribings scrawled on eggs," those tracings of ancient gods? Rilke says that when the time is right the heart will teach you: when work of sight is done, it is time "for some heartwork on the images within." The most ancient images held within history are of the Great Mother—woman of endless variation—and it is to her now that we turn in the psyche's search for what is necessary.

3
A Mother Essay in Images

Pregnancy of Stone

In China a seed is thought of as a "pregnant" stone. Ezra Pound says it in his *Cantos:* "the stone is alive in my hand, crops will be thick in my death year" (Figure 4).

Womb as tomb and the other way also: all wandering is from the Mother, to the Mother, in the Mother. The movement is in space and space is a receptacle, a vessel, a matrix—as it were the mother or nurse of all becoming.[1]

Seen from slightly above (Figure 5), the Mother whose breasts never run dry, arms tapering off, resting on great rounds, and feet diminishing to the point where she has nothing to stand on, is what archaeologists call a fertility object. The subject is life abundant, radiating from her mid-region. Her head appears to be sightless and is curled or cultivated, an organic, close-fitting halo. Gertrude Rachel Levy, describing this figurine and several others of similar type, says that the slight bowing of the head "as if above an unseen child," gives the impression of "brooding maternity."[2] Given over to containing, she takes all things into herself and incubates them. Her body is thus heavy with the burden of creation.

Carved into the curve of rock (Figure 6), goddess-guardian of a cave sanctuary, still sightless, but gesturing this time, she raises the crescent horn of the hunters. She is not the huntress herself, but the one who lends her creative force. An archaic poem sings of her:

Go rejoicing . . .
in the countless wombs of Earth

Have you heard
of . . . [the] Healer and Mountain Mother
who fashioned Huntress-Moon-Queen?[3]

Ten thousand years later the huntress turns up in Crete as
Britomartis and later in Greece as Artemis. This perhaps is an
image of her early conception. Bison horn, bull horn, blood-filled
crescent, horn of the moon—turning toward it, she suggests that
the link to the power of the hunt is herself. A drawing etched in
stone in another cave shows a hunter with drawn bow crouching
toward the animals—behind him a larger figure of a woman
stands with upraised arms (her arms raised this way show that she
is a goddess or priestess, standing in the gesture of epiphany,
welcoming the holy or the "wholly other forces"). In between the
two stands a horned animal. Underscoring the animal there is a
line that runs directly from inside the woman to the man, from
genital to genital—a magical connection.[4]

Originally, the great cave Mother was painted with red ocher,
a faint stain hinting at the importance of blood in the transformation rites to come. Her left hand falls on her belly with a simple
gesture that draws attention toward center. Only later, under
Christian influence, do these gestures of pointing to parts of the
body (breast, belly, pubis) become gestures of shame. At this
early stage the gesture is one of emphasis, pointing to an awesome
exhibit.

Have you heard
of . . . Mother Earth who wandered in the great gulf
in search of her child to give us law?
The star roads
the reading of signs
the meaning of dreams[5]

FIGURE 4

FIGURE 5

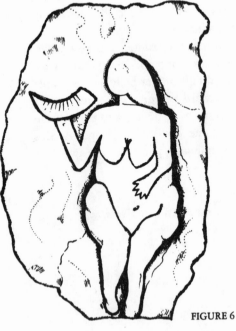

FIGURE 6

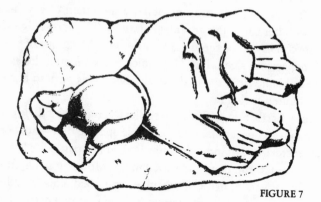

FIGURE 7

FIGURE 8

"Wide bosomed Earth, ever sure foundation of all!" (Hesiod). Bedrock of being, full and immobile, a mountain of a woman asleep with her ear to the ground (Figure 7). The knowledge she suggests comes out of repose, a knowledge stirring out of cave-deep unconscious sleep. Her law, which she wandered the earth to give us, came from the underworld. She gives birth to buried things, hidden meanings.

Mother Earth brings forth an endless variety of individuals, "she carries in her lap the seeds of those specific differentiations that characterize each individual female and her particular law."[6] The roots of law run deep and varied in our Mother tongue: from *lien*, to be prostrate; *ligger*, footbridge; *leger*, bed, couch, or lair —a place where animals put their young; *lager*, stored before use; *laghe*, what is laid down; *litter*, a portable bed, or the recently borne young of an animal (especially a sow), or the straw bedding that tends to become scattered rubbish; *lokhos*, a lying-in, hence childbirth.

Law, before it is hatched, is held deep within the body of the Mother. Her laws, the-way-she-lays-it-down, are primitive or basic. They remain after eons, even in the litter of past civilizations. Unlike the great changing law of the Father, which is based upon consciousness of self, property, and others, the Mother's laws are those of unvitiated nature. All things hang in the balance or "de-pend" upon her.

One New England winter Thoreau wrote that if God wanted to end the world all he would have to do would be to make it a little colder. It is one of the Mother's laws that warmth is necessary for life. There are fundamental laws of human experience that came, in time, to be represented by gods and goddesses, like "Strife is the Father of all things" (Ares) or "Necessity is the Mother of invention" (Anake). It was Ishtar's "law" that during the time of the dark of the moon male and female would be turned away from each other. The binding factor of such laws is not the threat of punishment or promise of cultural stability, but rather like the binding of electrons or of flesh to flesh—a natural, instinctual binding inherent in being (matter or energy) that lends cohesion, pattern, system, rhythm to the gradual wending of life toward death. Time does not change these universal laws of nature. The bed, as symbol of where the Great Mother's laws come from, is always, everywhere, the place of birth, of sleep and dreaming, of love, and of death.

Two of the scholars who did the most to reconnect us to Mother roots in the history of human culture, just at the turn of the century, J. J. Bachofen (as mentioned above) and Jane Ellen Harrison, were both students of law. When Bachofen was a young man, he went to Rome, where he kept reading symbols carved on stone tombs that forced the revelation in on him: there were customs recognized in Roman law that could never have originated in a patriarchal society. Increasingly, his interest took him into the unknown world intimated there. His search was for the spirit moving behind the law; he was after inner facts. Unlike other historians of law he was looking at the process of cultural maturation developmentally to determine the reasons for adherence to certain value systems. Why would one group of people condemn a social or religious practice that another group sanctions?

This search eventually led to the postulation of three major stages in the historical development of societies. The first he called "tellurian," of the earth. This stage was characterized by sexual promiscuity, and was represented by the luxuriant, unregulated wild plant life of the swamp. The second stage he called "lunar" and "matriarchal." This stage was characterized by the legal recognition of motherhood, and was represented by the tilled field, the beginnings of agriculture. The third stage he called "solar" and "patriarchal." Conjugal father right became predominant. Communal property gave way to individual ownership. Mother goddesses were worshiped during the first stages— first Aphroditic, then Demetrian.[7] Wild life was followed by cultivated life. The lunar-matriarchal stage that honored motherhood and the cultivation of seed recognized the archetypal mother-child unit as the formative factor in the plant and spread of human communities. He describes its "quality of natural truth":

Like childbearing motherhood, which is its physical image, matriarchy is entirely subservient to matter and to the phenomena of natural life from whence it derives its existence; more strongly than later generations, the matriarchal peoples feel the unity of all life, the harmony of the universe, which they have not yet out-grown. . . . They yearn more fervently for higher consolation, in the phenomena of natural life, and they relate this consolation to the generative womb, to conceiving, sheltering, nurturing mother love. No era has attached so much importance to outward form, to the sanctity of the body.[8]

Sanctity of the body. Body inviolate, fused with the earth (Figure 8). Prior to the Lady Under the Hill, whom we meet later in fairy tales, this Mother is the hill itself. She is a mountainous mass of earth whose headdress must seem to graze the heavens from the perspective of the small creature who depends upon her for food and support. She has one vocation: to be fully present to the passage of offspring from life to death—and the other way also.

Her Loins Articulated the Form of All Creatures

From time to time we are driven like the spirit of the salmon in this poem to swim against the current of history to seek our origins:

> *a spiritual urgency at the dark ladders leaping.*
>
> *This beauty is an inner persistence*
>   *toward the source*
> *striving against (within) down-rushet of the river,*
>   *a call we heard and answer*
> *in the lateness of the world*
>   *primordial bellowings*
> *from which the youngest world might spring. . . .*
> —ROBERT DUNCAN, *"Poetry, A Natural Thing"*

Bull-roaring, ever-rushing rivers have their source in the delta of the Mother—the deeply set triangle of her sex. This part, which

FIGURE 9

FIGURE 10

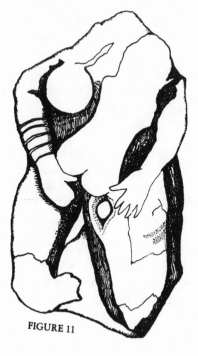

FIGURE 11

FIGURE 12

is exaggerated (Figure 9) on cave walls, bone engravings, cult figurines and statues, is a part that stands for the whole. Vulvular V's and the more abstracted triangle represent woman as fertile source. "The Pythagoreans held the triangle to be *Urgestalt* (original form), not only because of its perfect form, but also because it was the archetype of universal fecundity."[9] *Fecunda* is *femina*: fecund, or fertile, and female are one. The fertile woman bestows form through her own perfected form. The *mons veneris* of the Mother is the triangle of Aphrodite, the "mound of Venus," the mountain connecting man and woman, earth and sky.

In her fullness and immobility, sedentary and erect (Figure 10), the female is the "seat" of the human race. Eternally, maternally receptive, the body of the Mother became a throne. A chair with arms, backs, and legs. To be taken on her lap meant divine adoption.

Ruling kings take possession of the earth by "mounting the throne." A man becomes the god-king by enacting the double ceremony of becoming his mother's son and her lover. The lap, "from which the youngest world might spring"—what we know as the expanse of thigh—is related to labia and lip, the mouth of the mother vessel, river mouth, mouth of the womb.

Who shall ever praise sufficiently . . . those members of the body which are appointed for procreation? In the lap of the daughters of Jerusalem is the gate of the lord, and the righteous shall there go into the temple, even to the altar. And in the lap of the sons of the living god is the water pipe . . . which is a tube, like a rod with which to measure the temple and the altar.[10]

To "measure the altar" is to make love. The measure of the altar is the measure of a man. Olive Schreiner, in her book *Woman and Labor,* talks more specifically about the feminine "altar," the circular cervical os of the woman. She calls this passage "the great, central fact":

With each generation the entire race passes through the body of its womanhood as through a mold, reappearing with the indelible marks of that mold upon it. the *os cervix* of woman, through which the head of the human infant passes at birth, forms a ring, determining forever the size at birth of the human head, a size which could only increase if in the course of ages the *os cervix* of woman should itself slowly expand; and . . . so exactly the intellectual capacity, the physical vigor, the emotional depth of woman, forms also an untranscendable circle, circumscribing with each successive generation the limits of the expansion of the human race.[11]

Her loins articulated the form of all creatures (Figure 11). The untranscendable circle is the ring of matter itself—the mother's ring, the wedding ring, the shape of things to come.

Circle and triangle come together in the later figurines of Baubo who is primarily belly and vulvular V (Figure 12). It was intended that she be funny in order to lighten the labor of a mother who has lost her child.[12] She does not represent fertility —but rather an antique version of "the bearded lady," whose oddity is pronounced by being set apart or exposed to the view of others. One such sanctified bearded lady was called St. Unburdyne. It was to her that women prayed when they wanted to be relieved of the burden of husbands. She probably was a descendant of Aphrodite, who was sculpted with a beard in a statue of Venus Barbata on the island of Cyprus. She had a masculine name there, Aphroditos or Hermaphroditos. Some think the beard belonged to her masculine nature, to a warlike, marriage-repudiating goddess.[13] Others think of it as the pubic "beard" that naturally belongs to women. Baubo, who is related to Aphrodite, belonged more to women than to men. She danced and sang before Demeter, told obscene (filthy or piggy) stories, and gave birth to laughter—specifically "belly laughs."

Exhibitionism on the part of women for other women must have been central to the worship of certain deities whose purview we hardly understand. If women were not "raising their garments" to sympathetically "raise the flax," as happened along the

Danube for instance, what were they doing? If it is not fertility that is sought after in this peculiar way of venerating the goddess, it may be *venery,* the arousing and gratification of desire. In her poem "Belly Dancer," Diane Wakoski describes the dancer who wants to awaken desire in women, most of whom "frown, or look away, or laugh stiffly." She moves like a green silk snake, "awakening ancestors and relatives," confusing the women, exciting the men, who do not realize

> *how I scorn them;*
> *or how I dance for their frightened,*
> *unawakened, sweet*
> *women.*

She dances for the love of Venus. Veneration and venery belong to the same goddess. Venus-Aphrodite asks to be praised with "animal" lovemaking. Cats and other animals lie with exposed parts like the pig-riding Baubo, who comes with legs widespread, carrying a ladder.[14] This ladder-of-the-soul permits the initiate to go back and forth from the desirous mud realm of Baubo (her husband tended pigs) to the transcendent starry heaven of Venus. Women's worship connects the highest with the lowest, the maculate and the immaculate.

I mention cats not only because feline is everywhere regarded as feminine and because their sexual nature is unselfconscious, but because of a custom at Bubastis in the Delta of Egypt, where the cat-headed goddess Pasht was worshiped. Herodotus says that the pilgrims traveled downriver by boat to Bubastis, "men and women together, a great number of each in every boat." But whenever they came to riverside towns they would pull near the bank to allow the women pilgrims to perform before the women gathered on the shore. According to Herodotus, some of the women on the barge made noise and sang, "while some shout mockery of the women of the town; others dance, and others stand up and raising their garments expose their secret parts."[15]

Silly gestures are holy (*selig* in German). Baubo is a sacred imp of feminine licentiousness who is ever ready to oppose "straight-lipped" prudery. As the impulse of unrestrained life she may be constellated by restraint, overseriousness, emotional control, or depression. Consequently, she is the companion of the holy Mother who sits modestly with bowed head. Profanity is Baubo's saving grace. To be *pro fane* is to stand before the temple in the courtyard reserved for women. The path of the devout necessarily leads straight through the women to the inner altar. Reading between the loins (as James Joyce, who invented the "pudendascope," might have said), we are given to understand that profanity is essential to divinity.

"Hatch As Hatch Can" —JAMES JOYCE

Before the wind-borne bird became an attribute of goddesses (gray-eyed Athena with her owl, for example), the Great Mother was represented as all-bird. She bore the egg of creation in her buttocks (Figure 13), which gave her an odd "steatopygous"[16] look. Her face is beaked and neck elongated birdwise. Some of the small sculptures have holes around the head and shoulders for the insertion of feathers. Of all possible bird capacities—flying, seeing at night, molting, nest making, singing, escaping prey— the one most celebrated in these ancient figures is that of egg laying and incubating. Many cultures trace their origins to an egg cosmogony at the beginning of time. A simple story from the Upanishads:

In the beginning this was nonexistent. It became existent. It turned into an egg. The egg lay for the time of a year. The egg broke open.[17]

And then all things came from it: earth and sky, male and female, mist and mountain, silver and gold, rivers and sea. For neolithic man it may have been primarily a source of food that was sought

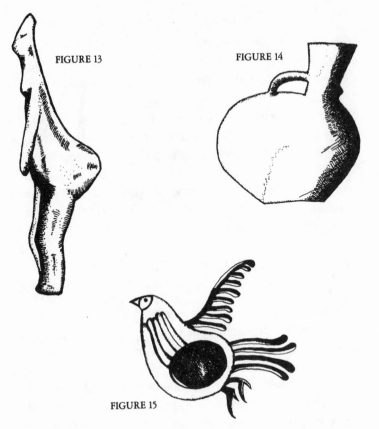

FIGURE 13

FIGURE 14

FIGURE 15

FIGURE 16 A

FIGURE 16 B

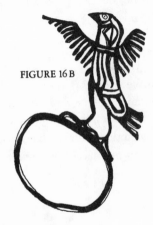

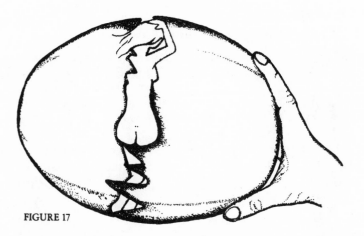

FIGURE 17

in making these representations, but the vessels modeled in egg-containing shapes suggest other ritual uses (Figure 14).

Now the white chick crawls out of the egg, we are as fresh-baked pots.

This is what people say when they have been "reborn" in rites of initiation.[18] Initiation as a feminine mystery implies submission to a natural process of transformation that is analogous to the "work" of a brood hen, whose warmth brings embryonic life out of an egg into the world. This ancient metaphor moved the hand that fashioned large and small pots in egg and womb shapes. Woman as vessel embodies this womb magic, and as bird vessel she performs the task of engendering matter. This means she is capable of giving birth to herself (matter = mother, or the primary matrix). Long before Plato's dinnertime discussion of the problem of which came first, the chicken or the egg, the great bird mothers were acting out the riddle.

The egg is in every respect the *arche genesis*. It comprises all parts of the material world: . . . the male and female potency of nature, the stream of becoming and that of passing away, the germ of all tellurian [earthly] organisms, of the higher and lower creation, and the whole world of gods who, of material origin like the entire tellurian world, have one and the same mother as men, animals and plants—namely, the dark egg.[19]

Bachofen is saying here that the darkness is our mother. A dark egg (Figure 15) would be one seen from the inside. Usually we think of eggs as white and golden, regular sunbursts of brightness. But, seen from the inside, an unhatched egg would be a lightless place where there would be no possibility of seeing with outward-looking eyes. Perhaps this is another reason why the egg symbolizes a phase of initiation—it is the dark before dawn. In rites of incubation darkness and dream sleep were the source of healing. Initiates who had been through a ritual descent into darkness as part of their instruction in mystery religions would, upon emerging, say: "I have seen the light." Closer to our own time and tradition in the West, baptism was depicted by an eleventh-century ecclesiastical artist as an angel lowering a person into the depths of an egg-shaped vessel. We speak of people being in dark moods or having black days—we don't say, "Today she is in her egg place," but we mean exactly that when we say someone is brooding or has withdrawn into her shell.

Thousands of years ago, the Chinese recognized the spiritual value of incubation. The sign for "Inner Truth" in the *I Ching* is identified with the image of brooding or incubating (Figure 16a, shown with a fragment of a Greek vase, Figure 16b). *Fu* (the character) is wind moving over water and represents the foot of a bird resting on an egg. In the Hebrew account of creation, God's movement over the waters is a brooding that precedes the birth of light and life. Warmth and concentration—like the child's discovery that directing rays of sun through a magnifying glass will start a fire—are the keys to birth transformation. In India this force is called *tapas,* the feminine mood of meditation that releases heat for hatching new life. Marie-Louise von Franz, discussing this process in her book on *Creation Myths,* says, "As soon as the image of the egg comes up it is associated with the idea of concentration: tapas, brooding, and with the birth of intelligence. . . . I have seen the same thing practically in analysis, where the motif of the egg very often appears in a state where one could say that the human being has, for the first time, a chance of reflecting on himself,"[20] where there is the possibility of giving birth to a new realization.

If something is to come of it, the egg must be broken (Figure 17). Open is broken; "there is no breakthrough without breakage.[21] This may be why there is a certain tap-tapping running through *Finnegans Wake* as a constant tip (or clue) to the world's renew-all. In many cultures children play a tapping game with their newfound Easter eggs—by tapping them together to see whose egg gets the most cracks. The best cracked-egg story is the one told by the Brothers Grimm in which the poor peasant woman came home one day to find a changeling (an unappealing fairy child) in place of her own baby. As it is said that one of the ways to get your own child back is to make the strange, ancient changeling laugh, she set about cracking and emptying an egg—and then proceeded to boil water in the two halves. This clever move happened to catch the attention of the changeling, who laughed and said he'd never, in his long life, seen such a thing:

> *Though old I be*
> *As forest tree,*
> *Cooking in an egg-shell never did I see!*

". . . And directly there came in a crowd of elves bringing in the right child; and they laid it near the hearth, and carried the changeling away with them."[22] It is laughter that frees the initiate from the lap of the mother Mnemosyne after the sojourn in the underworld. Perhaps the changeling is a way of representing the departures and returns we make to and from the hearth of self:

Mnemosyne, they named her, the
Mother with the whispering
feathered wings. Memory,
the great speckled bird who broods over the
nest of souls, and her egg,
the dream in which all things are living,
I return to, leaving my self.

I am beside myself with this
thought of the One in the World-Egg,
enclosed, in a shell of murmurings,
rimed round
sound-chamberd child.
—ROBERT DUNCAN, *"Tribal Memories: Passages 1"*

The poet is beside himself: an ecstasy of enclosure in the murmuring Mother. In another place he calls her Gaia—"murther, murmurer, demurrer." There is a certain maturity in demurring, related through the French *demorer* (backing off and lingering) to demure. To be demure is to be mature, ripe, or ready to hatch. The mother egg splits in two, she demurs, she recedes as her offspring advances. The eggborne child breaks out—into loud sound, laughter, mythy-speaking. The two parts of the broken egg are like the primal parents that had to be separated before any new thing could grow between them. In one variation of the broken-egg story, God splits his sides laughing. Six hearty laughs brought the gods and cosmic elements into being. Then he laughed for the seventh time "and while he was laughing he cried, and thus the soul came into being."[23] This divine expression of emotion was a breakthrough for humanity. Through his laughter and tears God bent down and whistled to Earth (Gaia, the demurrer) who opened up and brought forth the first human beings.

Helen's Breasts

> . . . and the wine cup that they wrought,
> called Helen's breast . . .
>
> —H. D.

Greek tradition has it that the first wine cup was modeled on the breast of Helen of Troy. Whereas the symbols of the belly are closed—egg, oven, cave, or pot—the symbols of the breast are generally open: wide-mouthed vessel, cup, bowl, goblet, chalice.

Wondrous things flowed from the accentuated breasts of Mother goddesses: fishes from her nipples, milk, water, and honey. Milk of heaven was called rain and was invoked by the fashioning of breasted vessels (Figure 18). In this one the breasts are set in bands depicting torrents of rain. Similar vessels appeal to the celestial cow to let down her maternal rain. An ancient Assyrian text concerning the infancy of a king might have been intoned to accompany the fashioning of four-breasted receptacles: "Little wast thou, Ashurbanipal, when I delivered thee to the queen of Nineveh; weak wast thou when thou didst sit upon her knees, four teats were set in thy mouth."[24]

Milk and honey require no preparation for eating. These foods, which were abundant in the Promised Land, are pure gifts of nature. Drinking mixtures of milk and honey was an important feature of initiation ceremonies because they are foods of the newborn and represent the neophyte's reliance on the Mother. With the symbol of the milk-giving breast, the mother moves from the sphere of containing to the sphere of nourishing, and the child—although still dependent—is already born and moving slowly toward independence. A Greek story tells that the Milky Way came from the forced independence of a young hero. Zeus laid his child Hercules (conceived of a mortal woman) at the breast of his sleeping wife, Hera. Had she let him suck his fill he

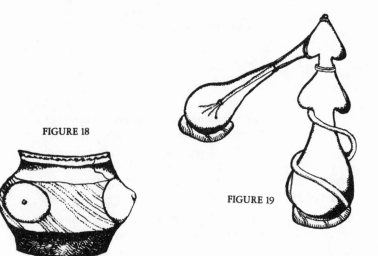

FIGURE 18

FIGURE 19

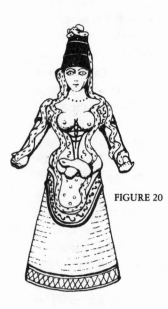

FIGURE 20

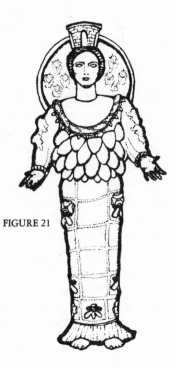

FIGURE 21

would have become immortal. But she awoke, and, seeing what was happening, angrily tore the child from her breast, thus spurting the sky with the milk that became our galaxy.

Spilled milk, like spilled male seed, means death or mortality. Sealing milk within the system (Figure 19) was a goal of alchemy, the science of elements prior to chemistry. Alchemists were concerned with immortality, with transmuting baser elements into higher elements: lead to gold ("our gold is not the vulgar gold"), or matter *(prima materia)* into spirit *(quinta essentia)*. The alchemists' texts show clearly that the work going on in the retort (Figure 19) was imitative of psychic creation. If the liquid flow of condensation and evaporation could be kept within the woman-shaped vessels it would approximate the creative cycle of universal nature.

Sealing in the breasts' vital essence is prerequisite to creation in other cultures as well. Among the Zuñi, breast-shaped pitchers are made by the women, who leave the nipple open to the last. The sealing of it is then "performed with the solemnity of a religious rite, with averted eyes. Unless this ritual were observed, the women would be barren."[25]

Such reverence for the numinous, awe before the ceremonial display of the body of the mother, later degenerated into embarrassment. Breast feeding became a hidden art, an occupation for the masses. During the Renaissance the Virgin became a lady:

The Virgin was moving back on to her pedestal in the fifteenth century, and a century later the distinction between a lady and a peasant in the matter of breast feeding was so unambiguously established that Clouet painted the king's favourite, Diane de Poitiers, naked in her bath, displaying her cool small rosy bosom while in the background a coarse wetnurse with a jolly and vulgar smile gives suck to a child from her swelling breast.[26]

Erotic nature gets split off from the maternal feminine. Mothers are supposed to be spiritual, Madonna-like—pale blue, creamy, and peaceful. Despite the complete giving over of the physical body demanded by childbirth, a mother's sensual experience becomes cloaked under the image of pure and selfless maternity. Before these instinctual strains become distinct, adolescent girls go through a period where spirituality and sensuality intermingle. When a girl's sexual nature awakens she often finds herself equally drawn to babies and to horses—to undomesticated libido. She will dream of bare-breasted women (or of being clothed except for the upper part of the body) at a time when both erotic and maternal instinct are newly emerging.

In Crete, it was adolescents and bulls that gave pleasure to the bare-breasted, welcoming priestess of the Mother (Figure 20). She is wrapped round by fecundating snakes, the masculine fertilizing power held in her sway. Here, at the height of a matriarchal religious era, you can see that the breasts of the mother were prized.

> . . . *her soft breasts*
> *were closed with delicate bark, her hair was leaves,*
> *Her arms were branches, and her speedy feet*
> *Rooted and held, and her head became a tree top,*
> *Everything gone except her grace, her shining.*
> *Apollo loved her still. He placed his hand*
> *Where he had hoped and felt the heart still beating*
> *Under the bark; and he embraced the branches*
> *As if they still were limbs, and kissed the wood,*
> *And the wood shrank from his kisses.*[27]

Not even a god can reach for her breast unless she permits his touch. If pursued unwillingly the girl will turn herself into a tree—beautiful, but remote, cold, and rooted. Many goddesses have their roots in tree soil. Most of them are virgin timber like Daphne (above) and Diana, or Artemis, whose desire is to remain untouched. It is said that a Roman of exceptional ability and distinction fell in love with an oak tree; he kissed it, embraced it, lay under it, poured wine over it.[28] His desire was to "husband" the tree or to marry the (unbending) goddess. Oak trees were especially sacred to Artemis, nocturnal, roving virgin goddess of the hunt, whose territory included all trees, mountains, wild animals, and nursing or childbearing women. Images of the "Huntress-Moon-Queen" were carved into trees surrounding the *temenos,* the holy center of her forest temples. This was probably a custom of marking off as an "attribute" of the goddess an object that once was the goddess herself. Earlier Mothers of animal and vegetable abundance stood immobile as trees: their legs trunks, arms branches, and breasts fruit yielding the milk of immortality.[29] Sometimes Artemis is shown as a date palm heavy with fruits like breasts. The goddess was the first tree of life, everybody's family tree in whom we find "the jets of blood, milk and rain commingling" (Robert Duncan).

In a late and famous Artemesian, a statue made for dedicating a place to the goddess, she appears as a stylized many-breasted tree or pillar (Figure 21). Her neck is hung round with a garland of leaves and acorns, the oak tree fruit that may have come to be her "breasts." And her trunk is flanked with rows of animal attendants: bees, bulls, stags, and lions. The bounty of breasts emphasizes her identification with animal life. Although she would never marry, she was indispensable for motherhood. She encouraged women to be fruitful and multiply and functioned as midwife to women in labor. She stood, like the queen bee who adorns her ankles, as a reminder of the instinctual intricacies of woman's dance of life. Honey was her balm, ambrosia for worshipful attendants. The gold of Artemis was a hidden gold unlike her brother Apollo's glaring gold of the midday sun—but both were known as healers.

Sometimes Artemis was an herb instead of a tree. Then her vital essence was found in the mugwort, an unlovely word that gains in translation: *artemesia* and *parthenium,* meaning "the virgin's plant."[30] The healing "milk of the virgin" in her case was the juice of this medicinal plant, which promoted conception, eased delivery, and encouraged the flow of milk.

The breasts of the goddess swell with the importance of transformation. Neumann calls the axial moments of transformation in the woman-retort "the three blood mysteries":

The transformation mysteries of the woman are primarily blood transformation mysteries that lead her to the experience of her own creativity and produce a numinous impression on the man. This phenomenon has its roots in psychobiological development. The transformation from girl to woman is far more accentuated than the corresponding development from boy to man. Menstruation, the first blood transformation mystery in woman, is in every respect a more important incident than the first emission of sperm in the male. The latter is seldom remembered, while the beginning of menstruation is everywhere rightly regarded as a fateful moment in the life of woman.

Pregnancy is the second blood mystery. According to the primitive view, the embryo is built up from the blood, which, as the cessation of menstruation indicates, does not flow outward in the period of pregnancy. . . .

After childbirth the woman's third blood mystery occurs: the transformation of blood into milk.[31]

A vessel of transformation, filled to the brim with life-sustaining liquid, the Mother offers her breast to the congregation of the faithful:

> *Drink ye of Mother's wine*
> *Drink, drink ye freely*
> *Drink ye of Mother's wine.*
> *It will make you limber,*
> *If it make you reel around*
> *If it make you fall down*
> *If it lay you on the floor*
> *Rise and drink a little more!*
>   *—Shaker song*

Everywoman

Every woman extends backward into her mother and forward into her daughter.

—C.G. JUNG

Crowned with her own creation (Figure 22), the Mother stands, silent image of herself becoming. Both of these figures have their mouths shut (no mouth) and arms crossed as if to say, "Don't ask me a thing, I am because I am." Many primitive sculpted objects, especially vessels, were made without mouths: perhaps because of the essential value of silence in feminine mysteries. *Mysteries* and *mysticism* share a common root related to things hidden, *myo,* meaning eyes and mouth shut. When a secret is shared with someone in the company of others, one puts a finger over one's mouth to imply this keeping silent. We say "my lips are sealed." But there is another kind of silence that is part of encountering the holy. When in the presence of something overwhelming one is silenced by the magnitude of the experience. It is mysterious because it is ineffable—there are simply no words to explain. Experience that cannot be articulated is generally undervalued in a world ignorant of the mysteries. Such a world creates psychic havoc for people whose mode of existence is feminine, for people who have given the greater part of their lives to woman's work—bearing children, caring for the living, and tending the dying. They are made to question their intrinsic worth because they haven't any words to convey the essence of primary experience. This small double statue stands almost defiant in the face of such a threat. She elevates her sense of self symbolically in the silent raising up of the child borne proudly on her head.

The child is father of the man. Or the child is mother of the woman. There is a tendency for a thing to become its opposite, a pendulum-swinging psychic law of energy called *enantiodromia:*

FIGURE 22

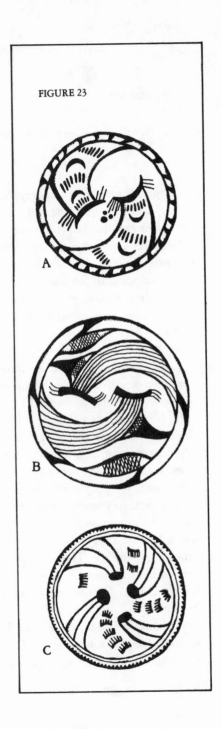

FIGURE 23

FIGURE 24

FIGURE 25

"Every psychological extreme secretly contains its own opposite or stands in some sort of intimate and essential relation to it. Indeed it is from this tension that it derives its peculiar dynamism. There is no hallowed custom that cannot on occasion turn into its opposite, and the more extreme a position is, the more easily may we expect an enantiodromia, a conversion of something into its opposite."[32] Jung cites the way God turns into the Devil in fairy tales, or the way a holy rite can become an orgy. Enantiodromia functions in personal psychology as well, where an attitude is too extreme: it is not uncommon for someone who lauds the use of drugs and promiscuous sexuality, for example, suddenly to be converted to a fundamentalist, moralistic, charismatic religion. Or, in a dream, for a child's loving mother to become a wicked witch. Or for the ferocious bear to turn into a young and handsome prince. But more obvious than any of these is the example of the moon: every opposed fact of the feminine is engaged in the moon's nighttime coursing across the sky. Constantly in movement, even when apparently standing slender and still, the moon daughter is moving toward becoming her mother just as the full mother moves toward the grandmother form and then down into darkness to be reborn. The growing and the diminishing, the wax and wane, provide the energy behind the movement.

The body of a doe, sacred moon animal, is stylized to a literal point in these bowls designed to show movement (Figure 23). Deer are transformed first into crescents and then as they whirl faster and faster around the center they seem to become cosmic points (comets?) trailing tails. An entire series of these bowls gives the impression of an accelerating yin-yang symbol. If one could hear the sound they make it would be the Ojibwa song of the moon deer:

(the deer's song)
my shining horns

Horns of the deer shine and drop off and spring up like horns of the moon. Hindus say that the moon "runs beautifully" and call it Mṛgāṅka: Marked-like-a-Deer. Spinning, shining (shouting) crescents cradle the full moon, rolling it over onto its other side. Curt Sachs describes a lunar round dance from middle Aryola:

The dancers join hands and whirl around in a circle; sometimes they take dainty steps towards the dancer opposite . . . and sometimes they sink to their knees, bend to right and left, and lean backwards. Then after a pause of a few seconds, they let out a deafening roar and rush to the center, throwing their arms high in the air and standing on their tiptoes. The entire group is charged with the highest ecstasy; then as though slowly tiring, as a result of their over-exertion, they sink to the ground with their eyes closed and touch the earth with their foreheads.[33]

In all this he sees common motifs of the moon dance: circling, facing one another, forming crescents by bending, rising suddenly with a shout, and sinking down.

Moon movement governs—or "steers the dancing steps"—of the feminine. Most moon dances consist of these contracting and expanding concentric circles, turning, passing into each other, sinking to the earth and rising. Understanding the mother and daughter as concentric circles, these movements describe the dynamic peculiar to the separation and reunion of Demeter and Persephone (Figure 24). (See Chapter 4.) Together with Hekate (Figure 25), who is the dark power of the moon, they form a whole whose parts are the various phases. The frieze of the poppy-bearing goddesses arrests them eternally in the moment of passing into each other. Sometimes the point of this passage is thought of as the Maiden Well, where Demeter sat grieving, awaiting "the flowering from the depths."[34] We know that dancers trod a circle around the well site at Eleusis, where the religious drama of mother and maid was performed. It was such a well that the Trittai, the "threefold maidens," dancing virgin daughters of an old king, overlooked and fell into. Earth took pity on them and sent forth a lovely threefold flower, thus preserving their connection with the Underworld but giving them back to Earth and Sky. Other names for these same maidens are the "brilliant," the "invoked," the "tumultuous"—and these, of course, are lunar associations. Women all over the world have broken their mystery silence tumultuously to greet the arriving moon. It is the *heuresis,* the finding-again, the reunion with a lost part of the self.

Hekate, Daughter of Night—the dark of the moon who dwelt in caves, walked the highways, stood threefold at the crossroads, and made love on the vast seas—was the force that moved the moon. Like gravity or the tide pull she drew the waning crescent down into herself and enabled the new moon to relight the black sky. She is the one who brought Demeter and Persephone together after their long separation. Her underworld realm is the one that sends up the poppy—flower of multiple seed, sleep, and forgetfulness. Again we encounter the motif of incubation—of going down into the dark of unconscious sleep—as a necessary step in the transformation cycle of maidens and mothers. Drugs and intoxicants, religiously and consciously used, were the Great Mother's way of inducing the required sleep-in-season. Once the source is forgotten and the narcotic is misused, the beauty of the poppy fades into blackness and stupor. Hekate becomes a witch whose power is magic rather than realization, and the passing of the phases or psychological states into each other is accomplished —if at all—by the use of too many "aids" (seeds, brew, grass, chemical), rendering the experience inaccessible and antipodal to consciousness. Hekate can poison as well as intoxicate, turn ecstasy into madness, and cause death where incubation—or a short journey—was intended.

One face of the Mother Goddess is not pleasant to gaze upon. In fact, it means certain extinction if you try. An Egyptian manuscript from 2000 B.C. says, "We must die because we have known them."[35] It is never wise in myths and fairy tales to look certain women, death, or gods in the face because their unmediated power is too great—like the sun in eclipse. The only way to see it without being blinded is to turn your back to it and look at the image it casts in reflections on leaves and trees. When approaching the terrible snake-haired Gorgon, the hero always has to look at her backward in a mirror or else be turned to stone. The Greek Mother of madness and intoxication, the maiden Semele, who gave birth to Dionysos, had asked to see her mysterious god-lover in his true form. He reluctantly visited her with the magnificent and terrible force of lightning, a fiery embrace that consumed the woman and brought forth the child.

Semele and her three sisters may have a primitive connection to the moon that has been lost. Each of them gave birth to a son who suffered either madness or dismemberment: Autonoë's son, the hunter Actaeon, was torn to pieces by his own hounds (hell-hounds of Hekate) for gazing upon the naked goddess (the lunar Diana-Artemis); Agave, transformed into a maenad (moon-mad maiden), unknowingly tore apart her own son, Pentheus, for daring to look upon the women's secret Dionysian rites (he suffered the same fate as Dionysos); Ino's son, Melikertes, was driven by madness (his mother) into the sea. Madness is everywhere associated with the moon. And some cultures describe the moon's fate as dismemberment: every month its bony body is torn limb from limb and then reassembled in the underworld darkness.

Assembling and disassembling, remembering and dismembering, tearing apart and putting back together again the body of our knowing: the moon, like the poppy flower, requires that your imagination enter into it in order to avoid the harm of possession. One has to give something to the death-dealing Mother, whose crown is adorned with the treacherous red-skirted flower—acknowledge her presence, leave a candle at the crossroads, admit your own shadow side to view. If you give a part of yourself to lunacy, she will permit you to pass to and from the realm of the moon's dark phase. Otherwise she will detain you. Stupor and blackness will possess you.

Often, when nearing the goal of rebirth of some kind, sleep will overtake the hero/heroine. We have seen that when Psyche has made her descent to hell (place of the moon's underworld residence) to meet the Queen and receive the sealed casket of beauty she cannot resist opening it and immediately falls into a profound slumber—just yards from the place where Eros lies waiting. When Sir Gawain sought the Holy Grail he fell asleep before asking the king the proper question, leaving his final task only half completed. And when Dorothy, in a more recent version of the ancient pattern, falls asleep in the witch's poppy-strewn field she is within sight of the Emerald City. The poppy-strewn field is a place of conversion. The adventurer turns to stone. The questing Psyche withdraws into a cocoon. Things turn into their opposites. Energy is converted. In the Mother's realm even time can reverse. There are no logical procedures but rather meaningful changes. Hekate looks backward and forward even as she watches you approach. Her threefold vision takes in where you have been, where you are at present, and where you are going.[36] The periods of sleep and darkness and silence that punctuate the journey are her contributions to the cadence of becoming.

4
Mothers and Daughters

In an old *National Geographic* there is a picture of Mary Leakey on her hands and knees in the Olduvai Gorge region of Africa looking for signs of primitive life by working the parched earth with a toothbrush. I have carried this picture of patience around with me for a long time and only thought of it twice in recent years: the first time was when a young woman told me her dream of being led along a path by an older woman who was showing her how to rake the sandy soil into tiny furrows. The second time was when I read the words of a medieval alchemist who said that psychic earth can only absorb a certain amount unless it has been worked: raked, rended, or raped. Mary Leakey's way was the most gentle raking—the earth yields different secrets to the field worker's brush than to the spade.

The surface I am interested in brushing—the field I want to work—is the Nysaean (as in Dionysian—where the god was born) field where the goddess Persephone played. This is essentially the field of the feminine, of the mother and daughter, first given attention by a poet in an ancient hymn.

One of the tasks of the poet—like the archaeologist or therapist —is a kind of excavation of the unknown. Martin Heidegger said it this way: that he was a poet in order "to attend, singing, to the trace of fugitive gods." Along with the gods that have gone into hiding is our animal life, perhaps? some instinct that has fled for safety? part of our personal and collective history that eludes us? and leaves only traces. . . .

Several important researchers in the field of the feminine left traces that are "telling" when read together. The editor of Irene de Castillejo's book *Knowing Woman* writes, at the end of the chapter "Woman as Mediator":

This chapter has been concerned with a woman's roles in her relationship with men. But the author wanted to add a further section about relationships between women, which she felt to be of great importance, and different in kind. She was pondering these additional pages during the last days of her life, but did not write her thoughts down.

And the editor of Erich Neumann's work on *The Child* picks up after the book ends in an unfinished sentence, saying:

The author did not live to complete the present work. It ends in the middle of the section concerning the relation between the self [and] the father archetype . . . and it does not reach the stage of development at which the girl child requires separate treatment.

And Rilke, prophesying an evolution or unfolding that he didn't live to see, said:

Some day there will be girls and women whose name will no longer signify merely an opposite of the masculine, but something in itself, something that makes one think, not of any complement and limit, but only of life and existence: the feminine human being.[1]

There is a void felt these days by women—and men—who suspect that their feminine nature, like Persephone, has gone to hell. Wherever there is such a void, such a gap or wound agape, healing must be sought in the blood of the wound itself. It is another of the old alchemical truths that "no solution should be made except in its own blood." (The cure of an emotional wound is in the wound itself.) So the female void cannot be cured by conjunction with the male, but rather by an internal conjunction, by an integration of its own parts, by a remembering or a putting back together of the mother-daughter body.

It helped me to visualize the symbol of the Tao, to adapt it this way; we're looking at the relationship between the parts on one side, and *not* the conjunction of external opposites:

FIGURE 26

My reason for going back to Greek and pre-Greek literature for the poet's recounting of the myth of Demeter and Persephone is that our sense of ourselves has its roots in that age. In the history of human consciousness, Father culture was replacing Mother culture when Hesiod and Homer were writing, which means, among other things, that in the history of sexual posture women were rarely on top anymore. The important point is that this psychological age is not new.

Wherever the domination of masculine values begins, as, for example, with the reigns of Yahweh and Zeus, complications of life for the feminine are taken up into the myths of the people. The main reason, then, for going back to those shepherd poets, who (according to Hesiod) had stories blown into their ears through reeds by wind-borne maidens, is that the plots and solutions of their tales *prefigure* the plight of the feminine in a patriarchate. Myths (to repeat) are not false stories but are complex and essential psychic facts. They arise out of the sleep cycle of a culture the way a dream comes up in the sleep of an individual.

This tale of the Mother Goddess and her daughter has to do with sleep, especially the sleep-in-season of embryonic life. Reading (and paraphrasing) now from the *Homeric Hymn to Demeter* (seventh century B.C.)[2]:

I begin to sing of rich-haired Demeter, awful goddess—of her and her trim-ankled daughter whom Aidoneus (Hades) rapt away, given to him by all-seeing Zeus the loud-thunderer.

Apart from Demeter, lady of the golden sword and glorious fruits, she was playing with the deep-bosomed daughters of Oceanus and gathering flowers over a soft meadow, roses and crocuses and beautiful violets, irises also and hyacinths and the narcissus, which Earth made to grow at the will of Zeus and to please the Host of Many, to be a snare for the bloomlike girl—a marvellous, radiant flower. It was a thing of awe whether for deathless gods or mortal men to see: from its root grew a hundred blooms and it smelled most sweetly, so that all wide heaven above and the whole earth and the sea's salt swell laughed for joy. And the girl was amazed and reached out with both hands to take the lovely toy; but the wide-pathed earth yawned there in the plain of Nysa, and the lord, Host of Many, with his immortal horses sprang out upon her—the Son of Cronos, He who has many names.

He caught her up reluctant on his golden car and bare her away lamenting. Then she cried out shrilly with her voice, calling upon her father, the Son of Cronos, who is most high and excellent. But no one, either of the deathless gods or of mortal men, heard her voice, nor yet the olive-trees bearing rich fruit: only tender-hearted Hecate, bright-coiffed, the daughter of Persaeus, heard the girl from her cave, and the lord Helios, Hyperion's bright son, as she cried to her father, the Son of Cronos. But he was sitting aloof, apart from the gods, in his temple where many pray, and receiving sweet offerings from mortal men. So he, that Son of Cronos, of many names, who is Ruler of Many and Host of Many, was bearing her away by leave of Zeus on his immortal chariot—his own brother's child and all unwilling.

And so long as she, the goddess, yet beheld earth and starry heaven and the strong-flowing sea where fishes shoal, and the rays of the sun, and still hoped to see her dear mother and the tribes of the eternal gods, so long hope calmed her great heart for all her trouble . . . and the heights of the mountains and the depths of the sea rang with her immortal voice: and her queenly mother heard her.

Bitter pain seized her heart, and she rent the covering upon her divine hair with her dear hands: her dark cloak she cast down from both her shoulders and sped, like the wild-bird, over the firm land and yielding sea, seeking her child. But no one would tell her the truth, neither god nor mortal man; and of the birds of omen none came with true news for her. Then for nine days queenly Deo wandered over the earth with flaming torches in her hands, so grieved that she never tasted ambrosia and the sweet draught of nectar, nor sprinkled her body with water. But when the tenth enlightening dawn had come, Hecate, with a torch in her hands, met her, and spoke to her and told her news:

"Queenly Demeter, bringer of seasons and giver of good gifts, what god of heaven or what mortal man has rapt away Persephone and pierced with sorrow your dear heart? For I heard her voice, yet saw not with my eyes who it was. But I tell you truly and shortly all I know."

Then the two torch-bearing goddesses fled to Helios, the sun, "who is watchman of both gods and men," and inquired of him: what happened to Persephone? He asked queenly Demeter to cease her loud lament, thinking Hades no unfitting husband for her daughter.

But grief yet more terrible and savage came into the heart of Demeter, and thereafter she was so angered with the dark-clouded Son of Cronos that she avoided the gathering of the gods and high Olympus, and went to the towns and rich fields of men, disfiguring her form a long while. And no one of men or deep-bosomed women knew her when they saw her, until she came to the house of wise Celeus who then was lord of fragrant Eleusis. Vexed in her dear heart, she sat near the wayside by the Maiden Well, from which the women of the place were used to draw water, in a shady place over which grew an olive shrub. And she was like an ancient woman who is cut off from childbearing and the gifts of garland-loving Aphrodite, like the nurses of king's children who deal justice, or like the housekeepers in their echoing halls. There the daughters of Celeus, son of Eleusis, saw her, as they were coming for easy-drawn water, to carry it in pitchers of bronze to their dear father's house: four were they and like goddesses in the flower of their girlhood, Callidice and Cleisdice and lovely Demo and Callithoë who was the eldest of them all. They knew her not,—for the gods are not easily discerned by mortals—, but standing near by her spoke winged words:

"Old mother, whence and who are you of folk born long ago? Why are you gone away from the city and do not draw near the houses? For there in the shady halls are women of just such age as you, and others younger; and they would welcome you both by word and by deed."

Then she tells them her made-up story about how she had been brought there unwillingly by pirates "over the sea's wide back." She fled secretly from them and rested only here and would welcome work in the master's house.

The maidens then tell her about their estate and invite her home to tend their mother's only son, recently born.

The goddess walked to the threshold: and her head reached the roof and she filled the doorway with a heavenly radiance. Then awe and reverence and pale fear took hold of Metaneira, and she bade her be seated. But Demeter, bringer of seasons and giver of perfect gifts, would not sit upon the bright couch, but stayed silent with lovely eyes cast down until careful Iambe placed a jointed seat for her and threw over it a silvery fleece. Then she sat down and held her veil in her hands before her face. A long time she sat upon the stool without speaking because of her sorrow, and greeted no one by word or by sign, but rested, never smiling, and tasting neither food nor drink, because she pined with longing for her deep-bosomed daughter, until careful Iambe —who pleased her moods in aftertime also—moved the holy lady with many a quip and jest to smile and laugh and cheer her heart. Then Metaneira filled a cup with sweet wine and offered it to her; but she refused it, for she said it was not lawful for her to drink red wine, but bade them mix meal and water with soft mint and give her to drink. And Metaneira mixed the draught and gave it to the goddess as she bade.[3] So the great queen Deo received it to observe the sacrament.

She is then introduced as nurse to the child, Demophoön, whom she proceeds to anoint with ambrosia by day and place in a fire by night—in order to make him like the deathless gods.

But well-girded Metaneira in her heedlessness spied on the

goddess. She cried out "and smote her two hips," fearful for her son, thus bringing the process to a disastrous and abrupt close. Demeter rose and spoke in her anger:

"Witless are you mortals and dull to foresee your lot, whether of good or evil, that comes upon you. For now in your heedlessness you have wrought folly past healing: for—be witness the oath of the gods, the relentless water of Styx—I would have made your dear son deathless and unaging all his days and would have bestowed on him everlasting honour, but now he can in no way escape death and the fates. Yet shall unfailing honour always rest upon him, because he lay upon my knees and slept in my arms. But, as the years move round and when he is in his prime, the sons of the Eleusinians shall ever wage war and dread strife with one another continually. Lo! I am that Demeter who has share of honour and is the greatest help and cause of joy to the undying gods and mortal men. But now, let all the people build me a great temple and an altar below it and beneath the city and its sheer wall upon a rising hillock above Callichorus. And I myself will teach my rites, that hereafter you may reverently perform them and so win the favour of my heart."

When she had so said, the goddess changed her stature and her looks, thrusting old age away from her: beauty spread round about her and a lovely fragrance was wafted from her sweet-smelling robes, and from the divine body of the goddess a light shone afar, while golden tresses spread down over her shoulders, so that the strong house was filled with brightness as with lightning. And so she went out from the palace.

The people sought to appease the glorious goddess by building her temple. . . .

But golden-haired Demeter sat there apart from all the blessed gods and stayed, wasting with yearning for her deep-bosomed daughter. Then she caused a most dreadful and cruel year for mankind over the all-nourishing earth: the ground would not make the seed sprout, for rich-crowned Demeter kept it hid. In the fields the oxen drew many a curved plough in vain, and much white barley was cast upon the land without avail. So she would have destroyed the whole race of man with cruel famine and have robbed them who dwell on Olympus of their glorious right of gifts and sacrifices, had not Zeus perceived and marked this in his heart.

After imploring her, in vain, to change her course, Zeus sent Hermes to the House of Hades to retrieve the maiden. Hades said to her:

"Go now, Persephone, to your dark-robed mother, go, and feel kindly in your heart towards me: be not so exceedingly cast down; for I shall be no unfitting husband for you among the deathless gods, that am own brother to father Zeus. And while you are here, you shall rule all that lives and moves and shall have the greatest rights among the deathless gods: those who defraud you and do not appease your power with offerings, reverently performing rites and paying fit gifts, shall be punished for evermore."

When he said this, wise Persephone was filled with joy and hastily sprang up for gladness. But he on his part secretly gave her sweet pomegranate seed to eat, taking care for himself that she might not remain continually with grave, dark-robed Demeter.

Persephone then flies to her mother, who asks her to relate all the details of her stay below. With some foreboding she asks, "My child, tell me, surely you have not tasted any food while you were below?" Persephone confesses that she has in fact eaten of Hades's seed, which means that Demeter will have to abandon her daughter to the mist and gloom of the underworld "for a third part of the circling year." Nonetheless, the goddess rejoices and "straightaway" makes the fruit to spring up so the whole earth is laden with leaves and flowers. She hides white grain in the furrows of the earth and then when springtime waned, the rich land was waving long ears of corn and in other places sheaves of grain were bound.

At the *Hymn*'s conclusion, Demeter goes to the leaders of the people to show them the conduct of her rites and to teach them her mysteries as she had promised. And this is the story of the beginning of the Eleusinian mystery rites that occupied a large part of the Western world for some two thousand years, only to be replaced by the worship of Mithras and then of Christ. (Eleusis, which is a suburb of Athens, means "arrival." It was said of initiates that they had arrived.) Central to the mysteries celebrated at Eleusis is the re-enactment of the mother's losing and finding of her daughter, Persephone, the Primordial Maiden, called the Kore.

The story gets its initial impetus from the heat and speed of the rape. Kore is dancing with her friends in the flowering fields. Usually she is pictured with Athena and Artemis, two other virgin goddesses, who were self-contained and perhaps rather taken with their own strength and beauty. Persephone especially became enraptured by an incredible exaggeration of beauty in the one-hundred-blossomed narcissus. As she reached out for it, the earth yawned and the Dark God of the Underworld rapt her away.

In a similar account from the Indonesian island of Ceram,[4] the maiden Rabie, who was wooed by the sun man, ran away from the village and stopped to rest on the roots of a tree, which then began to sink into the ground. She cried out to her people. They desperately tried to dig her out, but the roots only sank deeper until she disappeared. Before she was underground, she called to her mother to kill a pig and hold a three-day feast and on the last day to look for a new light in the sky. On the third day they all looked up and for the first time the full moon rose in the east.

When the islanders re-enact this story, the maiden stands near a pit in the center of a spiral of arm-linked men and women who "*dance* her into the ground." They then stamp the earth over her like a seed, the burial before the birth. She rises as the full moon or, as at Eleusis, the full ear of corn.

The rhythm of the dance separates the mother and the maiden. Rape, in Gabriel Marcel's words, is "substituting your rhythm for the rhythm of another." It is a question of power and pulse. A girl child grows up in accord with the rhythm of the mother; the blood bond of pregnancy has a hold on the girl, who is made in the image of her mother. A boy's journey is underscored by a different longing and a different adventure. His sense of being "other" makes separation from the mother more plausible. He may come back to her in every woman he meets. But a girl meets her mother in herself and in her reflections.

The Seduction

Seduction is a kind of education. When you are educated, or educed, you are led *out*. When you are seduced, you are led *aside*. A girl's first seduction is when the separation from her mother begins. The house of her fantasies is altered when Persephone finds herself in the cold and gloom of Hades's place—torn from the field of Demeter's warm and fertile embrace. The event of first enrapturement seduces one out of childhood. One is snatched or seized by a totally unfamiliar attitude, caught against one's will, it seems, by the recognition of something beyond mother. The Great Mother, the Mother of Mothers, is as jealous as she is all-embracing. Her emotions are extravagant and unrefined. She, like the cat, is as likely to eat her own offspring in the face of danger as she is to attack and kill the threatening thing itself. In this aspect, she is as anxious to keep her daughter from men as she is to keep her from other women.

Colette, in *Sido,* the book about her mother, tells a story of the beginnings of that separation:

Once when my mother and Adrienne were suckling their infants, a daughter and son respectively, they changed babes for fun. So occasionally Adrienne would laughingly challenge me with a: "You whom I once fed with my own milk!" At that I would blush so madly that my mother frowned and scanned my face to find out what could have made me so red. How was I to conceal from that clear gaze of hers, blade-grey and threatening, the image that tormented me, of Adrienne's swarthy breast and its hard, purple knob?

As I wandered about Adrienne's house, forgotten among the tottering piles of books, among the countless volumes of an old medical library that smelt like a cellar, among giant shells and half-dried medicinal herbs, bowls of cats' food gone sour, the dog Perdreau, and the black tom-cat with the white mask who was called Colette and ate plain chocolate, I would start at the sound of a call that came over the rose-fettered yews and the emaciated thuyas paralyzed by the python coils of a wistaria. My mother had suddenly appeared at a window in our house, as though to give the alarm for fire or burglars, and was calling my name. What a strange thing is the sense of guilt in a blameless child! I rushed home at once, putting on a guileless expression and the breathlessness of one taken by surprise.

"All this time at Adrienne's?"

That was all she said, but what a tone of voice! Sido's acute perception and jealousy on the one hand, and my excessive confusion on the other, led, as I grew older, to a cooling of the friendship between the two women. They never had any altercation, and no explanation ever took place between my mother and me. What was there for us to explain? Adrienne was careful never to entice me or detain me. One can be captivated without love. And I was already ten or eleven years old. It took me a very long time to associate a disturbing memory, a certain warmth in the heart, and the enchanted transformation of a person and her dwelling, with the idea of a first seduction.

Sido and my childhood were both, and because of each other, happy at the centre of that imaginary star whose eight points bear the names of the cardinal and collateral points of the compass. My twelfth year saw the beginning of misfortune, of departures and separations.[5]

This captivation, being "taken" by another ("you can be taken without love")—seduced, raped, or enraptured—opens a door that was never there before, into a limitless and often terrifying basement, where gravity of a kind defined by Chesterton is suspended. He calls the law of gravitation "that mad quickening rush by which all earth's creatures fly back to her heart when released."

But Persephone does not fly back to the mother—yet. The

separation has occurred and Demeter begins her grievous wandering. It is a barren time for the mother when she can no longer delight in her own creation. The goddess's weary depression is a paradigm of psychological depression. Her sadness is punctuated by three stopping places at Eleusis. One is the *omphalos,* or navel—a belly button mound of earth at the spot where Persephone disappeared. This so-called world navel is what the sibyls used to sit on when the voices of gods would speak through them (see Chapter 8). It is a point where two worlds meet and where one can be cut off—literally, the cord has been cut and the daughter is gone.

Another spot where Demeter, in her ugly guise, rests "vexed in her dear heart" is at the Maiden's Well. This well, where the girls of Eleusis came to draw water, was also called the "well of flowers" (the flowering from the depths took place here). It is still visible at Eleusis today—and the excavators could see circles traced in the stone pavement around the well where initiates danced during the Mystery Rites.

The third spot where Demeter stops is called the *agelastos petra,* the Laughless Rock. Her sorrow halts nature in its path; nothing grows, life is dead. She has hardened her heart. A pallor has come over her. A dark cloak covers her shining hair. Nothing of her fruitfulness is revealed, for her creativity (represented by the maiden) has gone into hiding. In dreams, the maiden often represents the potential self, the *becoming* part of the person, a possibility that is not yet real. It is like being pregnant in a dream: something has been conceived—a new attitude or idea, the seeds of a poem, an unknown strength, the courage to resist or create or die.

Demeter, in her wanderings, is described as past the age of childbearing. She takes on a different aspect of the Mother here by offering herself as nurse. Nursing is impersonal compared to mothering. A "mothering" attitude expects something—growth, a personal fate to emerge, specialness. Caring and hoping flow together. There is an obsession with how things will turn out. For a mother, the events around a child are matters of life and death. (Metaneira, seeing from her personal perspective, screamed when she saw Demeter putting Demophoön in the fire.) A nursing attitude, on the other hand, is less personally related. A nurse nourishes the child that is sick or helpless—it is not her child, so her history is not carried forward into the child, its life and death are not hers, her love for it is not complicated by a mother's fears and desires.[6] A nursing attitude accepts a child as it is, in its weaknesses, and does not spiderlike spin fantasies around it that can immobilize or make hazy the vision of the child.

This "distance" characteristic of the nurse type is what enables grandparents to relate to grandchildren in a freer-seeming and more-accepting way than with their own children. Demeter disguises herself as a grandmother. By her mourning, she puts quite a distance between herself and her daughter. Such distance—seeming so out of touch with her own life force—is one of the things that characterizes a depression. It may be that one needs the nurse attitude more than the mother attitude when suffering depression—you need to be left alone and paradoxically cared for as you are, rather than being personally hovered over and reminded that you are not being your old self.

Before any period of creative awakening, there is, as we have seen, an incubation period that feels gray, motionless, and utterly without passion. There is no horizon, no promise of its ending. Marie-Louise von Franz describes this state of being:

Before the birth of the hero or heroine, there is often a long period of sterility; and then the child is born supernaturally. Put into psychological language, we know that before a time of particular activity in the unconscious, there is a tendency toward a long period of complete sterility. It is, for instance, a normal condition in the creative personality that before some new piece of work in art, or a scientific idea, etc., people usually pass through a period of listlessness and depression and waiting; life is stale. If you analyze such people you see that the energy is meanwhile accumulating in the unconscious, evidenced in a feeling of depression and emptiness.

I remember a time when I felt desperate in this way. Then I dreamt that I was looking at a big railway station where shunting was going on, and new trains were being composed. The dream showed that the libido in the unconscious was readjusting itself; energy and instinctive patterns were rearranging. Before the outburst of a psychotic interval, there is also such a time when everything becomes stale. But then comes the explosion. Libido has been accumulating in the unconscious and comes out in a destructive explosion.

So these periods of sterility mean that something specific is in preparation in the unconscious.[7]

The three resting places of the goddess—the *omphalos* (navel), the Maiden Well, and the Laughless Rock—are all places where underworld and upperworld intersect. Each seat she sinks down onto in her desperation is a seething seat under which something is cooking or welling up. Consciousness has sunk so low that she is literally perched on the edge of the unconscious. It is the time "when woman does not know she is also who hunts for herself"; in the poet's words it is the time

> *(when Demeter has to be looked for . . .*
>
> *Oh, Woman:*
>
> *. . . That you may have cause again*
> *to seek yourself, to go out among flowers crying*
> *"Kore! Kore!," knowing*
>
> *the king of Hell*
> *also has you*
> —CHARLES OLSON, *"I Believe in You . . ."*

When the earth yawned and the girl sank down it happened that a herd of pigs fell in the chasm too. The pig, which is sacred to Demeter, was sacrificed for her in many agrarian fertility rites.

At the Thesmophoria, the women's festival held near Eleusis, three women buried a pig; later, its remains were uncovered and placed on the altar with grain and scattered on the field with seed corn.

Compost, corruption, and the fruitful decay—these are in the province of the feminine. "This is the region that feeds forth souls," the midden heap where god is hidden:

> *shards,*
> *scraps of leftover food, rottings,*
> *the Dump*
> *where we read history, larvae of all dead things,*
> *mixd seeds, waste, off-castings, despised*
> *treasure, vegetable putrefactions*
> *: from this adultery committed,*
>
> *the plant that provides, Corn*
> *that at Eleusis Kore brought*
> *out of Hell, health manifest.*
> —ROBERT DUNCAN, *"Nor Is the Past Pure"*

A necessary corruption. Corruption, from rupture, means to break entirely—a decomposition of matter, a falling apart of the mother-daughter body. The mother is broken in spirit, the daughter is broken in body—or impregnated.

Pigs were Demeter's fertility. Gravid sows were buried in the mystery pits. They were called the uterine animals of land, close to motherhood. (Dolphins were called pigs of the sea, the uterine animals of water. Poseidon was husband of Demeter, father of Persephone, in some accounts.) "Pig" in Greek and Latin was also "cunt" and it was sacred; pigs were not to be eaten during the rites. But pork becomes unclean and pigs become "disgusting" when the mother functions of the feminine, and the goddess of rotting and rutting and springing-to-life, are no longer revered. (As in the Christian tradition where we find, in one of the Apocryphal gospels, that Christ has come to destroy the works of woman: lust, birth, decay, and death.)

In the Mother realm, where the blackness of desire is not feared, where (with the moonstruck poet Levertov) "we rock and grunt, grunt and shine," the goddesses are all great, white, round maternal sows (Ishtar, Isis, Demeter, etc.). They are frequently depicted ritually exposing their genitals—in Crete, Babylon, Delphi—and in Egypt the goddess's companion Baubo comes riding spread-legged and bareback on a pig. According to an Orphic variant of the story, Iambe, the hearty serving maid who entertained Demeter at the house in Eleusis, is called Baubo (Figure 11), and her husband was the man tending the herd of pigs that fell into the chasm.

After the initiates at Eleusis bathed themselves and their sacrificial pigs in the sea near Athens, they formed a sorrowful procession along the Sacred Road to Eleusis. They—like the goddess—were heavy-hearted, searching for the lost maiden. When they came to the wide river separating them from the beginning of the sacred grounds, they had to cross over the Bridge of Jests, where they were entertained (as Demeter had been) by Baubo's suggestive dances, obscene gestures, and jokes. Baubo appeared before Demeter at the Laughless Rock —and, lifting her skirts, lifted Demeter's spirits. The modesty, the careful self-regulation, necessary in the search for our missing parts, is balanced by extreme immodesty. Likewise, sterility is countered by raucous sexuality.

To understand this little dancing "serving girl" we need to construct an archetypal history of the degenerate. The image of the dirty old woman was boisterously taken on by ancient women when celebrating the mystery rites in private. Degeneration implies a reversal—the power of profanation is in the swing from the sacred to its opposite. The dancing girl's service is to move the myth on, to assist in the swing from earth's degeneration to her regeneration.

The Ascent

Continuing on the road. The initiates enter the precinct of Eleusis, where the sacred drama, including the birth of the holy child, is enacted. A great light from a fire could be seen as far away as Athens—but otherwise we do not know exactly what they saw, because the Mystery was ineffable, unspeakable. We do know, though, from various accounts, that the fruit of the initiation was the vision of the eternal source of life. It was said of initiates that they were "blessed": "Blessed is he among men on earth who has beheld this. Never will he who has not been initiated into these ceremonies, who has had no part in them, share in such things. He will be as a dead man in sultry darkness."[8] And it was said by the Roman Cicero: "We have been given reason not only to live in joy but also to die with better hope."[9]

Any man or woman who spoke Greek and had not caused bloodshed could participate in the rites. Men, however, were given names with feminine endings. In later years (which means by about the fifth century B.C.) all the initiates wore white garments that were saved and used as swaddling clothes for new infants. Two priestesses presided over the rites, representing Demeter as the Mother of Life and Persephone as Queen of Death and Mistress of the Underworld—the light and dark sides of the moon.

The rites began in mid-September, coinciding with the Greek season for planting. "Bios" or, simply, life—the heart of matter—was the inexpressible mystery that Demeter shared when she taught mortals to plant seeds of grain and kernels of corn. It was her own daughter who was buried under earth, and yet the core of *herself* died with her and came back to life only when Persephone—flower sprout, grain sprout—rose again from the earth. ("Except a grain of wheat fall into the ground and die, it abideth alone; but if it die, it bringeth forth fruit," St. John. Cultivate your garden . . .)

The astonishing event and the event that made hope possible was that *death* itself (herself) had given birth. When Persephone accepts the seed of Hades, she becomes a mother herself, who in turn has a daughter who dies to her and then is reborn. "Every mother contains her daughter in herself and every daughter her mother—every woman extends backward into her mother and forward into her daughter."[10]

Every lass takes the leap. In *Finnegans Wake,* it is Nuvolleta, the daughter of the story, who finds herself fallen (like Persephone) in love and cries out to her mother, Anna Livia Plurabelle (who is all women in one woman): "Why, why, why! Weh, O weh! I'se so silly to be flowing but I no canna stay!"

There is no detaining the maiden's wending toward the death of what she has been. That imperative to move on, to create, pushes at us not only biologically, but psychically, to make something out of what we are. What can the Rites of Spring mean to us now in an age when Buckminster Fuller can make springtime come anytime in a dome? And what does menstruation signify when by extraction[11] a woman can end it before it starts? And what of fertility when conception can be put off at will? Does being "past the age of childbearing" still mean that a woman is "cut off from the gifts of garland-loving Aphrodite"?

First, the ability to make seeds sprout anytime in an air-regulated dome does not remove the need for periodic transformation—it just removes it to another realm of human experience. The ancient Latin poet who asks, "When will *my* springtime come?" does not wonder what season it is outside. Rites of seasonal and human passage are gone—the Mother-Daughter rites lasted for two thousand years, followed by another two thousand years of Father-Son rites that are fast disappearing. We are left without meaningful rules of ritual conduct—but the mystery remains. To be an initiate is to swaddle yourself against the world for a while, to be a candidate (dressed in pure white) for an entirely new experience of spiritual significance. An initiate re-enters the mother (De-meter, Earth Mother) to be remade.

Demeter's depression when she was "disfiguring her form a long while," the descent to the underworld, the barren period of waiting, and the long sorrowful procession on the road to Eleusis —imitating the Mother's search—these stages of the rite no longer have visible structures, symbols, or spaces to manifest in, but rather have themselves turned inward so that the initiation is an active entry into the dark terrain of an unknown self where we still search for the lost daughter, the feminine source of life.

Let me say this again another way. The rites are gone—yet the mystery remains. The unconscious self has an autonomous way of making itself known; if people do not gather anymore on a sacred road to search for their lost souls, the gathering together and the search will be translated into the movement and language of our interiors. Rites of passage have turned inward where they can be lived out as stages of psychic transformation.

A woman need not literally have a daughter to bear witness to the mystery of continuity—just as, I suppose, you need not bleed for four days to know the hold periodicity has on you. A child is as much the offspring of the body of your imagination, the treasure hard to attain, as it is the blood fruit of your womb.

It is essential also to let these daughters of imagination go from you—there are mothers in myth who would kill their own children if they proved a threat to their own individuality and passion. It takes great strength to let go of a thing you have created: a child, a work of art, a method, a situation where you are recognized, a string of words that work—but the estrangement, the giving up, the separation are often necessary in order for something fundamentally new to emerge.

When the last child leaves home, the void is filled only by the possibility of making something out of yourself. Demeter was past the age of childbearing and she returned to herself in a new form.

Perhaps that flowering of women, that gathering of women in our time who choose not to conceive literally, those who choose at a young age to be (paradoxically) *past* the age of childbearing, are those to whom the burden of a cultural labor has fallen. Like the vestal virgins who tended and carried the public fire, these women might be the bearers of a kind of illumination that we have not known before. Rather than be frightened by this force, those who have borne children or wish to be literal mothers need to recall their essential role at this point, for, if the mothers who conceive of new forms of language and culture forget their connection to the body, to the real female depth of tissue, to the earth (their Mother), the life they create will be sterile.

Among those urging us toward an unprecedented fertility are three Portuguese women, known as the three Marias, whose exchange of letters helped me reach my conclusion: "Out of whom," Maria asks, "if not your own mother within you are you creating yourself?" In this exercise of ours, she says, "those who draw nearer to us can already hear the pattern that each of us is tracing in her life, the surging tides of love that are swelling between us, tides not of nostalgia or of vengeance, but rather like those between mothers and daughters of one and the same house."[12]

And the last word from Seneca:

There are holy things that are not communicated all at once: Eleusis always keeps something back to show those who come again.

5
Spiritual Pregnancy

In India where ritual is still inseparable from life, Hindu mothers are culturally provided with a way of releasing their sons to the world. Somewhere around the boy's fifth year an observance begins. For one month every year, for an indeterminate number of years decided by the family's spiritual director, the woman sacrifices things that are of value to her, abstains from certain foods, and goes to the house of the guru to listen attentively to stories. Her sacrifice begins with her favorite fruits and advances to metals: iron, copper, bronze, and lastly gold—her precious ornaments. After the number of years has passed, the day comes for the final ceremony. Heinrich Zimmer describes that day:

The last, extreme stage of the sacrifice is a total fast: the woman presents fresh coconut milk to the guru and must then go thirsty all day. Brahmans, relatives and household attend this ceremony, representing the world to which the son must be given. At the end of the rite, twelve Brahmans and a few beggars belonging to the fifth caste, or "untouchables" are given ceremonial food: the highest and lowest caste, the summit and base of the social pyramid, symbolize the whole social world for which the matured boy must leave his home and sever his maternal bonds. . . . At the end of the ceremony, the guru declares that the mother is ready to perform the act of giving her son to the world. And then, silently and inwardly, she completes the sacrifice of her life's fruit.[1]

This beautiful way of marking the painful and necessary release of the child is called *phala* ("fruit"), *dāna* ("gift"), *vrata* ("observance")—the giving of her fruit to the world.

Gift giving should never be a thing that comes easily. A real gift should be so much a part of one that it leaves a hole when given. Being left with a vacant interior space is an irreversible experience of motherhood that leaves a woman more aware of the outside world (to which her "gift" has gone) and more aware of the inner world where the emptiness can be felt as either loss or potential. A hole can be something missing, a place to go into, a space to be filled.

Matriarchal consciousness, or the awareness of the world from the mother's point of view, proceeds from a state of pregnancy or total intersubjectivity. There are always two things happening at once, two meanings—life of mother and child-in-utero are inseparable, senses intermingle. When William Blake prayed to be saved from single vision, "May God us keep from single vision and Newton's sleep!" he was suggesting that the world be perceived on multiple levels simultaneously: "Now I a fourfold vision see,/And a fourfold vision is given to me. . . ." Vision itself can be pregnant, enabling the onlooker to see through the "four eyes" of mother and child at once. The mother opposes "single meaning." There is always the child to take into account—the child in the sentence, the hidden meaning. When we speak of a pregnant image or pregnant situation we mean that there is more to it than meets the eye.

When the mother is separated unwillingly from the child or when the fruit is *taken* from her rather than *given,* a certain understanding is lost, an organic bond severed that severs the mother from her own life's meaning. Such a moment in history is frozen in stone on a relief from Milan: the mother sits on her throne at the left of the picture. Her hand is raised almost to her mouth in a familiar gesture as if to stop a startled gasp. Her child has been taken from her and set on a rock at the far right with a nursing goat. In between the separated mother and child two young men dance with raised clashing shields. They performed the separation at the behest of the father: the patriarchate has begun. And "patriarchy," as Jane Ellen Harrison observes in the context of this picture, "once fully established, would fain dominate all things, would invade even the ancient prerogative of the mother, the right to rear the child she bore."[2]

In the Indian ceremony the fruit is allowed to ripen naturally —the time the ceremony takes is idio-rhythmic, according to the time it takes for the meaning to crystalize in an individual woman. Though the spiritual director is usually a man, the consciousness is matriarchal: patient, related, based on feeling and the "favorability" of time. Rilke, who lived with this sense of time, knew that meaning evolves when images are allowed to ripen in the mind:

INITIATION

Whoever you are, go out into the evening,
leaving your room, of which you know each bit;
your house is the last before the infinite,
whoever you are.

Then with your eyes that wearily
scarce lift themselves from the worn out door-stone
slowly you raise a shadowy black tree
and fix it on the sky: slender, alone.
And you have made the world (and it shall grow
and ripen as a word, unspoken, still).
When you have grasped its meaning with your will,
then tenderly your eyes will let it go. . . .

Imaginal thinking clears the blocked channels of energy that flow between creatures and things. In certain parts of the world when people feel creativity is blocked—when a conversation doesn't go anywhere or when an animal cannot give birth—they will say "the goddess sits before the door with her arms and legs crossed, we must change her attitude!" Her crossed limbs bind up the life force the way a restricted imagination cripples the psyche, leaving little energy available for ripening one's world in Rilke's sense.

In recent history (comparatively) such a poverty of imagination in the Western world came about under the stern and watchful eye of the Protestant forefathers, whose primary allegiance was to the letter of the law, to dogma, to definition—to words with restricted boundaries. When a people's religious symbols permit only one way of seeing—rather than initiating flights of faith and fancy—souls become weak, mere shades of their former selves. Protestant reformers re-formed the spiritual message of Christianity to leave out myth, allegory, symbolism. What was once seen as a fertile field producing a variety of meanings became a one-crop field with one meaning to be abided by resolutely (Calvin). Norman O. Brown says that the crux of Protestant literalism is the reduction of meaning to single meaning—univocation: "Luther's word is *Eindeutigkeit:* the single, simple, solid and stable meaning of scripture."[3] Reading with that kind of eye ("single vision") prepared the way for the characteristic reliance of modern scholarship on unimaginative, standardized texts. A return to symbolism, to a simultaneous awareness of several meanings, to the admission that words have undersides like poplar leaves, would spell the end of the Protestant/patriarchal era. "The letter killeth, but the spirit giveth life" (II Corinthians).

Those who have ceased to belong to a vital religious tradition endowed with images, rites, and myth are guided by the poets. Like priests and shamans, "the true poet—and there are not many —is the guardian of the archetypes of his culture's collective unconscious. His function is not to invent, but to rediscover and to animate."[4] The strata from which the meaning is recovered is necessarily deep (writing that takes in only the social horizon dies with it). It reaches to the beginning of personal and collective time—back to the mothering caves of memory.

> *Here we are; in the darkness,*
> *close to the very heart of Mother*
> *Earth,*
> *Where her blood flows in seams of shining coal,*
> *And our picks beat a rhythm to her*

heart,
Where her warm brown flesh encloses us
And her rocky bones trap us.

This poem was written by a twelve-year-old girl from New Zealand who probably never saw those representations of the huge-bellied, pendulous-breasted, wide-lapped women of the Stone Age. But to a miner's daughter the cave Mother would always be accessible. The Psalmist says:

For thou didst form my inward parts,
Thou didst knit me together in my mother's womb.
Thou knowest me right well;
my frame was not hidden from thee when I was being made
in secret, intricately wrought
in the depths of the earth.

The womb of the mother is our first home. Caves were the first homes of humankind. "Just as every adult was once inside the mother, every society was once inside the Great Mother."[5] Even though matriarchal consciousness grows out of the specific "cavity" of the mother's form and function, it is accessible to everyone who can find a taproot to primary experience. R. D. Laing says that he has now met "thousands" of people who can actually recall their intra-uterine existence and the traumatic experience of birth from their personal mothers.[6] I don't literally mean that life will be one-dimensional without recapturing that first memory—but rather that we have a chance of regaining a much-needed balance if we can learn to see things and feel things again from the point of view of our own childhood and the childhood of humanity.

In high school biology teachers used to relate the complicated theory that "ontogeny recapitulates phylogeny"—that individual genesis or development repeats phylum development. Every infant embryo goes through a process of development similar to the evolution of the entire species. At one point we all have ear slits like fish gills. Psychologically, this theory means all individuals, in their growth and development, repeat the stages of the development of consciousness, that we learn to talk first and then to reason: our first emotion is fear (like the "primitive") and our most highly developed function (like the most highly developed peoples) is abstract, analytical thinking. Reconstituting our collective selves—or putting the broken pieces of our fragmented individualism back together—requires an act of remembrance, discovering and embracing. "To recapitulate the phylogeny is to reconstitute the phylum, the unity of the human race; the atonement."[7] To return to the womb then would mean to rediscover and animate a lost infancy, a stage of culture held within the consciousness of the Mother.

Animation is another way of talking about pregnancy. It is a bestowal of life that Neumann describes as the matriarchal wisdom (or moon wisdom) "of waiting, accepting, ripening [that] admits everything into its totality and transforms it and, along with it, its own being. It is always concerned with wholeness, with shaping and realizing, with the creative . . . and every creative achievement, like a pregnancy, presupposes an attitude of patience and relatedness."[8] Giving life and breath to something, especially to dead cultural ideas and outworn habits, takes time. In the biblical story, Sarah waited ninety years to conceive. The barrenness and desolation of spiritual impoverishment, the absence of meaning that comes about when multiple meanings are denied, requires either a miracle or years of psychic cultivation to yield a child.

The slow course of seeding fresh perceptions is occasionally speeded up by the brilliant reminders of those who can see both ways. For example, the poet as interpreter of body, says: "the body itself by movement of its own tissues gives the data of depth" (Charles Olson).[9] There is much to learn about the nature of the feminine from the inner contours of a woman's body. We can befriend the body without getting trapped by a shallow physiological literalism. Nietzsche may have unwittingly furthered this particular sort of trap when he said: "Everything about a woman is a riddle, and everything about a woman has one solution. It is called pregnancy." He is also the one who wrote: "Woman is at best a bird or a bee or a cow."

There is nothing to learn from these statements if looked at with single vision. Birds, bees, and cows are attributes of the goddess—her attendants or her sacred guises. The Mother was surrounded by melissae, her bee maidens. She frequently (as Artemis, for example, Queen of Beasts) wore bird robes. The Teutonic Mother Hulda, disguised with a tail, visits herdsmen's pastures to mingle in their dances. Pasiphaë, in Crete, was a sacred white cow daughter of the moon. And Hathor appeared as the great Celestial Cow to the Egyptians. Birds and bees and cows abound in our mythology and come up repeatedly as archetypal expressions of the airborne and earthbound, spirit-and-body-nurturing aspects of the feminine principle.

But the "solution of pregnancy" is more difficult to interpret generously in a time when women are so easily (and rightly) offended. I have responded in part in the foregoing chapter on Demeter and Persephone ("A child is as much the offspring of the body of your imagination . . . as it is the blood fruit of your womb")—but I want to look more closely at the mysteries of conception and pregnancy here, as a student of Mother culture, to "study" them.

A studied approach to anatomy looks for meaning rather than facts, contemplates, researches without direction or strict purpose, and is willing to go in circles—to walk about the core, wandering and waiting like the sad woman in "The Nixie in the Mill Pond" (Grimms' tale), who has to circle the pond time and again until the moon is full. Organic life has its own time. It is moon related, slow, moist changing in the dark, periodically open —ready for new contents to enter—and periodically sealed off. The ovum (egg) is like this in a woman—it becomes immediately "sealed off" by an intricate latticelike network as soon as one male sperm has entered it. What has been conceived in time takes root (implants itself), grows, permeates the body in which it has found nourishment, and eventually "comes forth." Likewise, we speak of an idea whose time has come, or a ripe story. To conceive of an idea is to begin to understand it. Receptive listening, pregnant silence, bringing data to bear on a problematic situation—even aborted thoughts—are all feminine modes of consciousness.

The body-based metaphor extends to all realms of human and cosmic endeavor. All life was conceived in the ocean; in the Hebrew account it happened when God passed gently over the surface in the wind. Those infinitely small organisms that evolved into increasingly complex life forms were held within that great briny body and delivered on the sea's edge, as Whitman says it, "out of the cradle endlessly rocking." The sea precedes even the cave as our first home. There is the intra-uterine sea where the embryo dwells in the cavelike dark of every mother's womb.

I laughed when the midwife told me that the heartbeat of the infant embryo inside me would sound like "a horse galloping fast under water"—but then the sound resounded in my ears! It was overwhelmingly like being in an oceanic chamber, where I heard, not stillness, but the echoing sounds of life racing, feeding, multiplying. Whether or not a woman ever literally conceives, she always carries this vast ocean of possibilities within her. I heard a little girl's dream once about a seal in the ocean that gave birth to a baby seal. Then that newborn seal gave birth to another one and on and on. . . . Matriarchal consciousness recognizes this tie to ancestral experience not through genealogical charts but through the inheritance of body.

The moon expresses this eternally conceiving and bearing inheritance in the succession of phases: dark to new crescent to full to old crescent and down into dark again. The White Goddess or the Muse who inspires mortals to ecstatic speech, song, and dance is the moon in her fullness. Her full stage is symbolic of coming to creative fruition—when the fruit of the moon tree is ripe. In the waning stage the fruit is eaten away or withers. The dying crescent is absorbed into the blackness of the no-moon, under (or inner) worldly womb phase. This is the time of conception and increase. Looking at the moon in its visible phases—rising in the east, full overhead, diminishing in the west—consider again Jung's moon-reflective statement about feminine immortality: "Every mother contains her daughter in herself and every daughter her mother. Every woman extends backwards into her mother and forward into her daughter."

Recognition of the self as container of endless transformations is another way of understanding the meaning of pregnancy. Nietzsche did understand it metaphorically, I am sure, because he also said: "In a state of pregnancy we hide ourselves." Periods of necessary withdrawal often come over us without our knowing why. Conception happens this veiled way, in the dark. The moment of conception may not register consciously but the new inner activity has begun and it pulls us to sleep or solitude or moodiness or sickness. Growth needs invisibility. Perfection of form needs time. Horace said to hide a poem in your desk nine years before showing it to the world.

On the one hand, pregnancy is a nocturnal mystery characterized by hiddenness, veiling, submission, waiting, regenerative growth, interior harmony. On the other hand, it is a state that becomes increasingly obvious to others, one that forces the world to comprehend the creative process. Hiding behind pregnancy from this angle would be like the young celebrant who carried the water-filled vessel of the goddess (Isis) out in front of the raised phallus of the god (Osiris) in ritual procession. She was the bearer of life hidden behind the leading vessel. There would be no need for her to explain anything about herself, just as women who are actually pregnant and bearing the full vessels before them in public need not explain themselves.

There are times to hold our creations before us; we can hide behind them for periods of necessary incubation. Many fairy tales show women sitting through years of hiddenness, a kind of dark incubation in which something grows. Usually they have to weave or knit in the meantime, which shows that it is a period of life when children are being "intricately wrought." Such times are often marked by silence. Wordless ways of communicating develop not only between the mother and child or the writer and her poem—but between the one who creates and those whom she seeks to have around her. In a poem that shows how silence and gestures are natural to life stirring in an inner sanctuary, Rilke describes a meeting of mothers:

VISITATION OF THE VIRGIN

At first it all went easily with her,
but oftentimes in climbing she already
felt the wonder stirring in her body—
and panting then she stood upon the lofty

Judean hills. Not by the land below,
she was encompassed by her plenitude;
walking, she felt that no one ever could
surpass the bigness she was feeling now.

She had to lay her hand upon the other
woman's body, still more ripe than hers.
And they both tottered toward one another
and touched each other's garments and hair.

Each, with a sanctuary in her keeping,
sought refuge with her closest woman kin.
Ah, the Savior in her was just in bloom,
but joy already in her cousin's womb
had quickened the little Baptist into leaping.

Sharing a period of withdrawal or incubation is a paradox. These moments or days or years cannot be shared with an unsympathetic companion who would break the stillness with inappropriate inquiry or just a different sense of timing. Neumann, in keeping with the moon metaphor, writes: "While patriarchal consciousness annihilates time and outstrips nature's slow processes of transformation and evolution by its purposive use of experi-

ment and calculation, matriarchal consciousness remains caught in
the spell of the changing moon. Like the moon, its illumination
and luminosity are bound to the flow of time and to periodicity.
It must wait for time to ripen, while with time, like sown seed,
comprehension ripens too."[10] Patriarchal timing is quantitative,
measuring space in equal sections. Matriarchal timing is qualita-
tive, subjective, experiencing the length of a moment according
to feelings. It is heart centered rather than head centered. A
woman's experience of herself in pregnancy draws her to other
women who know what it means to carry the fruit of the night
under one's heart. Their shared knowledge proceeds from traveling through similar interior terrain—a terrain that is extraor-
dinarily different from masculine physical territory, which is un-
changing according to this noblewoman from Abyssinia:

How can a man know what a woman's life is? A woman's life is
quite different from a man's. God has ordered it so. A man is the
same from the time of his circumcision to the time of his wither-
ing. He is the same before he has sought out a woman for the first
time, and afterwards. But the day when a woman enjoys her first
love cuts her in two. She becomes another woman on that day.
The man is the same after his first love as he was before. The
woman is from the day of her first love another. That continues
so all through life. The man spends a night by a woman and goes
away. His life and body are always the same. The woman conceives. As a mother she is another person than the woman without
child. She carries the fruit of the night for nine months in her
body. Something grows. Something grows into her life that never
again departs from it. She is a mother. She is and remains a mother
even though her child die, though all her children die. For at one
time she carried the child under her heart. And it does not go out
of her heart ever again. Not even when it is dead. All this the man
does not know; he knows nothing. He does not know the difference before love and after love, before motherhood and after
motherhood. He can know nothing. Only a woman can know that
and speak of that. That is why we won't be told what to do by our
husbands. A woman can only do one thing. She can respect herself. She can keep herself decent. She must always be as her nature

is. She must always be maiden and always be mother. Before every love she is a maiden, after every love she is a mother. In this you can see whether she is a good woman or not.[11]

Motherhood is in some sense a preparation for maidenhood. Pregnancy is a preparation for virginity. Withdrawal is a preparation for emergence. Aphrodite, who is called the Emerging One, renewed her virginity every morning by bathing in the sea of Paphos. Before every love she was a maiden. How is it that a woman makes herself a maiden again? The Abyssinian woman suggests the "solution of pregnancy": only when a woman has been split in two can she know what it is to be whole. A woman may feel returned to the complex, unsplit virgin nature at different times in her life after particularly difficult labors. It is in the nature of the mother to feel alternately burdened, closed, possessed and lightened, receptive, virginal.

Matriarchal consciousness would find the solution to impoverishment of spirit or psyche in spiritual pregnancy—pregnancy proceeding from a virgin's willingness to meet every stranger as a god in disguise. Once you have been a mother, once you have given birth to something uniquely of yourself, borne some fruit to the world, one is in a position to *go back* to a state of readiness prior to conception. A woman begins the normal phases of ovulation again shortly after a child is born and weaned. She cannot actually be twelve again, and we cannot relive the Stone Age—but one can bring those stages of their own and their ancestors' life to consciousness. The Babylonians would say that one can only sit in the temple of Aphrodite once:

The Babylonians have one most shameful custom. Every woman born in the country must once in her life go and sit down in the precinct of Aphrodite, and there have intercourse with a stranger. Many of the wealthier sort, who are too proud to mix with the others, drive in covered carriages to the precinct, followed by a goodly train of attendants, and there take their station. But the larger number seat themselves within the holy enclosure with wreaths of string about their heads, and here there is always a great crowd, some coming and others going; lines of cord mark out paths in all directions among the women, and the strangers pass along them to make their choice. A woman who has once taken her seat is not allowed to return home till one of the strangers throws a silver coin into her lap, and takes her with him beyond the holy ground. When he throws the coin he says these words, "I summon you in the name of the goddess Mylitta." (Aphrodite is called Mylitta by the Assyrians.) The silver coin may be of any size; it cannot be refused, for that is forbidden by the law, since once thrown it is sacred. The woman goes with the first man who throws her money, and rejects no one. When she has had intercourse with him, and so satisfied the goddess, she returns home, and from that time on no gift however great will prevail with her. Such of the women as are tall and beautiful are soon released, but others who are ugly have to stay a long time before they can fulfill the law. Some have waited three or four years in the precinct. A custom very much like this is found also in certain parts of the island of Cyprus.[12]

Certainly this manner of sacred prostitution can occur repeatedly in the psychic life of an individual. Sometimes one is the beautiful woman waiting briefly. Sometimes one is the ugly one who waits for years. Sometimes one is the stranger with the coin. Sitting in those labyrinths of cord means to be in a timeless place that has (like a woven cord) no beginning and no end. In the wreaths of string "they carry the inadvertent love affair woven through their hair like a celibate braid."[13] Men and women were not starting a new relationship outside the temple grounds (regulations were that the stranger be gone before daylight), but enacting a sacred union in honor of the goddess. The women were giving themselves in order to be given to. Dedication of womanly need or instinct to the goddess would ensure fulfillment and fertility. Some women chose to stay and serve the goddess instead of going back to town (see Chapter 7, Hetaira, for further discussion). They were then regarded as virgin priestesses, or "joy maidens." They had other duties than ritual congress with strangers—tending the sacred fire, performing water rites. But even these tasks represented the dedication of their powers of production and reproduction to the goddess. Children born of a temple priestess were called "divine" because they were born of these "holy virgins."

The free woman, who is archetypally both virgin and prostitute, is bound to her own instinct (or the law of the goddess) in a way that makes her appear to be the ultimate anima, the veiled, beautiful, beckoning soul of a man. This is because she is completely "other," unknowable and thus unattainable: the Eskimo mother goddess is called "She who will not have a husband" and one of the oldest goddesses in the world, the goddess of Saïs, says, "No man has lifted my veil." There is an extraordinary attraction to a self-sufficient nature that will not permit violation. These goddesses (to repeat) are not saying that they will not give themselves sexually—but rather that they will not be taken or possessed by another being. Their abundant fertility, like a virgin's erotic exuberance, is not dependent upon being fertilized in the male sexual embrace because it is a spiritual pregnancy that fills from within. A woman experiencing this facet of her femininity may feel an affinity with the chastised "profligate" woman who, with extravagance and abandon, poured the precious oil and kisses on the feet of Christ. This was extravagance of affection. In fairy tales like the one about Mother Hulda and the girl who drops her spindle into the well, this "pouring out" motif is represented in the shower of gold that falls upon the girl.

Abandonment is necessary for redemption. In order to become pregnant with the potential of realizing unknown faces—or facets —of one's self, one must be open to the strange fertilizing powers of the imagination.

Too often women get caught in a restrictive, single vision. Instead of realizing, a woman will concretize. Instead of admitting everything into her totality—waiting, accepting, ripening, transforming, and being transformed—a woman will literally conceive and bear a child. One woman of this type who repeatedly gave herself over to childbearing, whether or not her deepest feelings were in accord, dreamt that she was a whore visited by a mailman. She took the letter carrier literally—thinking that to be open to the male meant receiving him sexually and bearing the consequences.

In a culture where there is no ruling principle of love, no goddess to whom the first fruits of labor are dedicated, it happens that the father is the one to take the virginity of a girl. Some cultures have ritually sanctioned this "paternal defloration," but in our culture it is, for the most part, a covert operation that happens in the mind of a girl. It happens not because individual fathers will it, but because Zeus ordered the separation of the infant from the enthroned mother in that ancient frieze. Since then girls have grown up as extensions of the father's property—bearing his name, wearing his coat of armor in the world. In order to leave home then, a girl has to sacrifice her virginity to him (or to God) rather than to the Mother Goddess or the strangers and priests acting on her behalf. The father's law that she not be promiscuous (there are no promiscuous boys) leaves her unfree to choose. Consequently, her "virginity" is an unconscious, unchosen, and restricted experience.

Where matriarchal consciousness flourishes (as it does in certain receptive familial and cultural pockets) a way of being grows organically out of a certain watchfulness. The mother attitude watches and dreams and admits all sides of a thing to view without judging or discriminating according to sets of abstract principles. It sees things patiently and paradoxically. It is an inclusive attitude that always takes an other into account. Consciousness of relationship, of the inexpressible bond between things, orders actions. This attached, accessible nature has this drawback: that one can perceive so many sides to an issue at once the freedom ends up muddle. But generally the attitude based on the intra-uterine-like interdependence of all life is the attitude that most successfully changes the course of the spirit.

Spiritual impoverishment, like impotence, can incapacitate a person for life. Von Franz says that she frequently deals with the problem of impotence in men by ignoring it—and looking instead at the things that seem to be blocking their creativity (what goddess sits cross-legged before his door?). In a similar way, when a woman has gone to that dark moon land of No-Return, into that unapproachable time of depression or detachment where nothing can be conceived (joy and relationship are especially inconceivable), she suffers from a monumental blockage of creative energy. In a more primitive culture this would be the time for her to undo every knot on her garments, unlock the doors, open windows, uncork bottles, untie shoelaces, unbraid her hair, set the cows out of their stall, free the chickens, free anything that is tied! And a man should also untie anything in the vicinity of his dwelling. He should take the axe out of the log in which it is stuck, unfasten the boat moored to a tree, withdraw cartridges from a gun, release the arrows from his crossbow.[14] I am not opposed to trying these things. There is wisdom in periodically releasing yourself from all personal ties—just leaving home for a while, or taking off from work. Maybe no one should embroider, knit, or sew at such times: unweave your tapestry like Penelope in order to be unavailable. (She unwove by night what she had woven by day so that none of her suitors could claim her.) Read poetry, walk outside, listen to music, leave things undone.

If imagination should remain unfertile and creativity blocked, then the situation is altogether more profound. Spiritual poverty has deep and lasting effects that cannot be eradicated by "techniques." It requires an attentiveness to your heart like the dramatic observances of the Indian woman who "worked" for years with a teacher whose wisdom she respected. Changing an attitude, in a time and place where spiritual guides are few, might require the radical gesture of going to sit in the sacred precinct of a healing god. In the ancient world that meant, as it could mean now, going to a place where sleep was deep and dreams spoke clearly.

Out of the dreams come heartfelt thoughts, images, and words to attend to—words that were, from the beginning, necessary for the birth of human being. Exchanging words is the essence of psychotherapy. Freud said that "words and magic were in the beginning one and the same thing and even today words retain much of their magical power. By words one of us can give to another the greatest happiness or utter despair. . . . Words call forth emotions and are universally the means by which we influence our fellow creatures. Therefore let us not despise the use of words in psychotherapy."[15] In other times and other cultures, where words were regarded as essential bits of the core of a person, a misspoken word could endanger a life. We still say "you had better take that back" when we feel threatened by someone else's words. God made Ezekiel eat his very words (which he had written on a scroll) because they were displeasing. When that same Old Testament God created the world he said "let there be" this-and-that, and then he said that "it was good," meaning "good enough to eat"—especially succulent and ripe.[16]

In Isak Dinesen's account of Fatima's labor in *Shadows on the Grass* a woman who is ripe and ready to deliver her first fruit is helped by the efficacious nature of the word:

The gentle midwives were busy, bending and again straightening up the girl and from time to time knocking her in the small of the back with their fists as if to knock out the child. For the time that I was there I saw them dealing out only one kind of medicine: a matron amongst them brought along an earthen ware dish, on the inner side of which a holy man of the town had drawn up, in charcoal, a text from the Koran; the lettering was washed off carefully with water, and the water poured into the mouth of the labouring young woman.

If taken seriously (swallowed whole) the word medicine of the matron compels birth.

Pregnant words serve the functions of both binding and severing. In contrast to the woman in the Indian story of the fruit-gift observance, whose separation from her child was so carefully mediated, the Aztec mother moves quickly toward severance—toward the establishing of the son's independence and the re-establishing of her own virgin nature:

WORDS SPOKEN BY A MOTHER TO HER NEWBORN SON AS SHE CUTS THE UMBILICAL CORD

I cut from your middle the navel string: know you, understand that your birthplace is not your home. . . . This house where you are born is but a nest. It is a way station to which you have come. It is your point of entrance into this world. Here you sprout, here you flower. Here you are severed from your mother, as the chip is struck from the stone.[17]

The hard and soft of this vision—the flower and stone—circumscribe the nature of the virgin Mother. Her pregnancies of body and spirit proceed from her capacity to give and to cut off. Unlike Artemis, the virgin goddess who oversees pregnancies as midwife but is never pregnant herself, the Mother's perspective is always from within the experience of being overtaken. Her movements are regulated by relationship to an other. Artemis, to whom we move now, is never overtaken. Where she strides, literal, punctual, straight to the point, the Mother moves metaphorically several ways at once, taking her time, walking, resting, rising "to attend to . . ." The mother place holds us in a rich embrace until her waters break and expel us. Afterward, human beings are poor and require nourishment and intimacy. How this particular problem of the impoverishment of the first human beings was countered by the gift of the old Eagle Mother is told in an Eskimo tale gathered by the mythologist and explorer Knud Rasmussen. The people needed words and needed friends to change the course of a pervasive poverty. In the bird mother's service, one of the sons of men restored a certain richness to human being. This story leads us over the border of the Mother's realm into the wilder country of Artemis. It is called "The sacred gift of song, dance and festivity comes to mankind":

Once upon a time a man and a woman lived near the sea. The man was a great hunter, sometimes hunting game inland, sometimes catching seals from his kayak. They begot a son, these two lonely ones at their house, and, when he grew up, his father made a small ptarmigan-bow for him, and soon he became a keen and skilful bowman. Then his father taught him how to catch caribou, and soon the son became as great a hunter as his father; they shared the hunting between them, the son hunting caribou up in the mountains, while the father paddled out to sea and hunted seals from his kayak. But one day the son did not return from the hunt. The parents waited in vain for him, in vain they searched for him, but they found not a trace. They begot another son; he grew up, became big and clever like his father; but he too disappeared mysteriously one day. The husband and wife then lived alone, and they grieved deeply at the loss of their sons. Then they begot a third son; he grew up like his brothers with a liking for all forms of manly pursuits, and even as a child was eager to go hunting. He was given his brother's weapons, first a little ptarmigan-bow, and afterwards the big, powerful bows for caribou, and so it was not long before he became as skilful an archer as his father. They brought much meat to the house, the father from the sea, the son from the land, and they had to build many large stages beside their house in order to have room for all the game they killed.

One day the son as usual was hunting in the interior when he caught sight of a large young eagle circling above him. Quickly he reached for his arrows, when the eagle descended and settled on the ground a short distance from him. Then it pushed its hood off its head and became a man, saying: "It was I who killed your two brothers, and I will kill you too, if you don't promise to hold a songfeast when you return home. Will you, or will you not?" "I would gladly, but I don't know what you mean. What is song? What is feast?" "Will you, or will you not?" "Willingly, but I don't know what it is." "If you come with me, my mother will teach you what you don't understand. Your two brothers disdained the gift of song and feast; they refused to learn it; that is why I killed them. Now you can go with me; and as soon as you have learned to put words together into a song and have learnt to sing them, and as soon as you have learnt to dance for joy, you shall be allowed to return freely to your house." "I'll go with you," said the young caribou hunter.

And so they went together up towards the tall mountains. The eagle was no longer a bird, but a big and strong man in a brilliant coat of eagle-skins. They walked and walked far, far in over the land, through ravines and valleys right over to the blue mountains. Here they came to a great mountain, which they began to climb. "Our house is high up on the top of this mountain," said the eagle. And they ascended the mountain, higher and higher, and had a view over the plains where men hunted caribou. But as they got near to the peak of the mountain they could hear a strange knocking sound, which grew louder and louder the nearer they came to the top. It was like the beating of enormous hammers, and it was so loud that the ears of the caribou hunter tingled. "Do you hear anything?" asked the eagle. "Yes, a deafening sound like the strokes of a hammer." "It is my mother's heart you hear beating," said the eagle. They reached the eagle's house, which was built right up on the peak. "I must prepare mother; wait till I come back," the eagle said and entered the house. A moment later he returned and led the caribou hunter inside. They came into a house that was built in the same way as the houses of men, and there on the platform, quite alone, sat the eagle's mother, decrepit and sorrowful. Then her son spoke and said: "This young man has promised to hold a songfeast when he gets home. But he knows nothing about putting words together into songs, he knows nothing of how to sing a song, nor does he understand beating a drum and dancing for joy. Mother! Men don't know how to feast and now this young man has come up to learn it." These words put life into the old eagle-mother; she became very pleased, expressed thanks and said: "But you must first build a festival house where many people can assemble."

So the two young men built a qagsse, a festival house, bigger and better built than ordinary houses. And the old eagle-mother taught them to make drums, both the ordinary drum consisting of a large wooden ring with a skin stretched over it, and the special ceremonial drum, the one used at the great present-giving feasts, made of four pieces of wood put together to form a hollow cavity, which gives a special clang when struck with a drum-stick, which is narrow at the handle and thicker and heavier at the other end. This festival drum had to have a deep, sonorous tone, reminiscent of the beating heart of an old eagle. Later the eagle-mother taught them to put words together for singing and to arrange tones together so that they became songs, and she showed them how to beat the drum in time with the songs; and finally she taught them how to dance. And when they had learned all this and could do it, she said: "But first you must gather a lot of meat, then many people, when you have built yourselves a festival house and composed your songs. Then you must hold a song-feast." "But we don't know anybody except ourselves," said the young caribou hunter. "Human beings are lonely because they have not the gift of festivity," said the eagle-mother; "make ready as I told you, and when everything is prepared, you must go out and look for people, and you will meet them two by two; but you must get them together until there are many, and invite them to the festival house; then you must hold a song-feast."

The young caribou hunter had now learned all that was necessary, and the eagle-mother told her son to take their guest down to the place where they met for the first time. The son drew on his coat, which was made of glittering eagle skins, and when they came out of the house and stood on the uppermost pinnacle of the mountain, he said to the young man: "Lie across my back, grip me round the neck and close your eyes; today we are going to travel quickly." He did so. He heard a swishing noise around him as he closed his eyes, and the young eagle flew with him away over the mountain tops. When it suddenly stopped he opened his eyes again and leaped down to the ground. It had all lasted no more than a moment, and yet they had already come to the place of their first meeting. They parted, and the caribou hunter returned home to his parents and told them all he had experienced; then he said: "Human beings are lonely, and they live alone, because they know nothing of the gift of festival, and I have promised the eagles to teach them how to feast."

Then father and son built a large festival house, and when it was ready they went hunting far away, the son in across the land, the father out on the sea, and they filled all their meat caches and all their stages with meat and furs. When they had sufficient of all that makes men happy, they composed songs, practised dancing, and made drums. They sang to it all, to the words, to the dance, and to the drum-beats.

When all the preparations for the great festival were made, the young man set out across all the valleys down through all the gullies and up over mountains, looking for guests to participate in man's first festival; for they were lonely and knew no other people. As the old eagle-mother had said, so it happened; now that he had gone out to invite folks to a festival he suddenly met people, in two's. Some of them had clothing of wolf-skins,—others of wolverine skins, and others again of fox skins—he met people two by two, dressed in different clothes. But he got them all together and invited them to feast in the big, newly built festival house, and with pleasure they followed him.

Then they held a song-feast. First they gave all their guests food, and when they could eat no more, they gave them splendid presents, both meat and furs. Then came the singing and the dancing. The father beat the special festival drum, the sound of which, deeply resounding and loud, was like the beating of the old eagle-mother's heart, as the son had heard it that time he was nearing the eagle's house on the summit of the mountain. They danced and they sang, and the guests learned their songs and their dances, and soon they had a large chorus which joined in the singing. They went on dancing and singing all through the night until day began to break. It was only then that the guests left the big festival house. But as they crowded out of the entrance passage they all fell forward on their hands and crawled out on all fours; then father and son realized for the first time that their guests had been wolves, wolverines, red foxes, white foxes, cross foxes and silver foxes in human shape. They were guests sent there by the old eagle, and so tremendous is the power of festivity that even animals can become human beings.

A little later the young caribou hunter was out looking for game when he met the eagle again. At once it pushed its hood back and became a man, whereupon they made their way together to the eagle-dwelling, as the old eagle-mother wished to see again the young man who had held man's first feast. High up on the top of the mountains the eagle-mother came to meet them in order to thank him. And behold, the decrepit old eagle had become young again; for when men feast, all old eagles become young, for which reason the eagle is the sacred bird of song, dance and festival.[18]

6
Artemis

The woman on the Amazon pole is unconventional in any culture: she is wild mountain woman, woman alone, fighter, hunter, dancer, lover of animals, protectress of all newborn sucking and roving creatures, a sister to men and teacher of women. Her heart, in the Eskimo folk story, was the first drum. She is set apart in the way of shamans, who induce ecstasy with drumbeat and dance. Shamans wore animal costumes: bird feathers, bearskins, wolves teeth, and were thought of as being in close spirit-proximity to the animals, their ancestors. At an intertribal pow-wow in Wisconsin one spring I saw a dance where this spirit was present: a solemn group danced in unison with a deliberate, pulsating kind of rhythm, moving a young girl out before them as if she were riding the crest of a huge slow wave. She wore a sacred feather in her hair to honor all the female relatives of men who had died in war and advanced with dignity uncommon in such a young girl. Her age was just that of the *arktoi,* the nine-year-old girls who went for a time into the bear cult of the goddess Artemis. In her sanctuary they were protected from the world, learned to hunt, wore saffron bear robes, and danced the dance of emerging animal life.

Dignity and abandon alternate in a kaleidoscopic aura around this goddess, who stands, in her pre-Greek and most ancient form, on a mountain in Asia Minor flanked by lions, adorned by snakes and flowers, and attended by bare-breasted women (like herself) who raise their arms to the heavens in a gesture of epiphany. The goddess reveals her essence as virgin queen of the universe, source of the drawing-down and rising-up energy of plants, planets, and people that is expressed in the rhythm of ritual dance. Periodic oscillation between repose and movement, tension and release, sinking and leaping, holding-back and letting-go could be observed, and minutely imitated, in the natural world. Stars dance, rabbits dance (in midnight moon circles), mountain chickens do solitary dances, apes do group dances with stamping movements around trees and even adorn themselves with vines and things that swing. Bees dance for food (in service of the queen mother) and cranes that became associated with the Cretan labyrinth do a stately weaving dance that was imitated for millennia by maze dancers who trod the difficult pattern of the labyrinth to its core. This particular dancing ground was said to have been built for Ariadne, sister of the monstrous Minotaur who was imprisoned there. Ariadne was only a princess then—a daughter of Queen Pasiphaë, who conceived Ariadne's brother by mating with a bull—but she was probably once herself a great queen, even the Mountain Mother, spirit kin to Artemis. (The sister-brother relationship between Ariadne and the Minotaur is related to the sister-brother bond of Artemis and Apollo, which I will discuss later.) For Ariadne, the labyrinth was like a uterine enclosure and the crane dance that wove its steps with her magic thread was the way to freedom.

Rhythm facilitates the passage from one realm to the next. A dancer's step can cross the border separating life from death. (As Charles Olson said it, "he who possesses rhythm possesses the universe.") The Lady-of-the-Wild-Things, as Artemis came to be called, is the goddess of perilous passage. Her skill at leading the dance is the same skill that makes her a competent midwife. Both are based on instinctual rhythm. Her domain included the leaping and begetting of all things, even to the leaping of the child in the womb. Every woman who has felt that embryonic dance and been present to the rhythm of her own labor knows a part of the power of this goddess. She is also present at the other end of life, where the passage is perhaps more perilous, into the realm of death. We have lost the instructions for that dance, but occasionally the faint beat will reassert itself in astonishing ways. Laurens van der Post, in *A Mantis Carol,* tells a beautiful story of a woman who danced the "dance of the great hunger" for a bushman who had become her unlikely friend in the middle of New York City:

The last time I visited him he was very ill in bed and I sat with him and held his hand while he was lying there breathing heavily, his old face looking more wrinkled than ever and his eyes firmly shut. I don't know how long I sat there except that I went on doing so gladly because I knew he knew I was there, so firmly was he holding my hand. Suddenly he opened his eyes and he smiled at me not as an old man but as he smiled when I first met him in the prime of his life. He said in a voice almost young with the note of gaiety in it, "Dolly, dance for me, please. Please dance for me, Dolly, I have so often danced for you." And the strange thing was that all my instincts were to get up and dance for him the dance of the great hunger, as you've called it, in the manner he had so often done for us, only I didn't know half the how of it, never having danced it myself. But his eyes were so full of expectation and so pleading that I thought: Oh heck, come what may and no matter what a fool I make of myself, I'll do my best for him.

I let his hand go, stood up, saw his eyes following me eagerly, kicked off my shoes, stepped into the centre of the room and turned my back on him, as he had always done, to begin with a great sideways stamping on the floor with his bare feet before he would whirl about to confront us with his face and hands thrown upwards. But in turning my back on him, I heard a strange sound, like the issue of some gust of great wind thrown at the door with such force that it passed thin and elongated through the key-hole into and out of the room. It was a sound I'd never heard before, but it filled me with alarm. I instantly whirled about, and Hans Taaibosch had gone.

I say gone, not as an evasion of fact but deliberately because I felt then, although I can only put it into words tonight because of what you have told me, that his spirit in that moment had recovered the freedom of movement so vital to it and gone on a great long walk-about of the universe which he had rehearsed so well and loved so much on earth, and that he was not, as the doctor who was immediately summoned declared him to be, dead.[1]

Freedom of movement and the undertaking of the great long walk-about are essential to the wilderness existence of Artemis. Her mountain-covering stride on earth is reflected in the heavens by the solitary and unimpeded passage of the moon. It may be that this goddess, who has no fear of the dark, or of wild animals, or of places uninhabited by men, is the force that sustains our attraction to the primitive and unknown. She can teach us how to make contact with the unconscious and survive. Artemis is energy: death-bridging energy, psychic energy, abundant energy, excess energy. Artemis organizes the hunt, slays beasts, conquers hunger, eliminates the barren places, moves the moon, and strides erect, exuberantly through the unmarked forests where fear and creaturely dark prevail. She carries the strength of the bow (*bios*, "life") in her forearm and the unerring death-dealing arrow in her hand. Like any divine being (or pure archetype of existence) she is formidable. But, when she lives through a person we can touch, her essence is approachable and may even suggest a way of restructuring our sense of reality to include access to hers. The people of Santa Barbara County, California, had this opportunity for a brief time in 1853, when the so-called "Lone Woman" of San Nicolas Island was found and brought back to the mainland.[2]

She had no name, but was called the Lone Woman because she had lived alone on that seven-mile island, some seventy miles off the coast, for eighteen years after her people had been evacuated (for unclear reasons). It was said that she was left behind or else jumped overboard because her child could not be found. She may have been searching in the mountains when the ship was forced by stormy seas to leave. Three years before she was finally discovered, a missionary priest who still believed she was alive (after fifteen years) sent a schooner to San Nicolas to find her. The sailors came back reporting no trace of the woman, except for a ghostly figure that ran up and down shore beckoning to them through the fog as they sailed away.

But the extensive beds of sea otter sustained their interest longer and another crew returned on a hunting and fishing expedition three years later. This time Captain Nidever saw a slender footprint in the sand and soon after one of the men in the party found her crouched in a small hut constructed of whale bones and animal skins. She was so intent on watching the search party fanned out on the shore below that she failed to notice his approach. When he finally stepped around to the front of her hut, she surprised him by rising slowly and intentionally without the slightest sign of alarm and came forward, addressing him in an unknown tongue.

She seemed to be between forty and fifty years of age, in fine physical condition, erect, with well-formed neck and arms and unwrinkled face. She was dressed in a tunic-shaped garment made of birds' plumage, low in the neck, sleeveless and reaching to the ankle. . . . As the men came up, she greeted them each in the same way she had met [the first], and with simple dignity, not without its effect on both Indians and white men, made them welcome and set about preparing food for them from her scanty store.[3]

She left the island gratefully, hoping to be reunited with her people. In sign language she told the story over and over again of losing her child—of her tireless search, her hope, and finally her despair and resignation. On the trip back to Santa Barbara she sat comfortably with the men, explaining her methods of hunting, eating their strange new food, and teaching them her way of sewing. Once back on the mainland she was cared for in the home of the Captain and his wife, where she in turn loved and tended the children in the family. Due to utter deflation from the failure to find any of her people and perhaps to the contraction of a severe case of dysentery, the Lone Woman died seven weeks later. In those short seven weeks she endeared herself to the local people and would occasionally put on her green satiny bird dress and make small movements with her feet and hands which the family called dancing.

There were, of course, those who reacted as if she were an

alien creature, a freak they wanted to exhibit to the public in San Francisco (this is exactly how Hans Taaibosch, the African bushman, got to New York; the curiosity raised by an anomaly can be staggering; some people respond to the unknown or "primitive" creations of the unconscious this way, as if a dream or fantasy were weird and curious—to be exhibited and kept at a safe distance), but most people responded to her with tenderness and rapt attention as if the lost woman had been a lost and miraculously recovered part of themselves. They gave her gifts and money, tokens of personal and collective energy, because there was no other way to express their feeling that she had given them something invaluable. Her self-sufficiency, her goddesslike bird gown, the ease with which she traveled with men, the way she could apparently speak to animals, and her love of young children, to whom she gave all the gifts and money, are all specific reminders of the ancient huntress Artemis. In the *Homeric Hymn,* that sounds stilted and stylized after the moving story of the Lone Woman, "the goddess with a bold heart" is invoked by the poet:

I sing of Artemis, whose shafts are of gold, who cheers on the hounds, the pure maiden, shooter of stags, who delights in archery, own sister to Apollo with the golden sword. Over the shadowy hills and windy peaks she draws her golden bow, rejoicing in the chase, and sends out her grievous shafts. The tops of the high mountains tremble and the tangled wood echoes awesomely with the outcry of beasts: earth quakes and the sea also where the fishes shoal. But the goddess with a bold heart turns every way destroying the race of wild beasts: and when she is satisfied and has cheered her heart, this huntress who delights in arrows slackens her supple bow and goes to the great house of her dear brother Phoebus Apollo, to the rich land of Delphi, there to order the lovely dance of the Muses .... There she hangs up her curved bow and her arrows, and heads and leads the dances, gracefully arrayed, while they all raise their heavenly voice, singing how neat-ankled Leto bare children supreme among the immortals.[4]

There is nothing very "human" or approachable in this song of the goddess, except perhaps the suggestion of her relationship to her brother and the description of her hanging up her weapons to dance after the hunt is over. Yet the goddess with the bold heart is familiar to contemporary hunting women, who feel the bloodlust coursing through their veins as described by Nancy Mitford in *The Ladies of Alderley:*

We had a splendid day yesterday and killed ten stags; three of them were brought to bay by the hounds and the Duchess shot them all with her rifle, which has made a proud woman of her.[5]

And instead of being described, as Artemis is in another hymn—wearing a saffron-colored knee-length, red-hemmed tunic—the Duchess, according to the papers that day, was wearing plaid trousers and short petticoats half way down her knees. In another place, Mitford goes on to describe the power of the chase, in a way that helps with understanding Artemis:

. . . more than anything in the world they loved hunting. It was in their blood and bones and in my blood and bones and nothing could eradicate it, though we knew it for a kind of original sin . . . . For three hours that day I forgot everything, except my body and my pony's body . . . . I forgot everything, I could hardly have told you my name. That must be the hold hunting has over people . . . It enforces absolute concentration, both mental and physical.[6]

One thing civilization takes from us, increasingly, is the chance to be engaged in any activity that totally absorbs both mind and body. Women who are extremely upset by problems in their emotional lives will consider giving up everything to study medi-cine—to choose a completely absorbing time-eradicating intellec-tual task. And men who are at a similar point of spiritual resigna-tion will say they are going to give up everything to join a road-construction crew—choosing back-breaking labor instead. It is because we are so split that healing comes legitimately in being able to go sit in the sun for a while or walk in the woods or take up an absorbing book. This vocation-vacation separation is unsound on the archetypal level where Artemis dwells. She knows the rhythm of alternating between hunt and dance in the *Homeric Hymn,* but running under all her activity is the absolute intermingling of tissue and intention, blood and will. There are no unnecessary movements; every action (inseparable from its emotion) is urgent. This must be, in part, the exhilaration in war (which is also part of the phenomenology of this pole: warrior women, Amazon queens, lady knights), but there is that other "wild" outlet, equally magnetic, as embodied in the Lone Woman from San Nicolas, of survival on a deserted island.

Being able to survive in the wilderness without comforts of home or city is the ability that Artemis knew she possessed even at the age of three. In an account of the goddess's girlhood, Callimachus gives a folktale version of how Artemis came into her natural realm: One day when Artemis was still quite little, Zeus asked her what presents she would like. She answered at once, saying:

"Pray give me eternal virginity; as many names as my brother Apollo; a bow and arrow like his; the office of bringing light; a saffron hunting tunic with a red hem reaching to my knees; sixty young ocean nymphs, all of the same age, as my maids of honor; twenty river nymphs from Amnisus in Crete, to take care of my buskins [boots] and feed my hounds when I am not out shooting; all the mountains in the world; and, lastly, any city you care to choose for me, but one will be enough, because I intend to live on mountains most of the time."[7]

Artemis knew that she would always be invoked by women in labor because Leto bore her without pain. She would also be thought of as protectress of infants and all sucking animals. Zeus apparently agreed to all this and appointed her guardian of roads and harbors as well.

This last gift of guarding highways and waterways connects her to Hekate, goddess of the dark moon, who is sometimes thought of as another form of Artemis. Then the sister-brother twins were called Artemis-Hekate and Apollo-Hekatos. They were both *hekaergos* or "workers-at-a-distance." I will come back to this magical aspect later.

Long before Zeus deigned to grant the girl the gifts she requested, Artemis (like Hekate) was a wild, wandering mountain goddess whose realm naturally included beasts and labor. Her mother, Leto, who some say was a goddess who came the arduous way from Asia, disguised herself as a wolf in order to protect herself in the last burdened months of childbearing. In a later version Artemis's mother disguised herself in order to escape the jealous Hera, wife of Zeus, who exiled Leto and pursued her relentlessly with the decree that she should give birth in a land where the sun never shone. She was to give birth in a time of utter blackness, or "when only wolves could see." The hour of the wolf is the time between night and dawn. It is the hour when most people die, when sleep is deepest, when nightmares are most palpable, when ghosts and demons hold sway. The hour of the wolf is also the hour when most children are born.[8]

A Polynesian naming poem chants it this way:

NIGHT BIRTHS

The slime, this was the source of the earth
The source of the darkness that made darkness
The source of the night that made night
The intense darkness, the deep darkness
Darkness of the sun, darkness of the night
  Nothing but night

. . . The little ones seek the dark places
Very dark is the ocean and obscure. . . .
With a dancing motion they go creeping and crawling. . . .

Born to the two, child of Night-falling-away
Born to the two, child of Night-creeping-away

The little child creeps as it moves
The little child moves with a spring . . .
A tiny child born as the darkness falls away
A springing child born as the darkness creeps away
Child of the dark and child in the night now here
  Still it is night

Fear falls upon me on the mountain top
Fear of the passing night
Fear of the night approaching
Fear of the pregnant night
Fear of the breach of law
Dread of the place of offering and the narrow trail
Dread of the food and the waste part remaining
Dread of the receding night
Awe of the night approaching
Awe of the dog child of Night-creeping-away . . . .[9]

To the natives raising this chant, the dog child was a shape-shifting god to be feared. Frequently Artemis-Hekate appears accompanied by hounds or a terrifying three-headed dog. The goddess is a shape shifter: she and her brother both—the two lights of heaven, moon and sun, born out of utter darkness ("children of Night-creeping-away"), are children of endless transformations. They inspire sudden changes, especially into animal forms. Artemis favored stags and she-wolves and bears. All-animal Artemis could be a dreadful goddess taking vengeance upon man by killing, dismemberment, and devouring. Blood giving and blood letting, she rules deep in the untamed forests of the human psyche. To heed her call meant "to go berserk"—to don the thick coat of the bear. Berserkers, the mad warriors and werewolves of the North, were exempt from laws and social order and were feared because of the animal frenzy that might overcome them at any time, even off the battlefield.[10]

With Artemis the frenzy feared was more the frenzy of *estrus* —of animal heat or rutting. Where she was called Wolf One, in

Attica, she gave sanctuary to young girls nearing the age of puberty. The nine- to twelve-year-old "she-bears" lived in that wilderness for a while (a place we would call a wild-life refuge) and went through a period of initiation known as "bear-service." The goddess they served left them free to hunt and roam under the guidance of a female pack leader whose intent was partially to keep the "she-bears" from men and boys. In Sparta, where boys and girls were sent out hungry, together, at dawn to hunt for their food, they were still not permitted to "share the couch" because early pregnancies would incapacitate a girl for sport and dance.[11]

> *I am, thou woost, yet of the company*
> *A maide, and love hunting and venerye*
> *And for to walken in the wodes wild*
> *And noght to ben a wyf and be with child*
> —CHAUCER

Girls at this young age—as well as women at certain self-conserving stages of culture—prefer the virgin sense of belonging to themselves or to other girls. A friend told me once that after she and her girlfriends heard how children were born they gathered at their small island hideaway and swore a blood-sister pact that they would never do "that." Artemis exacted similar promises from her nymph companions. Once Britomartis (from Crete) ran and hid from a pursuer for nine months until, unable to hide any longer, she threw herself into the sea. Her escape is not unlike the chilling historical account of the Greek mothers and daughters who, when faced by enemy Turks, sang and danced the sacred *romaika* and hurled themselves one by one into an abyss.[12] They would rather throw themselves to their deaths from a cliff than submit to the treacherous hands of enemy men. Britomartis was saved, however. Fishermen caught her in their nets below so she was thereafter called Britomartis Diktyma, "of the nets"— another name of Artemis.

The length of the nymph's terror-stricken run toward the sea suggests that she really had broken the pact and was about to deliver irrefutable evidence of having slept with a man. Artemis (paradoxical as it sounds for a goddess associated with childbirth —but for everything there is a season, a time when she grants permission and a time when she denies) was infuriated at the sight of a pregnant nymph. Once while bathing with Kallisto, "the beautiful one," Artemis noticed her companion was burgeoning and angrily transformed her into a bear for the transgression. Apparently Kallisto thought she had been making love to Artemis but it was Zeus or perhaps Apollo who had taken on the guise of a woman to seduce her. When she heard this the goddess's anger gave way—not enough to restore Kallisto to her woman form, but enough to raise her to the heavens, where she lumbers still in the constellation of the Great Bear.

> In the hell holes and the heavenly meadows
>   she appears.
> From far away she is coming coming
> —MERIDEL LE SUEUR, *"Behold This and Always Love It"*

In *Rites of Ancient Ripening,* Le Sueur calls up the goddess "Changing Woman" from a distance. Artemis, her brother Apollo, and her other image, Hekate, all share this capacity for coming powerfully from afar. Like the bow and arrows of the twins, Hekate's magic can be made to strike far from home. The essence of magic is operating at a distance. Hekate's birds and Artemis's feathered shafts are used for magic and divination because of their similar far-ranging, airborne movement. Using magic effectively removes the operator from the target, which is aimed at from afar. Even though personal aims are met, the process itself is impersonal, not-quite-human, actually unrelated. The "long-winged moon" (Hesiod) oversees magic because its light is cold and distancing. When Medea, the enraged wife of Jason, who had taken another king's daughter to his bed, decided to move on her desire for revenge, she tells us she has "chosen Hekate for a partner." She is gifted with magical power and uses it to torture the new "bride" of her husband by sending her innocent children—like golden arrows—with the enchanted robe that will cling to the princess's flesh burning her to a gruesome death. Her magic is "black magic" here, operating at a distance in service of her own ego or destructive will power. When magic comes up in this connection, as protection against inevitable conflict, the conflict is not fully suffered and there can be no conscious realization of the meaning of the situation and generally not much chance of coming through it intact.[13] In Medea's case, she was compelled to kill her own children and then drove herself into gloomy exile to end her life cut off from all life she had known.

Jung tells a Medea story about a woman who committed murder:

"She put poison in the soup of another woman who was in love with her lover, and she was not found out. She came to confession absolutely destroyed. She felt cut-off, for people had begun to avoid her without knowing why. She lost all her maids and servants and nobody wanted to live near her. She lived quite alone. She rode everyday, but then the horse would bolt and would not carry her, and when one morning she called her dog and the dog put its tail between its legs and slunk away, she had to confess. She was slowly and cruelly ruined from within."[14]

(Silver turns black and has to be worked hard to shine again. The beneficent face of the moon maiden turns black and deadly. During this phase people should leave cakes lighted with candles for Hekate at the crossroads as a way of praying for the return of her light side.)

Confession—which in itself can be extremely difficult work—enables the movement out of exile. It is the first stage of analysis,[15] which functions like a bucket drawing up unlit slime—"source of earth, source of darkness":

> Out from the slime come rootlets
> Out from the slime comes young growth
> Out from the slime come branching leaves

Out from the slime comes outgrowth
Born in the time when men came from afar
Still it is night[16]

Yet the birth begins. And always it comes into being in the animal place: in the animal cradle of evolution; in the lowly stable or goats' cave where the first breath of divine children is warmed by the animals; in the animal nature that finally showed the woman in Jung's story that it was time to turn from her path of death and self-destruction. The other side of the treacherous magic that darkly illumines a facet of Hekate is the vital intuition of animal nature flowing through Artemis. She was born with eyes like a wolf, capable of seeing in the wave-sheltered darkness of Delos. The island describes itself in the *Homeric Hymn to Apollo* as a place lacking in people, where many-footed creatures of the sea and black seals make their dwellings undisturbed. As soon as Leto bore her in that desolate place the young goddess sprang to her mother's assistance and worked as midwife in the midnight delivery of her twin brother Apollo. Artemis knew the ways of woman's animal body without being taught. She literally stood at both ends of her mother in labor—the ready goddess at the knees and a date palm (a many-breasted tree, or Artemis as protectress of mothers and infants) at her head. Leto labored a full nine days and nine nights when the pains of childbirth seized her "and she longed to bring forth; so she cast her arms about a palm tree and kneeled on the soft meadow while the earth laughed for joy beneath. Then the child leapt toward the light and the goddesses raised a cry."[17] This was a birth out of exile:

Exiled I cried along the rivers
caged in time and loss,
Empty pod I longed for winged seeds.
Till merged in earth's agony of birth
leapt bridge
struck lyre

Impaled on earth and flesh's spring,
  budded with child.
—MERIDEL LE SUEUR, *"Budded with Child"*

Artemis never bears children herself; she is rather a tender of
birth like contemporary lesbians who breed animals and work as
midwives, or old women past the age of childbearing who choose
to nurse the young. Artemis brings certain caged aspects of feminine nature out of exile. When she puts on bird wings she is
woman liberated and her name then is Nemesis, another daughter of Night, who is "righteous anger directed against those who
have violated order," especially the laws and order of nature.[18]
Nature's law and order is quite different from that of civilization.
It is the law of untamed instinct, the virgin's order of open territory where the divisions are made according to animal need and
strength and not according to a man-made sense of justice.

In keeping with the undomesticated nature of her territory,
Artemis's way of knowing what goes on is primarily intuitive,
unschooled, "not trained in libraries or fed up in Attic academies
and porticoes . . . [but] simple and rude, uncultured and untaught
. . . of the road, the street, the workshop."[19] She is the guardian
of these places, guardian of experience, from *ex-periculum,* which
means moving "through peril" or "out of fear." One is drawn
toward the perilous places, with Artemis striding alongside. Instinctual nature seeks its source or goes to find the experience that
will make it aware of itself.[20]

> *Sister, I too beside the sea complain,*
>   *A bird that hath no wing.*
> *Oh for a kind market-place again,*
> *For Artemis that healeth woman's pain;*
>   *Here I stand hungering.*[21]

Hungers appeased by Artemis are many and varied—but she
does not feed you until you have made an essential sacrifice. She
is more demanding than some of the gods and leads one far from

the comfortable Olympian palace where delights follow so quickly upon the heels of desire. Artemis represents adventure, the tendency for striking out on your own. Following that instinct, which often comes up inconveniently in mid-life, means leaving the security of the city, of the home, family, and possibly even relationship, and finding a lone path that leads over the familiar hill of surroundings into a place where the only company is oneself as reflected in water, animals, and the surface of leaves. (In a poem called "Craving" [the hunger here is for a new way of speaking, for saying what is really meant], Denise Levertov says that the leaves on the tree tremble in speech: "Poplars tremble and speak if you draw near them." Poplars were known in the ancient world as borderland trees because of the striking contrast between the dark upper and light under surface of their leaves.[22] They, like Artemis-Hekate, stood as gateways between shadows and light, between the underworld, where the dark moon abides for a time, and the upper world, where we see the moon translate itself across the horizon.)

Another hunger increasingly felt, and one that Hekate satisfies in the story of Demeter and Persephone, is for the reunion with lost parts of the self, for the bringing together of sister parts again. That story (Chapter 4 above) begins with Persephone dancing on the flower-strewn meadow with her friends, including Artemis. Their circle is invaded by the fearsome King of the Underworld, who severs Persephone from the company of her mother and friends. She is cut off, as so frequently happens, by the circumstances of marriage. Her virginal nature, the hymen—"the heart of the boy in the woman"—was pierced that long night. (A hymeneal is the wedding song celebrating the loosening of that tissue; Hymenaios was a young boy god who dressed as a girl and died in the bridal chamber.[23]) This particular night in the life of maidenhood is one that Persephone's friend Artemis never enters. She stands instead, in her full and glorious stature, at the other end of it, available to her sister in travail. In the *Homeric Hymn,* Artemis-Hekate is a split figure: Artemis loses Persephone, and Hekate finds her at the other end.

Hekate, who lives in a cave at the entrance to the nether-world, knows her way in the darkness; she is a torch-bearing goddess who wears a gleaming headdress of stars that light her going. Although she was older than Zeus, and had her share of earth and sky and sea, she was never "elevated" to Olympus. She who walked the highways and dwelt in caves was connected to the mortal life of women. It was probably because of this dwelling-in-between that she was the only one to hear the cries of Persephone when she was abducted. Hekate, the Distant One, being neither goddess nor mortal woman at this time, con-tains the peculiar force that draws together whose who have been torn apart. Demeter, the grieving mother, wanders hori-zontally.[24] Persephone's journey is vertical—like a seed sunk and risen—and Hekate, goddess of crossroads, is at the place where the two meet.

We can see places where this archetypal reunion is occurring in our time. For instance, it is the Artemis-Hekate women, those who let that facet of themselves live most fully or keep this orien-tation toward feminine experience active, who are able to wel-come women out of marriages that kept them too much in the dark, where they were only another possession of Hades, the god of buried wealth. Coming up out of the darkness where their senses have been unused, these women feel half dead and are not capable of the immediate apprehension of environment that char-acterizes Artemis. Lust and luster have dimmed, contact with the graspable world diminished. It is at the point of emerging that a woman needs to find her own capacity for illuminating and focus-ing in on unfamiliar surroundings—the tools she needs to find are Hekate's torch and the arrows of Artemis.

In order to work this good magic of giving women back to themselves—making sound sense kin again, as Joyce says—the Artemis-Hekate women have to attempt the kinds of relationships where the shadow is admitted to view. The shadow appears in dreams as one of the same sex as the dreamer—we project the unwanted, negative, hateful, unknown parts of ourselves onto a friend who may be closest. Establishing a circle of trust, like the "choirs" or roving bands of the goddess, can give people the strength to face the blackest truths about themselves. The Artemis-Hekate aspect of the feminine encourages independence and departures—leavetakings in time and space and departures from the norm. It is not that the goddess isn't jealous of friends and lovers—we have seen that she can be vengeful when her pacts are betrayed—but rather she has the confidence that sisters of the same flesh and blood often have in each other: that they will be there for each other at the end of their travels. It may be this very principle of relatedness that made the Lone Woman of San Nicolas Island so affectionate and accessible after eighteen years of complete oceanbound solitude.

There are still undiscovered territories, adventures that have not been tried—ventures to the interior of human experience. Sometimes the weight of culture and personal history drives a person to seek meaning in a new direction. For one woman the driving forces were her mother and grandmother "Renewal":

My mother, grandmother and I are riding in the front seat of a car. Mother is driving. Grandmother Newell is in the center. Mother is determined that I begin a journey that is somewhat frightening to me. I will be leaving everyone to go in a direction no one has gone.

Another woman—much older, but facing an intersection as crucial as the dreamer above—dreamt that she refused to have a breast cut off even though it was cancerous. She is a nurse and undoubtedly knows the real danger of such a refusal. In her case it is her maternal nature that is killing her—making it impossible for her to leave her home and husband to go in a new direction. Like the Amazons, the bow-carrying descendants of Artemis, whose name *A-mazon* means without-a-breast (supposedly one was removed in order to better draw and release the bow), she can't move freely until the breast is removed. She is in the second half of life and needs—in accordance with Toni Wolff's structure

—to develop the axial arm of the Amazon pole to give balance to her heavy mother experience.

An important possibility inherent in this pole or this person who chooses to recognize Artemis-Hekate in actual experience is the extension of her concern for women into similar relationships with men. Men are brothers as women are her sisters. She wants no man as husband but will join with them in the hunt and feast at the same table. She never seeks their protection—only occasional companionship as long as it is based on outer interests held in common: animals, battle, music, divination, dance. Her love for Apollo, her brother, or masculine counterpart, like her love for women is "barren" in the sense of not producing offspring. But her productivity is of another order. Rather than regard her companions as her children, or as mother/father figures (a trap Aphrodite falls into), she sees others as her equals or spurs them on to that footing by her sometimes ruthless, sometimes playful competition.

Artemis chooses always to keep men at a brother distance. She does not want to be seen without her pelt on—and when she is, by Actaeon the hunter, she angrily transforms him into a stag and then sets his own hunting dogs upon him to tear the doomed man limb from limb. In hunting societies where cohabitation was relatively public, the man would go to the hut of the woman he wanted, stick his staff into the ground there or hang his quiver on the door to announce that he was sexually engaged within. Artemis, who always carried her own quiver, would hang it by the door to her dwelling—and it would seem to all who pass that there was a man in there with her. She herself was called a mannish woman and her brother Apollo a womanish man. These twins are a complete quaternity whose union is heavenly: like the sun and moon they pursue and flee and reflect each other—but never touch. In a culture where brothers were permitted to cohabit with their sisters, it must have been the spirit of the virgin huntress who inspired one girl to fashion staffs like those of her seven brothers: she set each one out at intervals so that it would appear that one of the brothers was always with her.

Brother love and companionship can free woman to life as well as keep her from a life of her own. Closeness to a brother teaches a girl different things than relationship to sisters. With sisters she learns to identify and with brothers she learns to differentiate. Once you see that a thing is different, the tendency is to try to incorporate it or eliminate it. This archetypal tendency to save or kill the brother is evident in fairy tales and myths. Girls save their brothers from animal or bird possession, for example, like the little girl whose brothers are turned into swans by an evil step-mother and remain winged for six years until the girl completes sewing a star-flower shirt for each of them. Her passion and perseverance were directed toward reunion.

Maidens like Medea and Ariadne, on the other hand, murder their brothers to be rid of them. Ariadne helped Theseus slay the Minotaur, her detested half-bull/half-man brother who lived in the labyrinth, and then she escaped the dark kingdom of Crete with the new sun hero. Medea killed her brother in order to flee home with Jason, who promised to take her to a new "civilized" land. Medea, as we have seen, brought the darkness of home with her and ended up a woman in exile. Ariadne, at one point in her journey across the waters, was abandoned by her hero as well— but she became clear about it (on the island of Naxos, where Theseus left her, her name became Aridela, "utterly clear" or "illumined") and moved on to consummate a sacred marriage to Dionysos, a raging bull god whose potency, like wine, repre-sented the transformed nature of her slain brother. In other words, Ariadne recognized her brother in her own desires and merged with them.

In adolescence many girls dream of sexual relationships with their brothers. One young woman was embarrassed by her dream of being taken on her older brother's lap until more brother dreams starting coming in over a period of several years. They showed him as her companion on long and tortuous journeys through strange houses and fantastic countries. This same brother figured in her first memory at the age of two and a half: on a walk together in the woods he pointed out a ditch where dangerous snakes lived. Brothers can function this way as awakeners of psychic life in a girl. By the very fact of their difference they inspire curiosity and stimulating antagonism (if it doesn't turn mythically deadly), and the fact of being in the same family usually encourages a certain loyalty and gap-bridging affection to grow up. This is not always the case, yet archetypally the brother-sister pair is a source of both hatred and love.

A woman's relationship to her inner brother, which is partially formed by experiences with real brothers, is projected onto the complicated sphere of heterosexual love relationships more often than it is into the "amazonian" realm, where relationships to men are distant. The more distant the male becomes the more likely he is to turn up in psychic life as an unrelated evil pursuer—usually intent on murder or rape—almost never as the friendly, brotherly, helpful sort. A woman, who is lesbian and often pursued by evil dream brothers, came to the point of terminating therapy when these brothers finally changed. Her dream series took place in an alleyway behind her childhood home. In the beginning she was regularly threatened by black "brothers" who drove by in cars aiming for her. Eventually the gloom of the alley lifted; it became a sunlit place where she learned first to ride her brother's bike and then to play softball with him. The transformation of the alleyway—which in itself is a behind-the-scenes transition space—took about six months and corresponded to no change in her outer relationships with men. Although changes did occur months later, to the point where conversations and playing music with men were enjoyable, the important factor seemed to be a coming to peace with a part of herself that had been repressed to the point of becoming dangerous.

Artemis encourages women to express their masculine natures. At the Korythalia, a festival in her honor, women would dance with exaggerated phalli attached to their male costumes. In their imitation of men, women would enact male sexual gestures, letting the rhythm of the other half of the universe pass through them. In this way their power was increased, and hopefully the harvest. Curt Sachs says it aptly when he describes the intention of the dance as "lifting and bursting the bounds of sex."[25] One can still see this dance performed in summery backyards where little girls playing under the sprinkler will detach the garden hose from the sprinkler and prance about—if no adults are watching —with the hose between their legs. It is not so much penis envy here as it is a germinal androgynous delight in being all things. The spirit of Artemis does seem to function in this boundary-breaking way between girls, calling them into her service at an early age. They may leave her for marriage, the way the girls trained under Sappho left her and their circle of intimate friends, or the way Persephone left the dance on the meadow.

For those who do leave, the imperative to reconnect with the lost experience may come up later in life in the desire to make friendships with women more central (like Margaret Mead and her friends at Barnard who agreed never to break a date with a woman for a man). It may take the form of wanting suddenly "a room of one's own" in order to foster the feeling of knowing oneself (this is like going deep into the inner woods with the huntress). It may emerge in a conscious attempt to change the nature of the man-woman relationship so that sexuality becomes less important than companionship. Or it may "come out" in a woman's recognition of her desire to form love relationships with women.

In the final scene of a fresco series depicting an initiation ceremony for women painted on the wall of a villa in Pompeii, four women are shown together—almost as if they were one woman experiencing four aspects of herself: one kneels in submission with her head on the lap of an older priestess; next to this pair you see the elegant naked figure of the initiate dancing; around her circles another more solemn woman who brings her a purple robe and a staff. Rilke, as if addressing the ecstatic woman, says:

Dancer: o you transposing
do you not take possession of the
hard-swung year?
—*"Sonnets to Orpheus"*

Protected and served by the overarching feminine, the woman moves moonlike from submission to resurrection. She has gone under and come up again, where she is greeted by torch- (or robe-) bearing Hekate—the part of herself that never left home and can therefore direct her returning steps.

This beautiful picture of fourfold woman fits the experience of those who have gone the way of marriage and returned to the protective circle of the virgin, but it does not fit Artemis herself, who never submits. Artemis is the call-of-the-wild, the undomesticated one who draws women instinctively to themselves—like the call felt by the northern goddess Skadi, who left the mountains to marry Njord, a sea god: they found that neither was willing to live away from home so he returned to the sea and she to the mountains, where she hunted on skis with a bow. Her separation from the man is paradoxical. She embodies a masculine nature that makes her self-sufficient and distant: she dwells in another world—and yet the distance and objectivity that comes of it may make it possible for her to see the man more clearly than the woman who goes along with him. Edward Carpenter wrote a book called *Intermediate Types Among Primitive Folk* shortly before the turn of the century, in which he describes these women (and men) as forerunners of culture because of their "double nature," their "command of life in all its phases." He describes the intermediate sex, saying that

we all know women with a strong dash of the masculine temperament, and we all know men whose almost feminine sensibility and intuition seem to belie their bodily form. Nature, it might appear, in mixing the elements which go to compose each individual, does not always keep her two groups of ingredients—which represent the two sexes—properly apart, but often throws them crosswise in a somewhat baffling manner, now this way and now that; yet wisely, we must think—for if a severe distinction of elements were always maintained, the two sexes would soon drift into far latitudes and absolutely cease to understand each other. As it is, there are some remarkable and (we think) indispensable types of character, in whom there is such a union or balance of the feminine and masculine qualities that these people become to a great extent the interpreters of men and women to each other.[26]

Artemis, the bow carrier, and her brother Apollo, the "unmanly" lover of mime and music, who carries the lyre, reflect and interpret each other: the interpretation, as William Carlos Williams said it, is "an interpenetration both ways, it can't be otherwise." And Heraclitus, in another of his fragments, provides a way of seeing the instruments of the divine twins as symbols of the reconciliation of opposing natures arrived at through an act of reflection, or "bending back":

People do not understand how that which is at variance with itself agrees with itself. There is harmony in the bending back, as in the case of the bow and the lyre.

7

Hetaira

Thus we cover the universe with drawings we have lived.
—GASTON BACHELARD

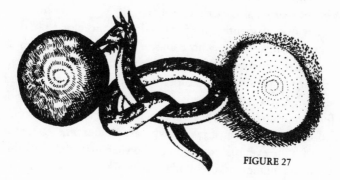

FIGURE 27

The drawing I have in mind is a series of circles representing stages of feminine development that are entered into, fully lived, and broken out of like eggs. There are three to start with[1]: first, the perfect, all-embracing circle of mother containment that shelters a child in darkness and warmth. Next to it there is a second, somewhat ominous circle wrapped round with a snake that arches back to break into the mother circle as if to draw out the contents of the egg. This is the circle of the father that draws a girl into the world. The first circle is a form of self-conservation. The second is a form of invasion and self-surrender. The third circle is one the woman draws around herself. It is a circle of self-realization that brushes up against the snake-entwined realm of the father as if it were still attracted to it and not quite able to spin on its own axis without the additional magnetic surge of positive and repellent contact. In this chapter I will try to describe the compelling nature of these highly charged points of contact, where the girl's life intersects the masculine principle which pulls her toward surrender and realization. The experience of self-surrender, which Artemis, the original "conservationist," does not know, characterizes the psychic life of the Hetaira (companion), the "father's daughter," whose surrender is inevitably to relationship.

Woman's original experience of herself in relationship to a mother is one of identity, a continuation of the blood bond of pregnancy. Unlike boys, who come to recognize themselves as "other," girls' discovery of self begins with a recognition of at-one-ness or sameness with motherliness, the source of life and protection. A girl's containment in this stage of identification with the female group (herself, her mother, her sisters) is often accompanied by the rejection of males, who are "different," so that it is only with the eventual intrusion of the alien masculine that this stage of containment-in-the-mother is broken. The depth psychologist's term for this is the "invasion of the paternal uroboros," the world-encircling snake.

Norse mythology tells how the giants threw the venomous world serpent to the edge of the earth, where it became the sea, completely circling the earth like the snake ring, called "uroboros" in alchemical tradition, that holds its tail in its mouth. Because of the open feminine mouth and the phallic tip of tail and the miraculous way it sloughs its skin in yearly regeneration, the uroboric snake is an enchanting creature containing all possibilities of male and female, beginning and end, life and death. Old European cartographers used to put a snake biting its tail in the corner of the map to mark the place where the unknown began, where the sea stretched into an unbroken horizon. They knew that Mother Earth was round and that the endlessly rocking movement of tidewaters meant that waves touching the shore would circle the earth to touch it again. (Some Mediterranean people called the ocean the "swift queen ever-turning back on herself.") "Uroboros," when used symbolically to represent a stage of child consciousness, is that quality of being cosmically "held" or protected within a magic circle that one is little capable of cracking until a door is opened from the outside, or until one sees something that forces a new way of thinking—one that urges breakthrough.

For a girl, this completely other thing is a boy—or the masculine principle. The original protected stage, experienced as one of psychic unity (one we look back upon as the experience of childlike wholeness) is broken into by the emergence of the archetype of the Great Father and his emissaries. Fairy tales usually depict this event in the coming of the king's son, the prince who represents the father.

In the story of Rapunzel, the girl is kept in prolonged mother captivity until the king's son comes by and happens to witness her predicament. The tower with no door and only one high window is the embrace of the enchanting witch mother who isolates the girl from the world. "Rapunzel" is another word for "rampion," a tuberous salad vegetable that was stolen from the witch's garden at the beginning of the story. Rapunzel's mother, who had long been barren, yearned for it during her pregnancy (perhaps it was used magically at some point in history to promote conception) and made her terrified husband steal it for her.

One day, as he climbed down the garden wall, the fearful enchantress was waiting for him: "How can you dare," said she with an angry look, "descend into my garden and steal my rampion like a thief? You shall suffer for it!" "Ah," answered he, "let mercy take the place of justice, I only made up my mind to do it out of necessity. My wife saw your rampion from the window, and felt such a longing for it that she would have died if she had not got some to eat." Then the enchantress allowed her anger to be softened, and said to him: "If the case be as you say, I will allow you to take away with you as much rampion as you will, only I make one condition, you must give me the child which your wife will bring into the world; it shall be well treated, and I will care for it like a mother." The man in his terror consented to everything, and when the woman was brought to childbed the enchantress appeared at once, gave the child the name of Rapunzel, and took it away with her. She would have her rampion back.

This is a way of saying that it is the archetypal Mother rather than the personal mother who holds a girl in the uroboric circle of the tower. (Frequently, when it is time to start leaving their mothers in a psychic sense, children will dream of their personal mothers as terrible witches—this compels a certain distancing that might not otherwise occur.) Rapunzel's golden hair grew and grew and grew so long and strong that she could wrap it around a hook outside the little window and drop it to the ground to make a braided ladder for the witch. It happened that the king's son, hiding in the surrounding thistle, figured out the riddle of the girl's inaccessibility by watching the witch mother calling out and climbing up. He then broke the mother hold on the girl by going up to her at twilight, time of changing worlds. She was terrified, for she had never before set eyes on a man, but he spoke to her so kindly that she lost her fear and surrendered her hand and then herself.

The story does not, however, end here. Hair, as time and custom testify, is a symbol for the soul because it grows out of the head—the place of consciousness. It grows again after it is cut and even continues growing after a person dies. Initiation rites usually include some form of hair cutting or alteration to symbolize a new orientation of the psyche. Rapunzel's hair had grown so long that it must have been time for a change—time to start another phase of life. Some of the stories say she was twelve when put in the tower and that the prince came a year or two later, which would mark the age of puberty with typical unconscious accuracy. The witch mother discovers the long-feared invasion of the male because the innocent girl asks why it is so much harder to pull the prince up by her hair than the old mother! She furiously cuts off the beautiful hair and takes Rapunzel away to an even lonelier desert. Meanwhile, the prince has fallen from the tower, been blinded by thorns in the thicket, and has set out wandering in search of his bride. Eventually, they are reunited: her tears of joy heal his eyes and twins are born to them out of the barren desert, and the cycle of containment and breakthrough can start once more.

In another story about this stage of feminine experience, the young girl is kept in a castle where she sees no one except for Lavarcham, the king's old "conversation woman," the helpful gossip of his kingdom. Deirdre escapes over the castle wall one night (she too is about fourteen), to follow a light in the forest where youths are encamped after hunting. This excerpt of an ancient tale retold illustrates the power of the first contact between princess and prince:

She stood forward a pace.
Had she really moved, or was she impelled! Surely a hand had taken her by the shoulder and pushed her forward! But in the moment that she moved panic seized her as suddenly and overwhelmingly as a hawk swoops upon a mouse. She lifted a hand to her breast so that her heart might not be snatched away, but the hand went on to her lips and covered them in terror lest they should call. She turned with one swift and flying gesture, but the foot that aimed for flight continued its motion, and the full circle held her again facing the terror. For he had already risen, lithe as a cat and as noiseless, and in three great strides he was standing beside her, standing over her, encompassing her about, not now to be retreated from or escaped from or eluded in any way.
And as her heart had leaped, so his leaped also, and they stood in an internal tumult, so loud, so intimate and violent that the uproar and rush of a storm was quietude in the comparison.
They could not speak. There were no words left in the world.

There were only eyes that plunged into and fled from each other, and a mighty hand that had gripped her arm. . . . A hand that pushed her backwards and backwards, away from the friendly logs that crackled and flamed, away from the quiet forms that might have rescued her but that lay as though slumbering in stone.[2]

The terror and fascination of this first encounter with the opposing masculine principle has the effect of seizing the feminine —an overwhelming effect that later becomes part of her sexuality. But at this stage the feeling of enrapture (rapt, raped), being swept off one's feet, is what comes to youth as a spiritual experience. You might not recall a hand literally seizing you in the dark woods night, but you might remember an awakening to a kind of intoxication mixed with awe or fear at the possibilities ahead— a sudden *enthusiasm,* which means having been seized by the god within. Dreamers at this stage are often overcome by animals (gods in disguise): a bull, a rambunctious goat, a great snake, or a bird as in Deirdre's feeling that a hawk was swooping down to snatch her heart. One young woman who was caught at this juncture, having severe difficulties with a relationship—due partially to her refusal to admit the desire to surrender to something more powerful than herself—dreamed that she and her lover were on top of a mountain looking in different directions: he was absorbed in examining a pile of moose droppings while she was watching with breathless excitement as an overwhelmingly large red and black hawk swooped from the heavens toward her. In her perception he was still engrossed in "the shit they kept dropping on each other" while she was about to be carried away by the spirit coming birdlike out of the blue. (Had the hawk actually seized her the relationship might have been saved.)

This element of woman's being carried away both spiritually and sexually is the main motif in Euripides's play *The Bacchae.* In this play the masculine principle is embodied in the divine form of Dionysos: god of wine, women, and song, the "god-who-comes." He comes into town and calls women away from their daily work at the looms to join him for a spell of mad dancing in the hills. The Bacchae, also known as maenads—mad minions of the moon—were periodically inspired to these wild orgiastic revels, to the horror of men. One of the few persons who understood was the aged Tiresias, who had been both male and female. The domesticated woman was taken over by a frenzied awakening to a dreadful part of herself. She nursed wild creatures instead of her own children, and tore animals apart with bare hands to fashion the fur pelts she wore in the hills. (Fashionable modern women dress symbolically like maenads in animal pelts and wear make-up —blood-red lipstick and nail polish—reminiscent of the maenads' exploits.)

This is an extreme example of the attraction to the irrupting archetype of the spirit father. It often takes a more pious form, as in a girl's dedication to God the father in the transcendent religious realm, or to an inspiring teacher in the realm of the intellect. It is evident also in a girl's experience of being drawn to priests, poets, and artists—creative men who represent the spiritual father. This stage is both marvelously creative and extremely dangerous because of the possibility of fixation—of becoming stuck in the generative father ground. A girl who becomes so rooted is called the *puella aeterna,* the eternal daughter, who lives within the thrall of the father, until the hero comes (either a real person or her own other side) to rescue her *to* consciousness.

Page Smith, who wrote *Daughters of the Promised Land,* makes us well aware of the benefits that come from a good father-daughter relationship in his discussion of the great women in American history. He notes a trend in this direction during the Protestant Reformation, when fathers took direct responsibility for the education of their daughters.

They had to be taught to read in order to enjoy the benefits of the Scriptures; when salvation might depend on literacy, education took on a new urgency. Fathers and daughters thus entered into a novel relationship out of which daughters acquired a new sense of personal dignity and worth. They were no longer simply dutiful and self-effacing servants of their masters, fathers or husbands, they were the children of God, precious in his eyes and filled with heretofore undisclosed or barely-hinted-at potential.[3]

Because girls were important for some reason other than marriage and childbearing, other kinds of attention could be freely turned on them. (Jonathan Edwards, the renowned preacher, had ten children, eight of them girls, to whom he gave tireless educational direction.)

Such intense and helpful relationships with fathers can free women to relate to men in highly charged fields of interest: emotional and practical or spiritual and intellectual. But if—as not infrequently happens—the natural undercurrent of attraction in the father-daughter relationship gets turned around on itself and goes unadmitted, an eroticism can develop that will hurt a girl as much as the encouraging attentive love helps her.[4] A girl learns about her effect on men at a very young age and often discovers that daughterly talent of attracting a man's most creative aspects. It is a mermaid's legacy, actually: once the male has drawn up to her rock side she turns the mirror toward him so that he sees himself excited or inspired.

The hetaira is a woman of this type, who can, depending upon her own strength (strength in this instance means knowing herself as hetaira), either play the role of awakening psychic life in a friend or companion or play the role of temptress and lure the other away from realistic adaptation to the world. She either enhances her partner's perception of himself or herself by exciting the psyche to new insights or she imprisons another by convincing him or her of some illusory talent, or latent potential, which would lead to losing a sense of what is and is not real about oneself. Circe, the sorceress in the Odyssey, was a hetaira who transformed her lovers into beasts. Seen psychologically, this would mean that through knowing her, their dark or unpresent-able shadow sides emerged with such violence or passion that it overwhelmed them. (This also might mean that in Homer's time men whose ugly sides showed were called "pigs.")

It is easy for the hetaira to become inflated with her own powers—to live beyond her station, or to suffer from "loss of earth" with her feet off the ground and her head in the clouds. In the story of "The Handless Maiden," a fairy tale which I want to give you in its entirety, the maiden—a *puella aeterna*—is so dedicated to her father that she loses not her footing or her roots but her hands, her very grasp of reality. The tale follows as Marie-Louise von Franz tells it in her book on *The Feminine in Fairy Tales:*

A miller had fallen by degrees into great poverty until he had nothing left but his mill and a large apple tree. One day when he was going into the forest to cut wood, an old man, whom he had never seen before, stepped up to him and said, "Why do you trouble yourself with chopping wood? I will make you rich if you will promise me what stands behind your mill."

The miller thought to himself that it could be nothing but his apple tree; so he said "Yes" and concluded the bargain. The other, however, laughed derisively, and said, "After three years I will come and fetch what belongs to me."

As soon as the miller got home, his wife asked him the origin of the sudden flow of gold which was coming to the house. The miller told her that it came from a man he had met in the forest to whom in return he had promised what stands behind the mill. "For," said the miller, "we can very well spare the great apple tree."

"Ah, my husband," exclaimed his wife, "it is the Evil Spirit whom you have seen. He did not mean the apple tree, but our daughter, who was behind the mill sweeping the yard."

The miller's daughter was a beautiful and pious maiden, and during all the three years lived in the fear of God. When the day came for the Evil One to fetch her, she washed herself quite clean and made a circle round herself with chalk, so that he could not approach her. In a rage he said to the miller, "Take her away from all water, that she may not be able to wash herself; else have I no power over her." The miller did so, for he was afraid. But the next morning when the Evil One came, the girl had wept upon her hands so that they were quite clean. He was baffled again and in his anger said to the miller, "Cut off both her hands, or else I cannot now obtain her."

The miller was horrified and said, "How can I cut off the hands of my own child?"

But the Evil One pressed him saying, "If you do not, you are mine, and I will take you yourself away!"

The miller told his daughter what the Evil One said and asked her to help him in his trouble and to forgive him for the wickedness he was about to do her. She replied, "Dear father, do with me what you will—I am your daughter." And her father cut her hands off.

For the third time now the Evil One came. But the maiden had let fall so many tears upon her arms that they were both quite clean. So he was obliged to give her up and after this lost all power over her.

The miller now said to her, "I have received so much good through you, my daughter, that I will care for you most dearly all your life long."

But she answered, "Here I cannot remain. I will wander forth into the world, where compassionate men will give me as much as I require."

Then she had her arms bound behind her back and at sunrise departed on her journey. In time she arrived at a royal garden and by the light of the moon she saw a tree standing which bore most beautiful fruits. She could not enter for there was water all round, but she was tormented by hunger, so she kneeled and prayed to God. All at once an angel came down, who made a passage through the water, so that the ground was dry for her to pass over. So she went into the garden, but the pears were all numbered. She stepped up and ate one to appease her hunger, but no more. The gardener perceived her do it, but because the angel stood by he was afraid, and thought the maiden was a spirit.

The next morning the king found that a pear was missing and asked the gardener whither it was gone. He replied, "Last night a spirit came, who had no hands, and ate the pear with her mouth."

The king then asked, "How did the spirit come through the

water? And whither did it go after it had eaten the pear?"

The gardener answered, "One clothed in snow-white garments came down from heaven and made a passage through the waters, so that the spirit walked over on dry land. And because it must have been an angel, I was afraid, and neither called out nor questioned it; and as soon as the spirit had finished the fruit, she returned as she came."

The king said, "If it be as you say, I will this night watch with you."

As soon as it was dark the king came into the garden, bringing with him a priest. At about midnight the maiden crept out from under the bushes and again ate with her mouth a pear off the tree, whilst the angel clothed in white stood by her. Then the priest went towards her and said, "Art thou come from God or from earth? Art thou a spirit or a human being?"

She replied, "I am no spirit, but a poor maiden, deserted by all, save God alone."

The king said, "If you are forsaken by all the world, yet will I not forsake you," and he took her with him to his royal palace. Because she was so beautiful and pious, he loved her with all his heart, ordered silver hands to be made for her, and made her his bride.

After a year had passed, the king was obliged to go to war and left the young queen to the care of his mother. Soon afterwards a boy was born and the old mother wrote a letter to her son containing the joyful news. But the messenger rested and fell asleep on his way and the Evil One changed the letter for another saying that the queen had brought a changeling into the world. As soon as the king had read this letter, he was frightened and much troubled, but he wrote to his mother that she should take great care of the queen until his arrival. But the messenger again fell asleep on the way and the Evil One put a letter in his pocket saying that the queen and her child should be killed. When the old mother received this letter, she was struck with horror and wrote another letter to the king, but received no answer. Rather the Evil One placed another false letter for the mother into the messenger's pocket saying that she (the mother) should preserve the tongue and eyes of the queen as a sign that she had fulfilled the order.

The old mother was sorely grieved to shed innocent blood so she cut out the tongue and eyes of a calf and said to the queen,

"I cannot let you be killed as the king commands, but you must remain here no longer. Go forth with your child into the wide world and never return here again."

Thus saying, she bound the child upon the young queen's back, and the poor wife went away, weeping bitterly. Soon she entered a large forest and there she fell upon her knees and prayed to God. The angel appeared and led her to a little cottage, over the door of which was a shield inscribed with the words: "Here may everyone live freely."

Out of the house came a snow-white maiden who said, "Welcome, Lady Queen," and led her in and said she was an angel sent from God to tend her and her child. In this cottage the queen lived for seven years and was well cared for; through God's mercy to her, on account of her piety, her hands grew again as before.

Meanwhile the king had come home again, and his first thought was to see his wife and child. Then his mother began to weep and said, "You wicked husband, why did you write me that I should put to death two innocent souls?" And showing him the two letters which the Evil One had forged, she continued, "I have done as you commanded," and she brought him the tokens—the two eyes and the tongue.

The king then began to weep so bitterly for his dear wife and son that the old mother pitied him, and said, "Be comforted, she lives yet! I caused a calf to be slain, from whom I took these tokens; but the child I bound upon your wife's back, and I bade them go forth into the wide world, and she promised never to return here because you were so wrathful against her."

"So far as heaven is blue," exclaimed the king, "I will go; and neither will I eat nor drink until I have found again my dear wife and child—if they have not perished of hunger by this time."

Thereupon the king set out, and for seven long years sought his wife in every stony cleft and rocky cave, but found her not—and began to think she must have perished.

But God sustained him, and at last he came to the large forest and little cottage. Out of the house came the white maiden and leading him in said, "Be welcome, great king! Whence comest thou?"

He replied, "For seven long years have I sought everywhere for my wife and child; but I have not succeeded."

Then the angel offered him food and drink, but he refused them both and lay down to sleep, and covered his face with a napkin.

Now went the angel into the chamber where sat the queen, with her son, whom she usually called "Sorrowful" and said to her, "Come down with your child. Your husband is here." So she went to where he lay, and the napkin fell from off his face.

So the queen said: "Sorrowful, pick up the napkin, and cover again your father's face." The child did as he was bid, and the king, who heard in his slumber what passed, let the napkin again fall from off his face.

At this the boy became impatient and said, "Dear mother, how can I cover my father's face? Have I indeed a father on the earth? I have learned the prayer, 'Our Father which art in heaven'; and you have told me my father was in heaven—the good God. How can I talk to this wild man? He is not my father."

As the king heard this, he raised himself and asked the queen who she was. The queen replied, "I am your wife, and this your son, Sorrowful."

But when he saw her human hands, he said, "My wife had silver hands."

"The merciful God," said the queen, "has caused my hands to grow again"; and the angel going into her chamber, brought out the silver hands and showed them to him.

Now he perceived that they were certainly his dear wife and child and kissed them gladly, saying, "A heavy stone is taken from my heart." After eating a meal together with the angel, they went home to the king's mother.

Their arrival caused great rejoicings everywhere; and the king and queen celebrated their marriage again and lived happily together until the end of their lives.[5]

This story is like a two-sided mirror—it can be looked at as the story of a man who mistreats his anima and the circuitous route toward re-establishing that sacred marriage, or it can be looked at from the point of view of a maiden who sacrifices her own development because of her devotion to the father. This latter side seems to best capture the fairy tale's images. The girl suffers because the father is willing to sacrifice his soul to the devil for money. He has become "poorer by degrees" until he has nothing left but the mill and the blossoming apple tree, which, it turns out, is synonymous with the blossoming girl. Economic values have taken priority over personal values—the mill stands before the tree—so that the miller's capacity for loving his daughter has degenerated into his willing substitution of her to save himself. "The Devil take her" is his unconscious attitude.

A girl who has not been given her father's attention (who has not felt his love for life over and above his desire for wealth or concern for his work) may have a void created in her, a vacancy that tends to fill up with obsessive, devilish impulses. These are then acted upon in order to get the father's attention or else kept completely out of touch by the girl's assumption of piety. She retreats into a melancholy passivity in the complete avoidance of the life of the spirit. This is the choice of the duty-bound girl in the story. She has her hands cut off, thus giving up any control she may have had and giving in to the feeling that she can't "handle things" anymore. Even the Devil is kept away by her purity. She is untouched and incapable of touching—there is no soul there for the Devil to take.

At this point, the father attempts to recognize the girl. But it is too late and, she suspects, insincere. She must leave the circle of parental containment and move on to the next circle of containment in the embrace of the spiritual father represented by the watery circle (moat) around the palace. She arrives there hungry, with her arms tied behind her back. She has accepted her fate but found no solution to the problem of being out of touch. Marriage is only a temporary solution. The king loves her and makes her a pair of silver hands. (Silver is a feminine metal, the color of the new moon, recipient of other [planetary] influences, symbol of new birth and purity. It has the magical quality of keeping away evil. It is cold, distancing, reflective.) But her marriage can only restore part of what had been lost. She still has to get her hands out of her father's hands to learn not only who she is as true wife to the king but who she is as a whole woman aware of herself as "rich in sorrows."

In *Knowing Woman*, Irene de Castillejo describes the animus (in its negative form) as capable of disastrously cutting off a woman's participation in life. It often gives one the feeling of being separated, tortured, unable to go on. At these times, the animus may take on the frightening countenance of the father who would sever his daughter's connections with the outside world. The violence done to her drives the handless maiden into nature, or into a deep introversion in the forest—"the place of unconventional inner life."[6] She retreats into her own loneliness with Sorrow, the child of her marriage. It is a painful place of separation but at least here she can live freely apart from her father's (and the collective) opinions about who she is and how she should behave.

It is at this point that many women who are terrified of being alone reject the angel's invitation to solitary retreat and go out instead into the streets again (or back home), seeking people and ways to fill the awful emptiness. This way, the work of finding your own law or the entrance to your own "cave of inner being" (literally, an *ethic*) is put off. Turning away from the world to discover whether you are really alive is unquestionably painful. But it is in the conscious acceptance of loneliness—when there is nothing else to do—that a natural process of healing occurs.

There are many versions of "The Handless Maiden" but the maiden's regaining of the ability to touch others or to be in touch with the world is always a natural (and, therefore, miraculous) healing. Once it happens that the maiden's hands are regenerated when she puts her arms around a tree. Another time she is told to reach into the water for her lost child—and her hands grow back as she does it. Often the period of handlessness lasts many years. This is the hardest part: just waiting. Letting things come of their own accord, or grow in their own time, often looks and feels like complete stagnation. But angels come out of those still depths. Having gone into the introversion and living through her time of incubation, the woman gains a sense of strength and spirit which enables her to participate again in the world of men and children. As Jung put it: a part of life was lost but the meaning has been saved.[7]

Weaving a cocoon out of the substance of one's own life is the

necessary prerequisite for the emergence of psyche: in withdraw-
ing we prepare a way out. Any of the feminine types on the
structural poles can go through this experience of withdrawal in
service of the emergence of self, but it is the hetaira who would
be thrown into this experience as a result of her dedication to the
father.

The hetaira more frequently becomes the "mistress" or the
extramarital companion than the wife and mother. Her closeness
to that forest realm of unconventional inner life calls her onto a
path of emotional wanderings and tentative attachments. Marriage for this type of woman—who values personal relationships
over any kind of tie to a family or profession—would look like
the marriage of the goddess Aphrodite, one which, because of her
energy and unending variety of desires, permitted her freedom
to explore numerous relationships with gods and mortals. She
also had the tendency to make her children into secret lovers (i.e.,
Eros) and to look for her father in the men she desired.

Aphrodite's origin is a remarkable story of a father-daughter
relationship. It happened that Uranos, or Sky, came, "longing for
love," to lie once again over wide-bosomed Earth. She was groan-
ing already under the affliction of his habitually stuffing the children deep back into her after they were born. His refusal to let
their children see the light of day finally incensed her into action:
she brought forth iron, fashioned a sickle out of it, and asked for
help from any of the many children. No one answered except
Cronos (who later became the father of Zeus); he took the
weapon in hand, crept up on his father where he lay, castrated
him, and threw his members into the sea. Up from his members
sprang the foam-born love goddess, Aphrodite. Since she de-
spised marriage it became her duty among gods and men to
make-love or re-member.

So the lovely pale maiden who steps lightly from her shell boat
onto the flowery isle in Botticelli's famous painting is the transformed phallus of the father. She is the cut-off fruit of his man-
hood. Robert Graves points out an ancient Hittite parallel to this

story: Kumarbi bites off the phallus of the god Anu, swallows the seed, and then spits some of it up on a mountain—thus giving birth to a new goddess.[8] The "springing up" of these goddesses and the self-willed movement characteristic of Aphrodite's night-time liaisons are both masculine, or attributes of the phallus itself. The gravity-defying, spontaneously generating member rises of its own accord like the sea swell in response to the call of its daughter, Desire. Desire in one sense means "to regret the absence of"—this must be the father's sense of it—and in another sense it means "away from a star," *de sidere.* Aphrodite's star is, of course, Venus, the wishing star of morning and evening that rises so close to the crescent moon. From the maiden's point of view, then, she has been cut off from the father and seeks always to close the distance between heavenly and earthly bodies. She herself is the connection, the power to make the wish come true, the body of water touching shore to shore, the movement of desire from quiver to heart. She is as much the arrow of Eros as she was the once virile shaft of the father.

These motifs of being cut off, foam risen, seaborne, and connecting distant shores are all present to me now as I remember the first dream I recorded (first day of college, first day "away from home"). It took place on the edge of the sea. A very beautiful Native American man with a craggy carved face and a red scarf tied around his hair stood on my right in a hunting jacket. Further ahead on my left stood my father knee deep in foam, in front of a group of people whom he was helping across the breakers. I approached and took his hand for support as the great wave came in—and I rose higher and higher and higher—frightened save for the hand . . . but I made it, with his help, over the rise and broke away to start swimming across the sea. I was hesitant to leave because I knew my father would die of a heart attack helping all those people across. A plain brown envelope passed between us (I gave it back to him for safekeeping?). He urged me to go on. I began swimming toward a white-shining crystal city on the far shore.

Our physical connection was severed forever as I passed through the gate of the fathers—both personal and archetypal. I left my native shore, but only after the genetic code, the sexual information in the plain brown wrapper, the inter-office envelope, had been passed between us. It seems the goddesses were always discussing their "offices" with their fathers. An office was like a charge, a public duty to perform as emissary, missionary, or emission of the father.

In a patriarchate we are born from our fathers at a much later stage than from our mothers, when we have reached the "age of discretion" or when we are capable of certain kinds of thinking. It remains true for everyone that birth from the mother is the first, indisputable "fact" of experience. We see her and feel her as basic matter, shelterer, nourisher, the place and house of generation. But the recognition of fatherhood takes an abstract thought, a leap of faith. Bachofen describes the distance of father conception: as begetter, the father belongs to the offspring only through the mediation of the mother; he stands in no visible relation to the child and thus always appears the remoter potency.[9] We are bound to the father by an invisible thread in contrast to the flesh and blood umbilical bond of pregnancy. "Seeing" the father's connection to his children, recognizing the reality of the invisible, or accepting the unknown behind the known signals the birth of spirit, of metaphor, of the capacity for creative thought. This may be clearer in the context of Athene's birth from the head of Zeus than in the birth of Aphrodite. But Athene's story is told by the next generation of the gods and represents a "higher" masculine conception—a birth from the upper head as opposed to a birth from the lower head ("As above, so below . . .").

According to the circular scheme of feminine development mentioned above, my sea's edge dream can be considered a prefiguring of the third circle. We move from the circle of mother containment to the circle of father containment, to break out again into the circle of potential self-realization. We leave home to find it. Just as every maiden who leaves her mother is Persephone, every girl who leaves her father is Aphrodite—out to seek what she can find across the sea. Persephone's split is healed when she herself becomes a mother. Becoming your own father, or Aphrodite's cure, would mean becoming self-generating, father to your own experience, capable of independent thought and action, especially in the realms of love.

Aphrodite's father-given "office" is sexuality. She is feminine sexuality (whether married, unmarried, widow, nymph, or crone) and feminine sensuousness, which can take many forms to heighten self-awareness and awareness of others. Smiles, loveliness, stately carriage, cheerful songs, the beauty of bodies, the joy of love, laughter, and the taming of wild animals (she mates the lion with the lamb)—these are all in her province. Her capacity to delight is countered by her tendency to lead astray. She has this dual potency—to bestow sight and to blind, both in the service of love. When someone is awakened by love, they see things within and without as if for the first time. Aphrodite teaches the secrets of the heart. She shows the value of spontaneous feeling and opens an undisclosed cache of creativity and imagination in both lover and loved. Gary Snyder, in a poem called "Wave," written to his wife, catches this hetaira aspect of the goddess in midair:

> Ah, trembling spreading radiating wyf
> racing zebra
> catch me and fling me wide
> to the dancing grain of things
> of my mind!

The flights of the hetaira, full of great swoops and soarings—fluctuations according to the mood of relationship—gain their momentum, not from winged promises of love that the betrothed make to each other, but from the sense of search and freedom that compels her. Olive Schreiner, in her book *Dreams,* envisioned it this way:

I saw a woman sleeping. In her sleep she dreamt Life stood before her, and held in each hand a gift—in the one Love, in the other Freedom. And she said to the woman, "Choose!"

And the woman waited long: and she said, "Freedom!" And Life said, "Thou has well chosen. If thou hadst said 'love,' I would have given thee that what thou didst ask for; and I would have gone from thee and returned no more. Now, the day will come when I shall return. In that day I shall bear both gifts in one hand."

I heard the woman laugh in her sleep.[10]

The wise hetaira takes the relationship between love and freedom into account. She is the woman who would rather struggle to keep her loves unbound by convention.

The other side of the wise hetaira is the foolish virgin who lives in the thrall of a daemonic freedom: she belongs to no man because she still belongs to her father; her sacrifices are for him as idol and ideal. She is free to be cared for by many people but rarely free enough to make a room of her own. In this sense she never grows up; she remains the *puella aeterna,* the girl or princess incapable of commitment because she does not know her own mind and heart. Her development is sacrificed in her dedication to the other: either to the man who cuts off her hands and would keep her at home, or to the father phallus that urges her constantly to express a sexual freedom that stunts her psychically. No matter how fecund or promiscuous, a woman remains uncreative until she arouses Eros in herself. (In the tale of Psyche's Lamp, Eros, the winged companion-son of Aphrodite, represents the capacity for relationship over and above the sexual union.) The fate of the hetaira as seductress is to remain enchained or encircled by her dependence upon admiration. Of course she admires others but there is self-enhancing purpose in it.

The hetaira does not respect social roles, nor does her erotic energy respect the categories of wife, husband, teacher, servant, son, and so on. Consequently, she generates great excitement, and fear as well. Her tendency, which is often unconscious and then all the more compelling, is to break up any institutional form of relationship. Where there is such a pattern, her nature is at work: when the girl falls in love with the priest (or nun), analysand with analyst, or student with professor, when a woman finds herself always moving into situations where marriage is disrupted or simply where friendships are treasured—that in itself can be quite disruptive in our couple-insulated society. Her attention releases contradictory tides of insight, creativity, compassion, jealousy, impotence, and sometimes death. Since she is not emerging with a restricted persona like "mistress" or "concubine" anymore, her energy flows across boundaries, and where it meets people who have not reshaped themselves to receive it, her energy can break them. Awareness has this advantage: choice of channel. The hetaira is often unaware of the emotional recesses her words, her work, and/or her presence can reach. As awakener of desire, she has a countertendency to leave a wake of resignation and despair.

Transitions from circle to circle or movement between ways of being can occur at any age. Vestal virgins, who were the young girls chosen in ancient Rome to be hetairae within the sacred precinct of the goddess, could make a choice around the age of forty: in mid-life (in those days perhaps it was late in life) they could choose to remain in the temple and so instruct the younger virgin keepers of the fire, or they could leave and go to the life of the world. Yeats has written of the moon, "Before the full it sought itself and afterwards the world." But the hetaira would probably stay. So-called realistic adaptation to the world is not interesting. She would rather bear the pain of her pole than the pain of wife and mother.

When Toni Wolff wrote her essay in 1932 on the structural poles, she said that our time seems to place emphasis on the Mother and Amazon. The Hetaira and Medial women were held in greater esteem in the Middle Ages and perhaps during the Renaissance. Once again it looks as if the part, or pole, that is repressed returns with great unwelcome force and confusion. Few are the mothers or elders who have taught us the ways of the hetaira, or to value her consciously. Nonetheless, as tired masks and roles fall away, it may be that "she of the sea," the love goddess who can be educated or drawn to the work of relationship, is floating up to disembark again in our culture.

A certain negative cultural exploitation of this emergent aspect of feminine consciousness is visible now in the human potential movement, where the mermaid's mirror rather than Psyche's lamp seems to be the favored instrument of perception. Taking up Psyche's lamp means the beginning of a long and lonely journey relieved at rare points by communion with the gods and the utter absorption of having to complete nearly impossible tasks. The mermaid, on the other hand, is more magical, more "tricky"; the work of her mirror is instantaneous. She entices one to acquire a new self-image by staring into other people's eyes, touching fingertips, intoning group mantras, playing mind games, exercising the left side of one's brain, clarifying values, and so on. Unfortunately, the mermaid has a tail sunk deep into the unconscious. Beneath the surface of her gift-bestowing water-mirror there stretches a vast, not yet human, unevolved, insidiously seductive realm. In fairy tales the tragedy often incurred by taking up with a mermaid is the loss of one's child—and the child everywhere represents human potential.

The danger of the shallow emphasis is that the hetaira nature will not evolve into the fullness of relationship of which it is capable. Although *hetaira* came to mean royal concubine or privileged prostitute, it actually means comrade or companion. A mermaid is incapable of being a companion—she is only an apparent companion in the moment of mutual inspiration, which does not see below the conscious surface. The mermaid, like the *puella aeterna,* is either sad because she knows that the source of her allure will keep her from being truly recognized or she is frightened because she feels deeply resistant to looking into her own nature. It takes great courage for a woman to begin to pull her "fish nature" up into the air where it can be seen. This would mean revealing the coldness concealed beneath her charm. Or the selfishness behind her apparent ability to please everybody. When a woman can too easily change her hue, her costume, her face value to suit the desires of an onlooker, she comes to experience herself as "slippery" and ultimately unembraceable. If she can tolerate turning the depth-revealing mirror toward herself she may be able to break the enchantment. (Having to be enchanting can be a terrible curse. To be *glamourous* means to act in a witch-like manner, to "bewitch.") The hetairic aspect of the feminine principle remains immature until surrender becomes possible: not the surrender of the first stage to an intruding masculine principle, but a surrender to the full impact of unrealized self. The *puella aeterna* grows up when she takes hold of herself; this occurs when she is excited by her own latent possibility without having to rely on the gaze of father or lover to move her. She is, paradoxically, then capable of companionship. Having once taken hold of herself she is able to give herself completely to the work of relationship.

This is especially the case in young life. The flow toward world blocked by a father fixation can be freed by showing a girl the values specific to the feminine, or by redirecting the father-held energy into a love relationship. But later in life, as Amy Allenby points out in her essay on the father archetype, "the situation is different and demands a different solution. In the second half of life . . . liberation from the past is not enough; a solution can only come through the experience and acceptance of the problem of opposites."[11] Jung called this element that comes into play later in life the "transcendent function." It takes one outside the confining patterns of social self-expression into an inner realm where symbols of the heights and depths actively weld together fragments of conscious and unconscious experience. Tensions between known and unknown, conscious and unconscious, energy and content are overcome or transcended by the fabrication of a new image or value that unites what was broken and scattered. "Collect the fragments of the splintered glass," H. D. instructs:

and of your fire and breath,
melt down and integrate,

re-invoke, re-create
opal, onyx, obsidian,

now scattered in the shards
men tread upon.
    —*"Tribute to the Angels"*

In the case study of an older woman written by Allenby, the work of re-creation took the time-consuming form of recasting the image of the father from a hideously distorted man who kept her from life by throwing boulders to block her way to a Chinese emperor who "exalted the inner world into a cosmic principle."[12] Her actual father was of course long dead, so this work of recasting took place in her dreams. The original containment in the diabolical embrace of the actual father was transformed into a sacred marriage with a symbolic father. One of the symbols delineated by her dreams as her father became clearer and less threatening was that of hands. Like the maiden in the fairy tale, this woman's hands "grew back." She was able to make contact with the world again from a self-made place. An archetype that exerts profound influence on a child is likely to continue to do so forever. Memories fade from consciousness but are held in the unconscious. Allenby ends her case description with this sober picture relevant to our study of the hetaira:

One final word about the patient herself. The richness and profundity of the unconscious material should not mislead one into inferring a correspondingly richly equipped personality. She, like every other patient who produces a wealth of unconscious imagery, remained in some sense the person that she had always been. The relative instability of her ego, and her difficulties of relationship had not disappeared. But her attitudes had changed, and so life also had changed for her. She had become aware of a personal centre from which to go out . . . without losing herself, a centre guarded by the parental images in their beneficent aspect. The father archetype had revealed itself as the cosmic source of creative power which no longer destroyed but contained . . . yet in a sense she still was, and may always remain, conditioned by her early involvement with her father. In her case even the hands are not so much a symbol of personal relationship as instruments for relating her to the impersonal sphere of matter.[13]

For the older woman it was not relationship to another person that became her primary focus but rather relationship to work—"to the impersonal sphere of matter," represented by clay, paints, and brushes, the material of an artist. The hetaira often turns this way. Her relationship to an actual father is transformed into a relationship to the "genius" of her work, a transcendent spirit that inspires her in much the way the muse inspires the man. There are those for whom these necessities come together—where the search for meaning involves the complete surrender to an "other" power or person. Hunger for essential work and vital relationship meld:

> *Love and hunger: all is done in these signs or never*
> *Done.*
>
> > *Or done wrong . . .*
>
> *And when work goes wrong, love goes wrong.*
> > *And the other way also.*
>
> —TOM MCGRATH, *"Letter to an Imaginary Friend"*

Two women whose spirits were melded by these necessities, for whom love and work became inseparable, Lou Andreas-Salome and H. D., were both imprinted by the archetype of the father. Lou Andreas-Salome, psychoanalyst and companion of Freud, Rilke, and Nietzsche, married a man who was her teacher, never slept with him, and used their "arrangement" as a base for extraordinary ventures into the realms of eros and intellect. And H. D., who describes herself as unable to work unless in love, was engaged to Ezra Pound at one time, eventually married Richard

Aldington "for convenience," and then left him to live with a woman named Bryher, who was also a writer. Listen to the voice of an aging hetaira who was "not cheated," as Jung said, "out of the late blossoming."

> *Why did you come*
> *to trouble my decline?*
> *I am old (I was old till you came);*
>
> *the reddest rose unfolds,*
> *(which is ridiculous*
> *in this time, this place,*
>
> *unseemly, impossible,*
> *even slightly scandalous),*
> *the reddest rose unfolds;*
>
> *(nobody can stop that,*
> *no immanent threat from the air,*
> *not even the weather,*
>
> *blighting our summer fruit),*
> *the reddest rose unfolds,*
> *(they've got to take that into account).*
> —H. D., "Red Rose and a Beggar"*

And from the "Grove of Academe," she writes about the worn hand touched again. This was also written shortly before her death in 1961:

> *I did not cheat*
> *nor fake inspiration,*
> *what I wrote was right then,*
>
> *auguries, hermetic definition;*
> *yet, I would have left initiates, many times,*
> *for a red rose and a beggar,*
>
> *but something sustained me,*
> *and when you greeted me,*
> *I was paid fully*

for the long search
and the meagre lamp;
there was no ecstasy, vision, trance,

no years between,
only an end to the whole adventure,
it stops here;

there is no striving for strange ships,
Adamic delights;
I have tasted the apple;

my hand worn with endeavour,
our curious pre-occupation with stylus and pencil,
was re-born at your touch.

Being reborn by falling in love with someone who shares your life's vocation is a hetaeric expression of life at any age. This particular orientation toward seeking companionship in the search for meaning ("the long search and the meagre lamp") was given impetus in H. D.'s case by the energy it took to break away from those original uroboric circles of mother and father containment. "What is this mother-father to tear at our entrails? what is this unsatisfied duality . . . ?" she asked. Her second year in college marked her leavetaking:

I don't suppose it was the fault of Bryn Mawr that I didn't like it. My second year was broken into or across by my affair with E. P., who after all, at that time, proved a stimulus and was the scorpionic sting or urge that got me away—at that time it was essential. I felt there I had fallen between two stools, what with my mother's musical connection and my father's and half-brother's stars! I did find my path—thanks partly to E. P., also R. A., (D. H.) Lawrence and the rest.[14]

The father she left, Charles Doolittle, brilliant mathematician and astronomer, was replaced in part by another more brilliant, more famous father-professor, her analyst, Sigmund Freud.

H. D. came to Freud after a period of visionary wandering. She had been cut off from a reality that she wanted to touch again. Like all the maidens in the tales told here, being cut off—and its other face, breaking away—are essential parts of her narrative. Rapunzel's hair was cut off. She and Deirdre both were cut off from the possibility of relationship with men. The pious maiden's hands were cut off. Aphrodite was literally cut off from the body of her father. Each maiden psyche in turn is then set upon a path of wandering—in desert, forest, sea—out of which it emerges open to love, and in H. D.'s case reborn to work. The purpose of the *puella*'s long way around is reconnection with a father principle: he who once blocked her way becomes a source of energy and inspiration. All wandering is (in this case) back to the Father. Her search is for her own roots in the invisible and leads her back the way the river runs in *Finnegans Wake* past the city of Dublin ("double-ends-joined") out to sea to meet her father:

. . . weary I go back to you, my cold father, my cold mad father, my cold mad feary father, till the near sight of the mere size of him, the moyles and moyles of it, moananoaning, makes me sea-silt saltsick and I rush, my only, into your arms.[15]

8
Medial Feminine: Sibyl

Images of women are given and taken back in time by a great archetypal undercurrent that sends seemingly new creations to wash up on shore, the way Aphrodite did, molded to move in the culture they arrive in. Some of these forms are always welcome (especially the Mother), while others appear to get lost, or to be hidden from view, or to be generally less accessible in nonreceptive cultures. Two such forms hidden by the convolutions of recent history are those of the sibyl and the wise woman: women who were the embodiments of specific powers of transformation that have been called magical, spiritual, and psychic. These feminine forces still move among us. But where and in what form? What guise does this aspect of feminine nature assume in the Age of the Fathers? Rilke, who is certain of the birth of a new femininity, describes his vision in a time of transition (1934):

The girl and the woman, in their new, their own unfolding, will but in passing be imitators of masculine ways and repeaters of masculine professions. After the uncertainty of such transitions it will become apparent that women were only going through the profusion and the vicissitude of those (often ridiculous) disguises in order to cleanse their most characteristic nature of the distorting influences of the other sex. . . . This humanity of woman, borne its full time in suffering and humiliation, will come to light when she will have stripped off the conventions of mere femininity in the mutations of her outward status, and those men who do not yet feel it approaching today will be surprised and struck by it . . . some day there will be girls and women whose name will no longer signify merely an opposite of the masculine, but something in itself, something that makes one think, not of any complement and limit, but only of life and existence: the feminine human being.[1]

Beneath "the conventions of mere femininity" there runs a deeper, truer, stronger strain of being where gods and spirits are alive—a layer of history and a stratum of experience where women speak the language of animals, wear mud and feathers, live secluded with other women and children, prophesy over steaming cauldrons, wash clothes in the river, turn into hags, invent healing remedies, and dance through full moon nights after sleepless nights and days of necessary labor:

> *Women who were turned inside-out*
> *Ten times over by childbirth*
>
> *On the wind-washed lonely islands*
> *Lead the circle of* obon *dancers*
> *Through a full moon night in August*
>
> *The youngest girl last;*
>
> *Women who were up since last night*
> *Scaling and cleaning the flying fish*
>
> *Sing about love.*
>
> *Over and over,*
> *Sing about love.*
> —GARY SNYDER, *"Love," Suwa-no-se Island*

Women who are in touch with this essential life-sustaining stratum of experience know that dance and song are as necessary for survival as food preparation. They work themselves into the gaps between culture and nature like a kind of glue that binds together apparently disparate realms. They bring the unattached moon and the flying fish down to earth.

In contrast to this culture-creating alternation between love and work of which the women in the poem are capable, Freud declared women to be "enemies of civilization." Because woman is "little capable of instinctual repression" (moved by the moon to sing about love!) she is unable to sublimate libido or channel that sexual energy into works of government, art, and so on. In a disintegrated patriarchal world, where the masculine drive for efficiency and objectification preclude the feminine energy that would take love into account, in such a danceless world (familiar to us) where "strife," as Heraclitus said it, "is the Father of all things and war the King," we find that mothers are enemies to the progress of the state—especially the kind of mothers who got together during the Vietnam war to declare (on posters and stationery and Christmas cards and bookmarks and banners) that "war is unhealthy for children and other living things." In such a world we would have to agree with Freud and then go a step further to encourage the uprising of the so-called enemy: mothers and children, madmen, poets, and any minority that remembers its roots in the unconscious, where a different rhythm anterior to current civilization prevails.

Robert Briffault, French scholar and ethnologist, contemporary of Freud, who wrote the massive three-volume work on *The Mothers,* opposed Freud's conclusion fundamentally. Rather than seeing women as destroyers of culture, he discovered that early culture is in a very high degree the *product* of the female group, and that the relative sedentariness of the matriarchal community of mothers and children was bound to provide a biological, psychological, and sociological force for the "ennoblement of the original state."

Briffault was looking at remnants of archaic cultures in Africa, Micronesia, and Italy. He was also part of the growing movement of people (of which Gary Snyder is a living descendant) who developed ways of "reading" instead of just cataloging artifacts of buried peoples and cultures. It was in this work of assemblage that the archaeology of the mind took root in a new profession called the psychology of the primitive, or anthropological psychology—invaluable for the search for psychic origins.

The means of humanity's ascent to consciousness are events of individual and group significance originating in the unconscious. We call these events rituals. A ritual cannot be created; it grows in accord with the need to make meaning. Every life passage—birth, marriage, death—and every important activity of primitive man has ritual foundations of expression: hunting, food preparation, eating, weaving, pottery making, the brewing of intoxicants, the fashioning of weapons and so on. If rite means "growth, becoming" then it has always been a matter of life and death. In primitive cultures, where thoughts and fears concerning physical survival constantly punctuated the days, rituals were tools of survival.

One manifestation of the ritual nature of an activity is the secretive way it is handed down from generation to generation. The spark of life is in it and must be carefully tended in the passing on. Rituals are often secret because they are life mysteries —they cannot be talked about because articulation divorces the speaker from the experience. Thus the ritual, having a spectator, would have become drama and would lose its internal efficacy.

Even though details are lost to us, it takes no great stretch of the imagination to associate rituals with decisive events like naming the newborn or gathering in the last sheaf of wheat. In earlier times the things we now consider mundane (a child's learning to recite her ABCs, for instance) were often highly charged. The alphabet in northern Europe was transmitted in secret by generations of Celtic bards who sang riddles, notched trees, and made hand gestures containing the letters that could only be guessed by those who were learned in the mysteries of words. In *Finnegans Wake,* Joyce invites the reader to remember the mystery of ABCs: be "abcedminded" . . . "Stoop to this claybook," to the dirt underfoot, "to this alaphbed" and read its world.

Ritual acts—such as crossing oneself or spitting in one's palms in the morning and holding one's hands up to the sun—are often simple gestures, but they invoke a complex emotional response to the world. This aspect of rite was captured beautifully in the film *Black Orpheus:* when the hero died two little Brazilian boys

ran for his guitar in a desperate attempt to get it out to the cliff
before sunrise. They had listened to the older man play his sunrise
tune for years and thought that if it wasn't played the sun would
not rise. In the last scene, one boy hesitantly picks the strings
while the other anxiously points out chords as the sun rises, a
glorious frame for their small forms.

Where there is an urgency about enacting these connections to
nature and spirit in a community, ritual is alive. For the most part
we see only vestiges of this urge in public ceremonies, religious
gatherings, holiday observances, family traditions (even the
guarded passing on of family recipes), political demonstrations,
and mass musical events like rock concerts. I use the word "vestiges" because I think the urge to connect has vacated its outward
appurtenances. The religious impulse seems to have "come
home" or been withdrawn from outer world to inner world,
where rituals, especially those pertaining to crucial life passages,
are experienced as stages of psychic transformation. Puberty for
girls is no longer bridged with tribal ceremony (or only in cheap
ways that draw a girl into a consumer-oriented, spirit-vacated
world), but every girl enacts certain blood rites of seclusion and
reincorporation in her dreams and fantasies. (The important fact
for me at the onset of menstruation was certainly not the "factual"
films shown to students in health class, but the fact that when the
blood flowed my words flowed. I mean that I stopped stammering
at that time—a certain halting way with words changed course at
puberty.) Another common passage inadequately marked with
outer forms in our culture is retirement. Older men (more often
than women) who have worked in one place for many years will
be fêted with gifts and speeches, but the ritual is a shallow one
that does not take note of the movement occurring in a man's
psyche at this age as he moves toward death. Sometimes a man
will mark the passage himself by beginning to develop an aspect
of his psyche that has long been dormant. (Jung commented once
that many men at work have a thinking capacity befitting their age
but that when they greet their wives at the end of the day their

capacity for feeling is at an adolescent, undeveloped level.) A man who has been primarily valued for his ability to be rational may find it possible to let his emotions flow more freely. He will turn to an inner spiritual source for affirmation and instruction or else remain one-sided, judging himself according to the standards of the business world that hired and retired him and feeling increasingly useless.

When a culture is so one-sided, ritual cannot be a vital force. It seeks a congregation whose reality is myth, as H. D. put it. Or a collective situation where spirit is recognized and transformation valued. For most of the "developed" world today there is no sense in the kinds of hunting rituals in which the hunter beseeched the spirit of the animal he was about to kill for food—if a deer hunter fails to bring home a deer his family will still be supplied by the supermarket. Or, if a gardener were to overlook the hanging and drying of the last ear of corn so that the seeds could not be blessed and planted first in next year's spring soil, no one would notice. In European farm villages, not so long ago, everyone would have noticed because the last ear of corn from the last harvested field was called the "old maid" and had to be displayed throughout the winter by that family as a sign of their being last to get their work done. Some who scrutinize the twentieth century for examples of modern ritual could call the annual fall preparation for deer hunting or the midwinter ordering of seeds from catalogs "rites"; but these activities are a far cry from the soul-felt, *necessary* enactments of the interrelationship between human beings and green-life, rock-life, animal-life, and planet-life. We are coming again to a point in our inhabitation of earth where these rituals respecting nature are necessary. We need ways to recognize collectively the spiritual dimension to water cycles and fuel cycles, for example—ways to recognize our essential dependence. Is there a way to re-enact the fact that a man is as much dependent upon and a part of the fossil fuel he burns as the primitive hunter was dependent upon and part of the deer he ate? Ancient fears of physical survival are coming up again out of necessity to balance the very great fears of psychic survival that characterize our time.

Each perception follows "instanter on another" (Charles Olson). We have barely begun to see how rites—especially rites of passage characterized by the elements of separation (from self or community), transition, and reincorporation[2]—have taken up their abode in an interior terrain (our psychic or spiritual lives) when we are called to look again at our part in the possible devastation and reconstruction of outer space, the world around us. Yet both of these enormous tasks, confronting our personal madness and disintegration, and recognizing our part in the world's decline, rest solidly on the basic need to recall old spirit connections. Several of the most advanced ecological and biological sciences are implicitly laying out this spiritual dimension in the ways of the old shamans who moved between spheres of matter and spirit without making any distinction. Depth psychology also recognizes the continuum of matter and spirit reflected in the borderless realm of the collective unconscious. "Blest be the tie that binds . . . ."

Scientist, therapist, and poet now urge us toward composing a symposium of the whole: the old excluded orders must be included: the feminine, the foreign, the animal and vegetative, the unconscious and unknown, the outcast and failure—all these that have been discarded "must return to be admitted in the creation of what we consider we are."[3] An underworld repressed, an outer world unexplored, a cauldron of collective energy, a mass of anonymous faces (like facets of yourself)—these are the sources for the conversion of spirit and human community.

There are times when only scattered individuals feel the imperative of change and times when the sights of a people are shaped by fear of the end of life and civilization as they know it. In such emergency times, symbolized by the reddening of the moon and blackening of the sun (Acts 2), lives take on another charge. It is as if the dark side of nature, which is normally negatively charged or valued—the sleepside or unconscious, nonrational, amoral, idio-rhythmic source of dreams and visions—emerges to effect the salvation of the breaking whole. Energy freed in such violent moments of changing worlds leaves the recesses of the soul exposed, endangered. Collective experiences such as the coming of messiahs, floods, wars, and stock-market crashes leave whole populations exposed, while individual experiences of the first menstruation, childbirth, a nightmare, a crucial realization, or retirement leave facets of the self exposed. It is at these points of exposure that certain "workers and collaborators in the universe" (Heraclitus) move to the fore. Shamans, for example, were not called to every ceremonial event but were indispensable when there was a potential crisis of the soul—when there was some danger of losing it. He or she would be there as a mediator between the forces of the visible and the invisible that created tension and trouble in the human world.

Mediation—as evident in the word itself—is the distinguishing characteristic of the medial feminine. This aspect of the feminine moves with facility through times of radical change because its network of information and connections goes so deep and wide that it seems to foresee change. Unfortunately, the word "medium," which is used to describe people with this uncanny ability, has been debased through association with the commercial images of fortunetellers, crystal ball, séance, and gypsy wagon. But underneath the commercial sheen of the medium, as so often happens with stereotyped characters, original meanings are preserved. There are essential mysteries held in stars and crystal formations (Jung came to describe the structure of an archetype in crystal language or analogy[4])—and the gypsy wagon is the best possible way to give an image to the idea of a roving *temenos*. A *temenos* is a sacred enclosure, a sanctuary, a square or ovular space where individuating or unfolding life is protected. These spaces must be "roving" now that our orientation toward spirit and the search for meaning are no longer attached to specific sacred stones, groves, mountains, or altars where the god dwells. God is indwelling. In His "indwellingness" the Hebrew god was called Shekinah, a feminine emanation and presence that wandered in and out of exile in accordance with the state of her temple or the brokenness of the world (Chapter 1 above). Men of mystical insight, in the eighteenth-century Hasidic movement, were said to have called upon her "to re-approach her source" in morally confusing situations. She was the spirit of clarification; her presence mediates the mystery to the man. This is an essential quality of the medial feminine that functions as clearly in men as it does in women. A woman who experiences herself as medium knows that she has not invented her visions but that she is capable of revealing hidden sources, showing people what they may already know but have hidden or never recognized.

We can discern sources of the medial woman's knowledge in the earliest mysteries or rites of the feminine, which revolved around the central elements of woman's life: birth, menstruation, conception, pregnancy, childbirth, menopause, and death. These elements of feminine existence were first identified with the wondrous metamorphoses of nature: kernel to corn, night to dawn, winter to spring, and then with the miracle of conversion of spirit from depression to animation, stasis to ecstasy. All great religious traditions hold out this essentially feminine promise of the possibility of rebirth. The work of woman is transformation: making something out of nothing: giving form to formless energy. Her instruments in this work are tripod and cauldron, her elements blood and milk—both liquids held within her are organic, "that with which one works." She is both container and contained at this stage. She transforms matter and is herself transformed. She is the procession of forms and the forms of the process.

Blood has had a magical significance everywhere because it "contains the soul." (As recently as 1628, when William Harvey's treatise on the circulation of blood was published, the blood's coursing was called spiritual movement.) It is the most necessary element for the work of a priestess, who, like a priest when he elevates the host in the Mass, is *set apart* from others in order to raise certain objects and events to new heights of meaning, to endow with significance, to make sacred, to consecrate, and to bless. Our word "blessing" comes from the Old English *bloedsen* or "bleeding." The necessity of its use rests on the matriarchal belief that even in the womb no life can be built up without blood. No doubt one of the first things woman knew about herself was that when blood flow stopped it was feeding and creating a child within. First the blood has to flow to make new life possible. One of the earliest Western records we have of the relationship between blood and basin (or kettle or cauldron) is in the twenty-fourth chapter of Exodus where Moses sacrificed bulls (in the wilderness of Sinai) and filled large basins with the blood, which was then sprinkled on altar and worshipers alike. All this at the foot of what had once been called the Mountain of the Moon.

The moon, among Native Americans, is called the First Woman and is said to "sicken" or be menstruating in the waning period of her cycle. The folktale motif of red rain or snow falling from the sky has to do with this "moon blood." Due to the similarity between woman's monthly cycle and the lunar cycle, the moon and the phenomenon of woman's bleeding became inseparable. This connection made the menstruating woman universally taboo. "Taboo" means variously unclean, holy, and set apart. There is something numinous, mysterious, awe-provoking in the ability of women to bleed regularly without dying—much as the moon diminishes and finally dies away, but returns from her death. This blood that is an indication of the miracle of life— because the woman does not die, and because it means she can bear children—has so much power in it that women were required to remove themselves from village premises when menstruating. Esther Harding suggests that it was either the bleeding or "rutting" that brought about the separation. The period of animal heat or *estrus,* the Greek word for "frenzied," brought on a state of sexual possession which seems to often correspond with the days around a woman's period—which would be another reason to keep her away from routine village life, where a woman's desire can be a man's undoing (for example, hunters who met a menstruating woman would toss up their spears and run; all was lost). From a primitive Australian woman's point of view, menstruation and separation came on because of too frequent intercourse:

The Mara Tribe has a legend according to which the menstrual period was brought on, in the first instance, because in the Alcheringa (the heroic age) a number of bandicoot men who were making ceremonies had too frequent intercourse with a lubra. (Bandicoot and lubra are the totem names of intermarrying clans, but men of the bandicoot totem may not marry a bandicoot woman.) This brought on a great discharge and the woman said, "I think I will not walk about a lubra any more, but a bandicoot," and so she stuck grass all over herself, and went away and hid in a hole, so that the men could not find her, and ever since then women have had monthly periods.[5]

There are many stories about the origins of menstruation—this one emphasizes not only its supposed relationship to phallic penetration but also the habit of seclusion. In this case it is woman's choice, not an imposed rule, to remain hidden in the time of her bleeding. This particular ritual could provide a good example of what I meant when talking about the internalization of the holy impulses of primitive peoples. Modern woman needs a way to hide herself from the constant demands of social and sexual life. She needs a private space or a private time to retire to be alone—or, in some cases, to be alone with other women. Increasing freedom from the body means that it is easy for her to forget this psychic need of periodic seclusion. New contraptions for contraception and the elimination of menstrual periods by suction tools are literally "mixed blessings." We have already lost touch with the physical demand to separate ourselves by asserting that we too can work straight through the month "like men" and straight through labor even as a man would. This argument, unfortunately, only puts women in the position of imitating the masculine ignorance of the value of the feminine. Despite the fact that men also have "periods" or cycles (although they are less noticeable), the patriarchal culture which informs our thinking does not look favorably on personal time or sabbaths.

The word "sabbath" has its origin in this notion of feminine periodicity. *Sabbatu* means heart rest. It was the evil day of Ishtar's menstruation, which coincided in Babylonia with the full moon. On this day no one was supposed to do any work, eat cooked food, or go on a journey. The day of the moon's menstruation or the Sabbatu was observed once a month at first, according to the full moon, but came to be observed four times a month in accordance with the four quarters of the moon.[6]

This intimate connection between women and the sabbath (Sunday in Christian tradition) prompted me to ask a priest once a number of years ago whether the original relationship between menstrual taboo and sabbath observance wasn't enough to raise women to the status of Celebrant in the church. Neither this "fact," nor the related fact that the first communion—for the child Christ and ourselves alike—was the flesh and blood of the Mother, had any effect. Whenever the connection between blood and the Blood of Life (i.e., Christ's) has been suggested it has literally been regarded as heretical. A Valentinian sect (heretical) drank the blood of a virgin from a cup or grail symbolizing her womb. And the eighteenth-century Moravians in Pennsylvania equated menstrual blood with the blood that flowed from Christ's wound. Yet for most Christians the connection became metaphorical in the transition from blood sacrifice to drinking wine. Wine is pure spirit(s) and removed from the earthly realm of the mother (remember that when Demeter was searching for her lost daughter she refused the wine cup offered to her; she drinks a grain mixture instead). In another religious tradition, the cult of Isis, described by Apuleius in *The Golden Ass,* a male initiate was made to eat the blood, or bloom, of the goddess incarnate in the rose.

Because of the power in blood, especially the blood of a virgin, its effect can be both efficacious and harmful. There are many folk-tales and primitive proscriptions about not walking under a tree where a menstruating woman has been sitting for fear that a drop of blood will fall on you. Esther Harding relates it to the modern English superstition of not walking beneath ladders for fear that a drop of (red) paint will fall on you. (I suspect that this unlikely position of the woman in the tree has to do with the common perception of the moon "sitting in tree branches.") Blood once had the power to heal and was used medicinally. The first flow of a young girl was especially potent for healing extreme illness. Also, a naked woman "in this condition" who runs around a field can kill the insects in it, thereby ensuring the growth of the crop. It is the young woman who contains the useful blood but the old woman who takes it. The historian Strabo (born 63 B.C.) gives a hair-raising account of the old women among the Cimbri, a people from northern Europe:

Their women who traveled with them were accompanied by sacred priestesses, gray-haired, white-robed, with a linen scarf buckled over their shoulder and a girdle of brass, and walking barefooted. These priestesses, with a sword in their hand, met the prisoners of war when they were brought to the camp; and having crowned them, they led them to a brass basin as large as thirty amphorae. They had a ladder which the priestess mounted, and, standing over the basin, she cut the throat of each prisoner as he was handed up to her. With the blood that gushed into the basin they made a prophecy.[7]

There is a most intricate intertwining of blood and prophecy and moon and poetry that is essential to the archetypal nature of the medial feminine. Two figures especially make these connections clearer—both of them have the gift of being able to give shape to what lies beneath the surface—first the sibyl and then the wise woman.

A sibyl usually had a seat in a temple. At Delphi, where the oracle was respected as ultimate authority in ancient Greece, the oracular messages were delivered by a sibylline priestess called Pythia or the Pythoness. Her serpent nature is related to the sounds she made when in the ecstatic embrace of the gods, or trance—the strange sounds were likened to the hissing of snakes, also to whirrings and whistlings as of bats or a violent wind. Cassandra, the prophetess "kissed by Apollo," who predicted the fall of Troy, was said to have come by her extraordinary gift of prophecy when her parents became intoxicated at her birthday celebration and left her lying asleep in a corner of the temple of Apollo by mistake. In the morning she was found wrapped round with snakes licking her ears. By this she gained the powers of prophecy and speaking the language of animals. Drinking the blood of animals and facing into the full moon are among the ways to induce the trance state that gave way to utterances interpreted by the sibyls' attendant priests. The Pythia at Delphi bathed in the clear waters of the Castalian spring, drank of it, and then took her seat on the raised tripod over a deeply intoxicating vapor-emitting pit:

The day came, god's day, with which his festival opened, and I remember that morning very well. Never was there such a sunrise over these mountains—never, at least, that I have seen. I had fasted for three days and was light, weightless as a bird. I bathed in Castalia's spring; the water was fresh and I felt pure. . . . Led between two priests I passed the altar where his eternal fire was burning, entered the pilgrims' hall and went down the narrow, dim stairway into the holy of holies.

There was as little light there as before and it was some time before I could make out anything. But I noticed the stifling fumes from the cleft at once . . . I smelt the stench of goat too . . . stronger and more pungent. There must have been something burning there, for I could smell that as well. And then after a while I saw a glow in a bowl in the darkness, and a little man was crouching over it, fanning life into the embers with a bird's wing . . . A yellow-gray snake writhed past his foot and vanished swiftly in the darkness. This filled me with terror . . . Later I learned that they were always there and were much venerated because they were oracle beasts and had divine understanding. I also learned that the embers glowing in the bowl were pieces of laurel: the god's sacred tree, whose smoke the priestess must inhale to be filled with his spirit.[8]

Later in Pär Lagerkvist's story *The Sibyl*, the young woman describes the dizzying effect of inhaling the vapors, sitting high on the tripod over the sacrificial cleft, and the feeling of sinking down into the dark. Suddenly, she is overcome by the god:

. . . I felt my body beginning to writhe, to writhe in agony and torment; being tossed to and fro and strangled, as if I were to be suffocated, and instead I began to hiss forth dreadful, anguished sounds, utterly strange to me, and my lips moved without my will; it was not I who was doing this. And I heard shrieks, loud shrieks; I didn't understand them. They issued from my gaping mouth, though they were not mine.

Heraclitus says, "The sibyl with raving mouth utters solemn, unadorned, unlovely words—but she reaches out over a thousand years because of the god in her." Thousands of years later, a poet visits the sibyl's site:

> *At Delphi I prayed*
> *to Apollo*
> *that he maintain in me*
> *the flame of the poem*
>
> *and I drank of the brackish*
> *spring there, dazed by the*
> *gong beat of the sun*
> *mistaking it,*
>
> *as I shrank from the eagle's*
> *black shadow crossing*
> *that sky of cruel blue,*
> *for the Pierian Spring—*

and soon after
vomited my moussake
and then my guts writhed
for some hours with diarrhea

until at dusk
among the stones of the goatpaths
breathing dust
I questioned my faith, or

within it wondered
if the god mocked me.
But since then, though it flickers or
shrinks to a

blue bead on the wick,
there's that in me that
burns and chills, blackening
my heart with its soot,

flaring in laughter, stinging
my feet into a dance, so that
I think sometimes not Apollo heard me
but a different god.
—DENISE LEVERTOV, *"The Prayer"*

By "a different god" she means Dionysos—the black goat god of intoxication who stings your feet into dancing and your throat into laughing. His maenads (the maddened *thiasos* or band of devoted feminine followers) are always detectable on vases and wall paintings by the abandoned way their heads are thrown back over straightened necks. Like Apollo's sibyl, they are deeply stung by the spirit entering their bodies.

Dionysos was closer to women than Apollo even though both were called "womanish" men. Apollo slew the Python or the Delphyne—one a male serpent, the other a female dragon—the day he was born. Some say that he did it out of vengeance for his mother because the serpent would not let Leto rest to bear her children there. But it is more likely that this story tells about the masculine appropriation of an ancient feminine function. Delphi means "womb." A small herd of mountain goats discovered the womblike cleft in the earth that later became the Delphic temple site. They were feeding on Mount Parnassus and "came near a place which had a deep and long perforation. The steam which issued from the hole seemed to inspire the goats, and they played and frisked about in such an uncommon manner that the goatherd was tempted to lean over the hole and see what mysteries the place contained. He was immediately seized with a fit of enthusiasm, and his expressions were wild and extravagant, and passed for prophecies."[9]

Inhaling the vapors, like drinking the water or drinking sacrificed blood, is the act that connects one to the earth and the under-earth—source of springs and nature and daemons. In the tale of "Deirdre," the kept maiden finally runs away to live with Naoise and his brothers in the hills. The king, who had been taken by the extraordinary beauty of his ward, sought revenge and killed the boys, the sons of Usneach. He tracks them down; they are taken and beheaded. "Then Deirdre comes to where the children of Usneach lie and Deirdre dishevels her hair and begins to drink Naoise's blood and the color of burning embers comes into her cheeks. She sings the lament for the death of the brothers and after that throws herself into Naoise's grave, gives him three kisses and dies." It had been prophesied at her birth that the child would be the ruin of all Ireland. The king had stakes driven into their graves, but they grew into trees that intertwined.

Poetry and prophecy are thus intertwined in the foretelling of great events in history. Cassandra foretold the fall of Troy, the Erythraean sibyl foretold the birth of Christ. The first letter in each line of her utterance spelled out "Ichthys" or fish, the divine name and symbol of the one who was coming. Utterances at Delphi were always delivered into poetry until it was remarked that the god and patron of poetry (Apollo) was a most imperfect poet. After that the sibyl spoke in prose. In order for poetry to work, thoughts, images, and memories "have to be turned to blood within us, to glance and gesture, nameless and no longer distinguished from ourselves."[10] When it worked, the sibyl must have been a poet herself: "The voice is not that of a god," according to Plutarch, "nor the utterance, nor the diction, nor the metre. All these are the woman's; the god puts into her mind only the images, and creates a light in her soul."

Images are god-given gifts but the speech that translates them into poetry and song is fashioned by the person. The inspiration comes from the Muses, the musical daughters of Memory, who blow the images into the ears of poets through hollow reeds. They tell Hesiod, the shepherd poet, that they "know how to blow false stories and true"—they know what Memory teaches, that an old story brought to consciousness or an experience remembered can haunt or heal according to the state of the one who receives it. In Eskimo tradition preparation for receiving the inspiration begins with clearing the ears even though it is song bubbles that come instead of wind-blown stories. An old woman who swung her arms incessantly as she spoke told the story of the "Qarrtsiluni" to Knud Rasmussen. At the opening of each new hunting season the men would want new words to catch the spirit of the new whale. Wornout words, old songs would not do when men and women danced and sang in homage to the big quarry. All lamps had to be extinguished when they were finding new words. Darkness and stillness would reign in the festival house where they sat in deep silence, thinking:

For our forefathers believed that the songs were born in this stillness while all endeavoured to think of nothing, but of beautiful things. Then they (the songs) take shape in the minds of men and rise up like bubbles from the depths of the sea, bubbles seeking the air in order to burst. That is how the sacred songs are made![11]

"Qarrtsiluni" means "one waits for something to burst." Out of the dark wait and expectation comes the birth moment. Rilke calls it that most rare hour when the first word of a poem arises and goes forth. Whether it is gentle like this, or the more violent coming that the sibyl knows, the song, prophecy, or poem is always a breakthrough. The barrier between gods and mortals (or the unconscious and consciousness) is broken in the bestowal of form on formless content. In this sense poetry is incarnational and feminine, giving body and blood to the not-yet-born.

In his elaborate book *The White Goddess,* Robert Graves explains that women who are poets write out of the experience of themselves as "source." Inspiration comes from the cauldron of Cerridwen (a Celtic goddess who is herself the cauldron) that contains a mash of barley, acorns, honey, bull's blood, and the sacred herbs ivy and laurel. The poetry-inducing contents of the cauldron are brewed together with the intent of making your senses burst. Intoxication, like inspiration, can enlarge a person enough for the goddess to enter. She comes unexpectedly from above or below as the moon-faced sibyl or bloody one. It can be an uncomfortable inhabitation as expressed in these excerpts from Diane di Prima's *Loba:*

> *O lost moon sisters*
> *crescent in hair, sea underfoot do you wander . . .*
>
> *I walk the long night seeking you*
> *I climb the sea crest seeking you*
> *I lie on the prairie, batter at stone gates*
> *calling your names . . .*
>
> > *hard-substance-woman you whirl*
> > *you dance on subways*
> > *you sprawl in tenements*
> > *children lick at your tits*
>
> *you are the hills, the shape and color of mesa*
> *you are the tent, the lodge of skins, the hogan*
> *the buffalo robes, the quilt, the knitted afghan*
> *you are the cauldron and the evening star*
> *you rise over the sea, you ride the dark*

I move within you, light the evening fire
I dip my hand in you and eat your flesh
you are my mirror image and my sister
you disappear like smoke on misty hills
you lead me through dream forest on horseback
large gypsy mother, I lean my head on your back

I am you
and I must become you
I have been you
and I must become you
I am always you
I must become you

> *ay-a*
> *ay-a ah*
> *ay-a*
> *ay-a ah ah*
> *maya ma maya ma*
> *om star mother ma om*
> *maya ma ah . . .*

See how her tit drags on the ground.
She steps on it. She baaaa's
She keens, as an old black goat, waiting
blow of the ax. Feel head roll on
wet earth, blood spout (fountain)
from neck, strong as column.
See her dance.

See the young, black, naked woman riding
a dead white man. Her hair
greasy, she whips him & he flies
thru the smoky air. Her hand
is in her mouth, she is eating
flesh, it stinks, snakes wind
around her ankles. Her hand

touches the (wet) earth. Her hand
shakes a gourd rattle, she laughs, her fangs
flash white & red, they are set
with rubies.

see how old woman's tits hang down
on that young, lithe body, know the skull
in her hand your own, she eats
your eyes & then your brain . . .

Hush, the old-young woman
touches you, she is gold, she wears
a peaked cap, vines
grow out of it. Her tongue flicks
at the corners of her mouth. . . .

. . . .

If you do not come apart like bread
in her hands, she falls
like steel on your heart. The flesh
knows better than the spirit what the soul
has eyes for. Has she sunk
root in yr watering place, does she look
w/her wolf's eyes out of your head?

The old-young she-wolf in goat's clothing rides the fountain of
blood to dead center. She is at home in torn flesh and has the
dangerous tendency to possess her victim—to dwell within
("sunk root in yr watering place") in such a complete sense that
there is no escape. Her dance is the dance of death, the true
"Enemie" that makes the blood of birth and death indistinguish-
able:

> *now all things (including notions, or whatever*
> *were once validities,*
> *all things now stand*

(including the likes of you and me, all, all
must be born out of
(God knows you know, Old Goddess, and
tremendous Mother)
There is birth! there is
all over the place there is

And if I, in this smother, if I
smell out one thing sharp,
or another
(where his teeth
have been in me, there—
even you know, Enemie—

. . . . .

it is why there is so much blood
all over the place
        —CHARLES OLSON, *"Part Lost"*

Birth always involves blood sacrifice. But there is a tremendous difference in the giving freely of it to make a new life and the unnecessary spilling of it when the victim dies. When I was teaching a class at Santa Cruz in the early seventies, interest in witchcraft and demon cults (which are an expression of collective wolf possession) was at a frightening crest in California. Partially because of the paradoxical omnipresence of evil in that beautiful place, I became extremely uneasy on the day of our final meeting when we gathered in the redwoods for a Mother rebirth ceremony. We planned to plant a fig tree, bury a fish for fertilizer, crawl through an animal skin, invoke certain goddesses, and chant hymns in their praise. These things I knew about. What I had not planned on was a literal blood spilling that came about when the other teaching assistant brought a vial of human blood with her that a friend had gotten from a research laboratory where she worked.

Nothing dreadful came of it but I carried my discomfort

around with me until I was reminded by our professor of the transition from bloody to bloodless sacrifice: from the literal to the spiritual body. As he had said it in *Love's Body,* communion was the solution to the problem of bloodshed: "Abstain from things offered to idols (Moloch, the Old Testament child-eating monster) and from blood. The problem of war is the problem of idolatry . . . the opposite of true war is poetry."[12] I had wanted to see the spilling forth of poetry, of memories turned to blood. My fear was exaggerated (perhaps) by the environment: it was said that infants had been sacrificed and eaten that year in Santa Cruz County. By taking the sacrifice literally we could have opened a door (I thought) to the wolf prowling there. Before wine there was certainly blood; before communion there was crucifixion or human sacrifice. But our freedom from the old way is to be cherished here. Understanding means embracing or gathering around. Pouring out bottled blood was a regressive way to understand the Old Goddess because it did not necessitate any inner, conscious sacrifice or creation on the part of celebrants.

Although there was no human sacrifice to the sibyl, she was associated with the Old Goddess and tremendous Mother. This required that blood be at least present: perhaps in animal sacrifice but more definitely in the red representation of her interior feminine power. The old Mother cave figurines were stained with red ocher and the ground around the clefts where three ancient sibyls resided was red. One of these places colored by the Earth Mother's blood was Cumae, the western city visited by the Roman hero Aeneas after his victory at Troy. He visits the Cumaean sibyl in her woodland temple cave to ask if he might pass into the underworld to speak with the shade of his dead father. Before actually approaching her inner cave dwelling in the region of the red earth, Aeneas stands for a while at the temple gates "reading" a picture of a Cretan labyrinth inscribed there. (The Cretan labyrinth was mentioned above in connection with Ariadne—the one that Daedalus built to be her dancing ground and the prison for the Minotaur.) Labyrinths always have a double aspect: they exclude those who are unwanted and allow in those who know the way. Sibyls standing guard at entrances into the earth have this double aspect. Like the muses, who know how to whisper both false tales and true, the sibyl's voice reveals to some and conceals from others. (She shines in the dark and is dark in the day.)

Beyond the temple gates which the hero enters, as if into a new or another way of life, stand the underworld gates, one of ivory and one of horn—the gates of false dreams and true through which the man must pass to return to earth. It is no mere happenstance that Aeneas paused for a while to read the message of the maze before entering the sibyl's domain. In a parallel story from the island of Malekula, the realm of the underworld dead is protected by a guardian goddess and a great rock. When the dead man approaches, he is confused by the sight of her and loses his way for a while. In this time she has drawn an elaborate labyrinth or maze pattern in the sand with her finger and rubs out half of it when he finally comes close. He must know how to complete the drawing. If he succeeds he passes through the lines of the drawing into the cave. If he fails he is devoured by the goddess. Failure comes from not having learned "the path" in his lifetime.[13] Learning depends upon symbolic thinking. "For those who have the symbol the passage is easy" (alchemical saying).

Another account of passage through the medial realm is given by Plutarch in his description of Thespesius's guided tour of the underworld. I am giving the passage alluded to in Chapter 1 above:

Proceeding as far again, he saw in the distance what he took to be a large crater with streams pouring into it, one whiter than sea-foam or snow, another like the violet of the rainbow, and others of different tints, each having from afar a lustre of its own. On their approach the crater turned out to be a deep chasm in the ambient, and as the colours faded, the brightness, except for the white, disappeared. . . .

The guide of Thespesius' soul said that Orpheus had advanced thus far in his quest for the soul of his wife, and from faulty

memory had published among men a false report that at Delphi
there was an oracle held in common by Apollo and Night,—false,
as Night has partnership in nothing with Apollo. "This is instead," he pursued, "an oracle shared by Night and the Moon;
it has no outlet anywhere on earth nor any single seat, but roves
everywhere throughout mankind in dreams and visions; for this
is the source from which dreams derive and disseminate the unadorned and true, commingled, as you see, with the colourful and
deceptive . . .

. . . he endeavoured to draw Thespesius near and show him the
light that came (he said) from the tripod . . . but it was so bright
that Thespesius, for all his eagerness, did not see it. But he did
hear, as he passed by, a woman's high voice foretelling in verse
among other things the time (it appears) of his own death. The
voice was the Sibyl's, the daemon said, who sang of the future as
she was carried about on the face of the moon. He accordingly
desired to hear more, but was thrust back, as in an eddy, by the
onrush of the moon, and caught but little. Among this was a
prophecy about Mt. Vesuvius and the surge of flame that would
pass over [the city].[14]

We meet the moon-faced sibyl here in an account made difficult
by the author's colorful attempt to prove many things at once.
The many streams pouring into the mixing-bowl crater represent
polemics or diverse arguments about who "owned" the oracle
and the vat of dreams in which the false commingle with the true.
We know that streams were always present where a sibyl dwelled;
whether in the underworld of Malekulan mythical geography, or
in the recesses of Cumae where Aeneas met the ferryman. Vergil
describes the latter: "Cleft out is the flank of that rock into a
cavern terrific. To it a hundred broad accesses lead, a hundred
their mouthways. From it a hundred come the streams of sound,
the sibyl's answerings."[15] And there is a similar Celtic female rock
spirit called Roaring Mouth who is associated with rushing water,
mad whitewater. A sibyl's raving is uncontrollable in the way a
murmuring spring, fountain, or river is uncontrollable. William
Carlos Williams, in *Paterson,* catches this essential voice. He is

describing how the ear picks up the sounds of the waterfall through all the other Sunday-afternoon park sounds.

> *Voices!*
> *multiple and inarticulate   voices*
> *clattering loudly to the sun, to*
> *the clouds. Voices!*
> *assaulting the air gaily from all sides.*
>
> *—among which the ear strains to catch*
> *the movement of one voice among the rest*
> *—a reed-like voice*
>
> *of peculiar accent . . .*
>
> *—beyond the gap where the river*
> *plunges into the narrow gorge, unseen*
>
> *—and the imagination soars, as a voice*
> *beckons, a thundrous voice, endless*
> *—as sleep: the voice*
> *that has ineluctably called them—*
> *that unmoving roar!*

One voice among many, moving under all. The original utterance of seerdom is the language of water. The river runs tellingly through Lagerkvist's novel *The Sibyl.*

As to the ownership of the oracle, disputed quite late in its history, Plutarch makes it clear that in some sense it is collective property, or at least a property of the collective unconscious. The sibyl has no single seat "but roves everywhere throughout mankind in dreams and visions." We are all sibyls in our sleep—her seat being set deep in the place we best hide ourselves.

In an ancient hidden passageway the sibyl sat on an *omphalos,* the raised mound of earth, the world navel. From this vantage point, with an umbilical root reaching down into the earthly wisdom of the underworld, she was able to relay the plot of a life

to a seeker. To one who is willing to pause by her gate to read
the pattern of an interior maze she will teach the forgotten alphabet of transmutation:

> *Relearn the alphabet,*
> *relearn the world, the world*
> *understood anew only in doing, under-*
> *stood only as*
> *looked-up-into out of earth,*
> *the heart an eye looking,*
> *the heart a root*
> *planted in earth.*
> *Transmutation is not*
> *under the will's rule*
> —DENISE LEVERTOV, *"Relearning the Alphabet"*

And five thousand years earlier from *The Egyptian Book of the Dead:*

> *My heart, my mother;*
> *my heart, my mother!*
> *My heart of transformations.*

Having such a heart with a root planted in the mothering earth
is the secret of the medial woman, who has a route to information
that no one else can follow. Looking up into a relearned world
"out of earth" is the vision of the initiated—those who have made
the ritual entry into earth at the invitation of the sibyl. They have
"stepped on to" or "made entry" (from the Latin *inire,* hence
initiation) into a new life. I say "at the invitation of the sibyl"
because it is an entry, or a breakthrough, that cannot be willed.
When the Cumaean sibyl thought Aeneas had been studying the
pattern on the gates long enough she interrupted him to tell him
to make the appropriate sacrifices and come in. Dreams function
this way for us. When we are ready to see it, a new content will
emerge. Studying the labyrinth, in the deepest, essential sense, is
the only real preparation for medial eruption we can make. When

it happens, it feels like an uprising, a taking-over by some god or strange force within. This process has been so associated with women throughout history that the words "god" and "sibyl" have merged in the word "gossip." With this notion our vision shifts to the figure of the Old Wise Woman.

9
Medial Feminine: Old Wise Woman

An old Midwestern mother of poetry once told me that words have two uses: the first is for analysis and the second is "to heat you and move you."[1] When asked how to go about getting in on this second aspect of language she said to go and listen to the rhythm of country gossip. Gossip is worth listening to: it means "god speaking through a woman."

God and *sybbe* yield gossip. From *sybbe* come both sibyl and sibling. A *gossip* is one who has a contracted spiritual affinity with another especially at baptism, as a god-parent. A gossip is also a member of the congregation of childbirth—the invited female friends of a woman in labor. We see this particular configuration of a merry meeting of gossips in many fairy tales, where all the fairies or witches come to a child's birth to offer their various blessings and usually one curse from the uninvited, as in the story of "Sleeping Beauty." A gossip is also a giver of gifts, a namer, and a manner of unrestrained or sibylline speech.

The muses are gossips when described as the "ready-voiced daughters" of Memory. Hesiod, who gave us this way of seeing the muses, has a line elsewhere in the *Theogony*—his story of the origins of the gods—that translates literally from the Greek to read, "Enough of this talk of oak and stone." Modern translators, rendering the phrase into contemporary tongue, write, "Enough of this gossiping." (In *Finnegans Wake*, Joyce has the two gossiping washerwomen by the stream turn into an oak and a stone at the end of a day.) A warm drink of ale or wine mixed with gruel, eggs, sugar, and spices is called a "gossip's cup" or "caudle"— like "cauldron." Sipping such a drink frees the tongue. "Going to the neighbors to tell odd stories" is gossip. This manner of gossip was set in type or put in print in an English countryside gazette called the *Loom and Lugger:* a lugger is a storytelling tramp or sailor, a yarn spinner. And the loom is the instrument of spinning, especially used by the old gray gossips who spin the threads of flax and fate.

In the story of Sleeping Beauty it is the gossips and their wheel that spin the story. The beautiful child who falls asleep at fifteen is born to a queen who had long been barren. The joyful king prepared a great feast and invited not only all their friends and relatives, but the wise women, that they might be favorably and kindly disposed toward the child. There were thirteen of them in the kingdom, but as the king only had twelve golden plates for them to eat from one of the wise women (or fairies) went uninvited. There is always room for twelve.

This motif originates in the age-old embodiment of the spirit of the feminine in triadic groups: the three fates, the three weird sisters, the three norns, the three graces, the three or nine muses or valkyries, and the twelve fairies. There are three, or multiples of three, so that the past, present, and future are each represented. When a thirteenth fairy appears we know that there is an imbalance in the system, something is bound to go wrong. The left-out fairy corresponds to the littlest norn, who gets pushed off the bench in a Teutonic folktale: norns, the northern fates who were called "wish wives" or "weird ladies of the woods," used to emerge from their woodland habitations to visit the house of every newborn child in order to utter its doom or destiny.

Once, three norns came upon a house where a new baby lay in its cradle; a candle burned brightly over the sleeping child. The first two norns gave the child happiness and long life. But the third and youngest—who had been pushed off the bench and fallen onto the ground when the three took their seat—rose up in anger crying, "I cause that the child shall only live until the lighted candle burns out." The eldest norn quickly seized the candle, put it out, and warned the mother not to rekindle the flame until the last day of her son's life. Similarly in "Sleeping Beauty," the angry uninvited fairy appears suddenly while the other fairies are bestowing their gifts and wishes, and calls out in a loud voice, "The Princess shall prick herself with a distaff in her fifteenth year and shall fall down dead."

A distaff is the staff or pole that holds the flax or the wool to be spun into thread. The thread can be spun on a hand spindle or spinning wheel. Because of its identification with "woman's work," distaff came to mean female. The distaff side of the family would be the maternal side as opposed to the spear side, or paternal. Spindle easily turned into "spinster" with its varying connotations. The thirteenth fairy's curse carried a rather heavy ancestral weight with it, but fortunately, in our story, there was one little fairy left who had not yet spoken. She could not cancel the bad fairy's curse, she could only soften it: she is the one who wished a hundred years' sleep instead of death.

Norns and fairies and fates and fays—those who pronounce and decree destiny—seem always to balance their boons with a curse. The kindly dispositions are supplemented by an evil one; or, as in the Moravian story where the first two sisters stalk through the countryside with scythes, cutting off people's heads, and the third one follows behind teaching the medicinal secrets of roots and herbs, evil dispositions are supplemented by a kind one. Blessing and cursing seem peculiarly related to the feminine. Remember the bloody origin of "blessing" (from the Old English *bloedsen* or "bleeding") in connection with the way mothers of a certain generation call their monthly bleeding "the curse."

One of the famous Brothers Grimm, the fairy-tale collectors who laid the foundation for what we now regard as the science of folklore, wrote a curious account of the relationship between woman and the magical arts. This is part of his account written around 1840:

The various ways of naming magic have led us to the notions of doing, sacrificing, spying, soothsaying, singing, sign-making (secret writing), bewildering, dazzling, cooking, healing, casting lots. They shew that it was practiced by men as well as women. Yet even our earliest antiquities impute it preeminently to women.[2]

Then he lists some other forms of doing magic and does not translate the words for us. These apparently sexual, unnamable things are, in his words, "hardly applicable to any but female witchery."

For the reason of this [he continues] I look to all circumstances external and internal. To woman, not to man, was assigned the culling and concocting of powerful remedies, as well as the cooking of food. Her lithe soft hand could best prepare the salve, weave the lint, and dress the wound; the art of reading and writing is in the Middle Ages ascribed chiefly to women. The restless lives of men were filled up with war, hunting, agriculture, handcrafts; to women experience and convenient leisure lent every qualification for secret sorcery. Woman's imagination is warmer and more susceptible, and at all times an inner sacred power of divination was revered in her. Women were priestesses, prophetesses—their names and fame are embalmed alike in Old German and Norse tradition—and the faculty of somnambulism still shews itself most of all in women.

Then again . . . the art of magic must have been chiefly monopolized by old women who, dead to love and labour, fixed all their thoughts and endeavors on hidden science . . . (and fancy).[3]

The secrets of women in this view are inextricably bound up not only with their bodies and imagination but with the works of their hands. Grimm makes a jump I cannot follow from the long list of woman's works to the notion of her "convenient leisure"; nonetheless his characterization of the extent and effect of feminine education fits with the way it is seen in many cultures. Even from ancient Sumer, in a poem written four or five thousand years ago, we hear of the learned goddess Geshtinanna who understands letters and functions as the first scribe in literary history. When the shepherd poet Dumuzi has a terrifying dream he calls on his sister for help:

Bring me my sister, my Geshtinanna,
  she understands letters
bring my little sister, my scribe,
  she is the singer
who understands the song,
  bring me my sister.
Bring my wise girl,
  she can read visions,
bring me my sister, bring me
  the little one, she understands
the heart of the whole matter,
  O my sister!
Bring me my sister, I shall tell her
  all my dream.[4]

In addition to holding the pen, wise women, according to
Grimm's account, wield the distaff, which is related through
shape and symbol to the shepherd's crook, priest's crozier, fairy
wand, or measuring stick of the dead. And they have about them
other constant symbols of their work, the caudle cup and spoon,
spindle and thread. Caudle cup and spoon are diminutive forms
of the goddesses' cauldron and stirring stick that stir poets to
ecstatic speech. The spindle and especially the thread, which we
will pick up again here in connection with feminine wisdom,
represents the idea of continuity in opposition to breakthrough.
A thread broken means death:

These were people
Who broke the string for me.
  Therefore
This place became like this for me,
On account of it.
Because the string broke for me,
  Therefore
The place does not feel to me
As the place used to feel to me,
  On account of it.

The place feels as if it stood open before me,
Because the string has broken for me.
Therefore
The place does not feel pleasant to me
Because of it.[5]

—AFRICAN BUSHMAN

The "people who broke the string for me" are called the "fates" in Greek mythology. When the spinners break the thread of a person's life not even Zeus can prevent the inevitable death. If the decisive thread that Ariadne unrolled through the labyrinth had broken it would have meant the end of her life rather than "continuance: into that life beyond the dead-end . . ." (Denise Levertov). When continuity is threatened within a lifetime—when someone loses the thread of sense or meaning—there might be a dream of a broken circle or broken thread. A woman who was quite "broken in spirit" told me she dreamed that blue thread was falling off her spool in bits and pieces. The thread comes up again and again in the attempt to weave meaning.[6] (Ezra Pound says: "I am not being merely incoherent. I haven't 'lost my thread' . . . I need more than one string for a fabric.") There is no way to prevent the spinners' inevitable measuring of your threads ("firmly they fasten the threads of fate, to Northward Neri's daughter cast one of the bands, unbreakable"[7]) but there are accounts of bold heroes (even Apollo, patron of artists) who seduced them with drink in order to disorient them for a while.

One of the meanings of *work* is weaving: from the Old English *wircan* and Middle English *wrought*—"what hath God wrought?" is "what hath God woven?" He wove the world by throwing a shuttle into the loom of nature, where we (as in Psalms) were intricately wrought in the depths of Earth. Woman's time-worn work is weaving tissue to bone or crossing the genetic threads of ancestors. The work is always sexual.

Always and everywhere fate was regarded among the Germanic peoples as a feminine power. The womb of the primeval mother bears all things. The Norns hold destiny in their hands; they spin the thread, tear it off, and determine what is to come. Something of the Norns is at work in women; each of them as place of conception, growth, birth. . . . More than the man, the woman is able to foresee the course of events and give such advice as will bring human action into harmony with destiny. . . . Fate is the sacred center of life. From its womb flow wealth and want, happiness and unhappiness, life and death."[8]

Fate in Old Norse *(skop)* also means genitals. Once when a man dared to look through the peephole of a house the valkyries had disappeared into (it is a rare thing for a house in a dream not to represent the body of a woman) he beheld the grisly sight of twelve women weaving on a loom made of mens' entrails and weighted with severed heads. They filled in a background of gray spears with a weft of crimson, singing all the while: "Weave, weave, the web of spears."[9]

The gray-haired weavers take up their home in the blood-weaving womb of a woman. Norns, as with wise women everywhere, dealt in death but were also midwives—the old gossips present at the instant of birth whose vision encompassed the future. They span the distance between the child's emergence and the old, old woman who has almost forgotten:

The old women came from their caves to close the too many doors that lead into pastures. Thru which the children pass, and in the high grass build their rooms of green, kingdoms where they dwell under the will of grass-hopper, butterfly, snail, quail, thrush, mole and rabbit.

Old Woman, your eye searches the field like a scythe! The riches of the living green lie prepared for your store. Ah, but you come so near to the children! you have almost returned to them. Their voices float up from their faraway games where. The tunneled grass hides their clearings. Swords and blades cut the near blue of sky. Their voices surround you.

Old Woman, at last you have come so near you almost understand them.

Have you recalld then how the soul floats as the tiger-tongued butterfly or that sapphire, the humming-bird, does, where it will?

Lying in the grass, the world was all of the field, and I saw a kite on its string, tugging, bounding—far away as my grandmother—dance against the blue from its tie of invisible delight.

In the caves of blue within the blue the grandmothers bound, on the brink of freedom, to close the too many doors from which the rain falls.

Thus, the grass must give up new keys to rescue the living.
—ROBERT DUNCAN, *"The Structure of Rime VI"*

This is a boy's view of how far away a grandmother is. Bound on the brink of freedom she is bound for death. He says he sees "a kite on its string, tugging, bounding—far away as my grandmother." Meridel Le Sueur, in a poem about being luminous with age, says, "I tie myself to the children like a kite." Being on the edge of that blue, close to the horizon of dying, brings the grandmother full circle to understanding how the child sees it "new." In a sense you are never so close to life as when close to death, and there are many deaths to live through in the course of a single lifetime. One of the "deaths" experienced later in a woman's life is the death of the full woman to the withered woman represented by the crone crescent of the moon, which initiated a time of great fear among primitive peoples. We are perhaps no less frightened of the hag—of the prospect (specter?) of woman aging—and feel uneasy when Grimm speaks of old women "dead to love and labor" or when the *Homeric Hymn* describes the ancient Demeter as "cut-off from childbearing and the gifts of garland loving Aphrodite." But Le Sueur faces it surely in "Rites of Ancient Ripening":

> *Without child or man*
> *I turn I fall*
> *into shadows . . .*

There is another dying to live through in old age—a dying from a certain brightness of immediately apprehended experience into the patchy or dappled realm of remembering. It is a shadowy or shaded field the grandmothers come to, where those who act as midwives to the psyche dwell.

The medial woman's function is to be of assistance in times of difficult passage. As midwife to the psyche she is constellated in "emergency" situations where a spirit, a song, an alternative, a new being is emerging—whenever things appear to rise spontaneously from the depths of the unconscious. An unexpected storm, fury, passion, poetry, and excitement all share the common Gothic root *us-gais jan,* meaning "to bring someone out of himself."[10] The medial woman is evocative: she evokes or calls forth the inner spirit. She has not only the power to inspire, but also the power to intoxicate or induce stupor and sleep. The cultivation of the poppy seed, for example, for potions of forgetfulness, is one of her tasks. On the brink of sleep she is close to death: she weaves dreams and "knits up the ravell'd sleave of care."

It may seem like a long way around—but this thread leads back to the problem of Sleeping Beauty, whose going under and coming out were mediated by the feminine principle active in fairies, who are little and look young but in fact are ageless beings (like the Moirai or Graiai, the Greek spinners, who were "fair-cheeked" but had the gray hair of a spinster). To sleep for a hundred years because a spindle or distaff was turned against you would mean that you were "cursed" by the feminine side of the family. Although sleep is classically close to death (brothers Hypnos and Thanatos), the curse of sleep is not literally death-dealing, which indicates some hope for girls who fade into a sleep state at fifteen. Like Persephone, they can come up again out of their phase of sleep-in-season.

The "season" that puts the girls to sleep is the pubertal awakening. (The prick of the spindle drew the first blood.) Depending upon a girl's relationship to her mother and her mother's relationship to her own sexual nature the pubescent girl will bloom or suddenly fade. In our story the queen mother had been barren for many years. She had been unable to conceive. The kingdom was characterized by the repression of feminine fruitfulness. Finally, when the sterility is turned to creativity because the queen in her bath is visited by a frog (a little sperm-man, a croaking harbinger of spring, companion of midwives), there is a princess born in the kingdom—to give the kingdom another chance. It is said that the girl's father delighted in her—but the mother or maternal princi- ple in the story gets split up into conflicting feelings about the girl, represented by the wishes of the wise women. Consequently, she is nurtured and drained at once. She is fed by the good (con- scious) wishes of beauty, virtue, gentleness, and so on, but an opposite tendency pulls her toward death.

In describing the consequences of one type of "negative mother complex" in a girl, Jung says that an identification with the mother comes about which leads to the

paralysis of the daughter's feminine initiative. A complete projec- tion of her personality on to the mother then takes place . . . Everything which reminds her of motherhood, responsibility, personal relationships, and erotic demands arouses feelings of inferiority and compels her to run away—to her mother, natu- rally, who lives to perfection everything that seems unattainable to her daughter. . . . The daughter leads a shadow-existence, often visibly sucked dry by her mother. . . . These bloodless maidens are . . . so empty that a man is free to impute to them anything he fancies. In addition, they are so unconscious that the uncon- scious puts out countless invisible feelers. . . . The girl's notorious helplessness is a special attraction.[11]

Sleeping Beauty's "countless feelers" are deadly to the men who are drawn to rescue her—the feelers are thorns in the encir- cling hedge that pierce the men to death in the same way the girl was pricked to sleep. It is often the case that the bloodless maidens or somnolent young women unintentionally kill all possibility of relationship when a lover approaches. (This is related to the mother's curse of not wanting the girl to know herself as sexual being; the "way into" the girl becomes thorny—like the *vagina dentata* [12]—and only blooms after one hundred years to allow a man easy entry.) Such daughters also have the effect of putting those around them to sleep. As soon as Sleeping Beauty fell asleep on the couch, sleep extended over the whole palace:

The King and Queen who had just come home, and had entered the great hall, began to go to sleep, and the whole of the court with them. The horses, too, went to sleep in the stable, the dogs in the yard, the pigeons upon the roof, the flies on the wall; even the fire that was flaming on the hearth became quiet and slept, the roast meat left off frizzling, and the cook, who was just going to pull the hair of the scullery boy, because he had forgotten something, let him go, and went to sleep. And the wind fell, and on the trees before the castle not a leaf moved again.

When the wind falls the spirit (*pneuma,* wind or breath) dies down. There is no visible movement. All energy has been withdrawn: Demeter, the principle of awakening seed and soil, has withdrawn into a cave, covered her head, and gone into her grief. Earth lies dormant. Instinct, represented by the horses, dogs, pigeons, flies, and fire, is paralyzed. When such a deep sleep is carried into the consulting room it even puts the analyst to sleep. Von Franz describes such a woman, who had been pricked by her mother's deadly spirit (the mother moaned constantly that she should never have married or borne children):

The strange thing was that when she first came into analysis, I felt as if something had been put over my head and I was falling asleep. I always let myself go into such fantasies when I get an impression from an analysand. My feeling in this case was that I should get up and put my head under the cold water tap. There was quite a pleasant atmosphere, for she was like a little duckling in my hands and never contradicted or opposed me in any way. She interested me, and I felt sympathetic, and yet had this sleepiness, which depicted her own situation. She had not woken up to the fact that she had a right to live. For years the analysis consisted

in showing her in all the events of her life where she had uncon-
sciously, continually given in. We always came back to the same
thing.[13]

Von Franz goes on to say that sometimes working psychologically with people who disappear from the surface of reality is not
effective. Sleep is the curse, but it also heals. After a while (one
hundred years, a very long time—time enough for everything to
have changed) the person will reappear. The put-off sexuality will
emerge. A woman who was numb and inaccessible will thaw, the
thorns will turn to flowers. The only reason given for this is
miraculous, unexplainable. Suddenly, after years of princes' having perished miserably in the thorn hedge, it opens one day to
receive a prince who is, as far as we know from the story, of no
special merit: he just happens to come on the right day. But he
must be an instrument of the wise woman who softened the
original death curse to the sleep of one hundred years. It is she
who parts the hedge, permits access and the eye-opening kiss. The
old woman who spun the length of sleep is there at the awakening. Her presence is in the mediating function of the unconscious
that brings the girl "out of herself."

The old woman's presence on the edge of sleep is not always
so benevolent. Sometimes she brings you out riding the nightmare (about which I will say more soon); at other times she bears
a mixed message, both terrifying and helpful; but in every case
she comes with an autonomy characteristic of the medial feminine. In a dream of this type, a woman was visiting her analyst,
who was living in the basement of the dreamer's great grandmother's house, "where the past was held." The analyst offered
to act as a guide. They had a pleasant visit looking over all the
old things, and the dreamer got to choose one item to keep from
this store of precious items that linked her to her feminine ancestor. She chose a coverlet (a veil, or mantle). She was ready to
leave when the analyst suggested she honor the casket of the great
grandmother on the way out. It had never occurred to her that

the grandmother might actually be present in any way other than in memory and she was terrified. She tried to physically restrain the analyst from proceeding further, at which point a jar of the grandmother's fruit preserves jumped out of the analyst's hands at her.

The dreamer was in analysis to work (among other things) on discovering the roots of her femininity. I have often seen this—that women beginning the process of psyche's excavation will dream about choosing among or "digging through" their grandmother's possessions, trying on her old clothes and hats, or deciding which piece of furniture to keep. In many cases the women will have rejected, with good reason, the ways of their personal mothers and will be left floating, looking for some way to reestablish the continuity of life represented by physically linked generations. (Clothes, in this connection, are sometimes called "threads.")

The analyst or therapist is also often present in these dreams—perhaps as a way of saying that they provide a way of seeing into the past both collectively (into the past myth and history) and personally (into the basement/unconscious place in the dreamer "where the past is held"). What is valuable is the dreamer's newfound attitude toward the past. In this case it is the attitude of the initiate who has chosen to be veiled by a coverlet or mantle. Such a rich symbol points in many directions at once. In terms of the foregoing discussion of the sibyl who meets the one-who-seeks at the entrance to the underworld labyrinth, the attitude assumed by the dreamer is appropriate for stepping into, or making a ritual entry into, earth—the place where the dead live. Long before wearing a veil meant being a bride, it was a sign of humility, of accepting the darkness and of accepting a spiritual guide who would lead you through the mysteries. Nothing is more mysterious to mortals than meeting the dead. Aeneas requested safe passage to the underworld in order to speak with his male ancestor. The dreamer descends through the basement in order to see what was valuable in her inheritance. She does not realize that she has come into the place where the body of the past is literally held, in the casket which she must honor.

Honoring the dead has probably always been a vital factor in the religious and social life of human communities. (From burial sites we know that primitive cave dwellers buried their dead in the middle of their dwellings and slept with their heads toward the "graves.") Fear is of course a primary reason: we are afraid of ghosts and do not want them returning to haunt us, which they will do if unpropitiated or simply not recognized. We provide candy for ghosts and goblins at Halloween time in order to keep the spirit of the dead from returning to our door. If the dead are not recognized (more than merely remembered; they demand attention), they will return of their own accord. The jar of preserves will jump out at you. Fruit preserves of the great grandmother appearing suddenly as they do at the point of the dreamer's refusal to go on might mean that the spirit of the grandmother, her particular feminine fruitfulness, is coming to meet the woman part way. It has been taken out of the hands of the analyst so that the encounter is solely between the woman and her ancestor, the woman and a forgotten medial part of herself.

Getting beneath the surface of ordinary experience—opening the door to the mind's basement—becomes less difficult once you have found the omphalos, that mound on which the sibyl sits. For many people, dreams are the omphalos. Freud described dreams as mushrooms with vast networks of underground mycelia. Usually we only see the rounded cap above ground. Sometimes we know enough to follow certain of the roots to their intertwining sources. Many a legendary king depended upon old women as his primary source of hidden information. Like the mushroom, the wise women had gnarled roots sunk deep into the motherland so that they knew everything that was going on in the king's realm. In the Irish tale of Deirdre the young girl is kept by such a king's "conversation woman." She was godmother of the girl and gossip of the king. When she was not tending the girl or out among the people she sat near his raised throne on a stool set there for that purpose.

Conversation women with divinatory powers, called "spae-wives" (spying wives), who were not attached to a throne, used to travel about the farmlands in Norway and Iceland either alone or in companies, visiting farms and foretelling the future. They were welcomed into the homes they visited, fed, and given gifts at parting. They wore hooded garments, boots of calfskin, and gloves of catskin. It was said that cats accompanied these seeresses on their journey between this world and another much the way dogs accompanied Hekate in Greece. Cats and dogs, the two most frequently domesticated wild animals, are apt to carry the boundary between worlds on their backs. They are uncannily close to being human and yet are at home in the ways of a completely instinctual, natural realm desirable to, yet uninhabitable by, human beings. Traveling soothsayers were old women of the road, straying or wandering in the tradition of Hekate. Like Hekate they were thought of as being part goddesses. Tacitus the historian tells about a tower-dwelling seeress who would send her messages out via a relative who acted as interpreter. He says then that it was the custom of northern peoples to regard women endowed with the gift of prophecy "even as goddesses."[14] But there is another reason for this high regard that the connection to Hekate suggests. You will remember that Hekate was a very ancient goddess predating Olympus, and that by the time Zeus was in ascendancy she was regarded as only part goddess, a dweller-in-between. This brought her close to the side of women who, especially in childbirth, are close to the border realm of the gods. Snorri Sturluson, the gifted thirteenth-century poet, chieftain, and Icelandic historian, said that these women who traveled about the countryside may have been the final representatives of the fertility goddess, who "survived last of all the gods."[15]

These shapers of destiny survived last of all the gods because they came closest to home. Not many gods or goddesses were invited into the homes of humble people the way the norns were. These wise women, who were there at the cutting of the cord, spun that cord into the future, "fastening it in the middle beneath the hall of the moon" ("Song of Helgi"). Moonsickness and madness were also associated with their travels. As the gods diminished in grandeur and power in the eyes of men the medial powers of the old hooded wise women were repressed and came out in twisted and tortured forms of witchcraft and sorcery. The dark of the night and the dark of the moon (Hekate) encouraged these eruptions. One terrifying midnight phantom goddess who rode a horse would send out fearful apparitions called Empusae. An Empusa would come wrapped in a blood-swollen bladder and "rush out upon women and children from dark places."[16] In this form she was naturally not invited into homes, so she would make her nocturnal visits uninvited, frequently in the shape of a nightmare.

The other face of Hekate the wanderer is Hekate the prowler, whose dogs become carriers of infection and madness. She too rode a horse and inhabited the darkest corners of the mind. She became mother of all witchcraft and witches and guardians of the stables where nightmares are tethered and loosed. In Slavonic *mara* means "witch;" in Polish *mora* means "nightmare;" the Czech *mura* means both "nightmare" and "sphinx moth"—a winged creature that comes out at night. In discussing the origin of the word, Jung says that although there is a connection between *mar,* "nightmare," and *mähre,* "a female horse," the actual source of the word means "demonic treading."[17] A nightmare rhythmically rides or treads its victim, just as a cock treads the hen. The rhythm is sexual, but it is feminine. Di Prima called her the "large gypsy mother who leads us through dreamforest on horse back . . . [she is] the cauldron and evening star" who rides the dark. Hekate on horseback is sometimes accompanied by Priapus—the erect phallic god. She is known to have ridden men to death. A twelfth-century English chronicle states that the wife of King Edgar was accused of witchcraft and that she was accustomed to taking on the form of a horse to work her magic. A bishop saw her once "running and leaping hither and thither with horses and showing herself shamelessly to them."[18] Apparently this particular form of sexual mania afflicted queens and especially housewives, whose "god" was depicted as the generative organ of a horse.[19]

An *alp* is a Norse nightmare or night elf, a feminine creature that seizes you in the dark. According to the Grimms, when a woman is going to bed she must move her chair from the place where she has been sitting, or the *alp* will weigh upon her.[20] Another such piece of advice is that if the nightmare visits you—a big woman with long flying hair—bore a hole in the bottom of the door and fill it with sow bristles. (Sow bristles are witch's whiskers.) Then sleep in peace and if the nightmare returns promise her a present. She will leave you then and come back the next day, in human shape, for the promised gift.[21]

Many more faces of the *alp* are revealed in James Joyce's *Finnegans Wake,* where he calls the heroine ALP and the hero H.C.E. He is Here Comes Everybody, Humphrey Chimpden Earwicker, Howth Castle and Environs, the High Church of England. He is no man and everyman, the Lord and the Evil One. His wife is ALP, Anna Livia Plurabelle, mother of the Virgin, empress of Rome, all the beautiful women in the world. She is the River Liffey (which "leafy-speafs" or speaks like the sibyl) running like a thread through the book. She is water nymph, matronly river, delightfully pure and filthy as a hag. She is the shameless barmaid and the proper and generous widow: "Grampupus is fallen down but Grinny sprids the boord." But above all she is the "spae-wife," the cackling Mother Goose, or the earth-pecking hen, Biddy, who scratches the torn scraps of a gossipacious letter filled with the secrets of a woman's heart out of a dung heap.

Joyce tells us that he found the manuscript for his book—the manifesto or mamafesta—in those hens' scratching on the dung heap. He is also saying that history is passed on in the old wives' tale. (In an oddly related scrap of Icelandic history we are told that women who prophesied and sang about destiny sat high above their audiences on cushions stuffed with hens' feathers.[22])

The hen sitting on a tale-telling midden mound, like the sibyl sitting on the raised umbilical mound of mother earth or the muse sitting on a well, is in a position to tap buried information. Freud called it digging for oil, tunneling deep. The material dredged up is often garbage—"the compost and fruitful decay" that yields secrets of civilization and personal psyches. Things discarded as mistakes or misperceptions of childhood—our own or the childhood of humanity—are often *drawn up* again with startling intensity. At the women's rites called *Thesmophoria* in ancient Greece, certain of the participants were designated as "the drawers up" (see Chapter 10). It was their task to descend into a cleft in the ground in order to bring up the rotted remains of the animal sacrifice, which was then used for compost.

Many dreams and pieces of active imagination contain this motif of descent and ascent. In one instance, a young woman went down into the church basement looking for pork chops. She spoke with one of the "janitors of shadowland," who directed her upstairs again to a rummage sale, where she was to look through old women's clothes. The going down and coming up are essential parts of the search for self. The wandering goddess Demeter —who wanders in search of a lost part of herself—sits on the edge of the Maiden Well to await the uprising of her daughter self from the depths. Demeter had disguised herself as an aging woman. She was part mortal and part immortal, a dweller in between the world of women and of goddesses. Like the Norns, the Valkyries, the spae-wives, and wise women, she is at home on the edge of the depths of woods, water, and the unconscious—places where things can turn into their opposites.

> at strange turns of the minds road
> wrong turns that lead
> over the border into wonder,
>
> mistaken directions, forgotten signs
> all bringing the souls travels to a place

of origin, a well
under the lake where the muse moves."
—DENISE LEVERTOV, *"The Illustration"*

The place of origin is the well. The old Teutonic goddess Mother Hulda loved to haunt lake and fountain and could only be reached by descending through a well. Her story illustrates the psychic fact that "good" can come of unintended turns—of events, of a spindle, of a girl.

MOTHER HULDA

A widow had two daughters; one was pretty and industrious, the other was ugly and lazy. And as the ugly one was her own daughter, she loved her much the best, and the pretty one was made to do all the work, and be the drudge of the house. Every day the poor girl had to sit by a well on the high road and spin until her fingers bled. Now it happened once that as the spindle was bloody, she dipped it into the well to wash it; but it slipped out of her hand and fell in. Then she began to cry, and ran to her step-mother, and told her of her misfortune; and her step-mother scolded her without mercy, and said in her rage, "As you have let the spindle fall in, you must go and fetch it out again!"

Then the girl went back again to the well, not knowing what to do, and in the despair of her heart she jumped down into the well the same way the spindle had gone. After that she knew nothing; and when she came to herself she was in a beautiful meadow, and the sun was shining on the flowers that grew round her. And she walked on through the meadow until she came to a baker's oven that was full of bread; and the bread called out to her, "Oh, take me out, take me out, or I shall burn; I am baked enough already!"

Then she drew near, and with the baker's peel she took out all the loaves one after the other. And she went farther on till she came to a tree weighed down with apples, and it called out to her, "Oh, shake me, shake me, we apples are all of us ripe!" Then she shook the tree until the apples fell like rain, and she shook until there were no more to fall; and when she had gathered them together in a heap, she went on farther.

At last she came to a little house, and an old woman was

peeping out of it, but she had such great teeth that the girl was terrified and about to run away, only the old woman called her back. "What are you afraid of, my dear child? Come and live with me, and if you do the house-work well and orderly, things shall go well with you. You must take great pains to make my bed well, and shake it up thoroughly, so that the feathers fly about, and then in the world it snows, for I am Mother Hulda." As the old woman spoke so kindly, the girl took courage, consented, and went to her work. She did everything to the old woman's satisfaction, and shook the bed with such a will that the feathers flew about like snow-flakes: and so she led a good life, had never a cross word, but boiled and roast meat every day. When she had lived a long time with Mother Hulda, she began to feel sad, not knowing herself what ailed her; at last she began to think she must be home-sick; and although she was a thousand times better off than at home where she was, yet she had a great longing to go home. At last she said to her mistress, "I am home-sick, and although I am very well off here, I cannot stay any longer; l must go back to my own home." Mother Hulda answered, "It pleases me well that you should wish to go home, and, as you have served me faithfully, I will undertake to send you there!"

She took her by the hand and led her to a large door standing open, and as she was passing through it there fell upon her a heavy shower of gold, and the gold hung all about her, so that she was covered with it. "All this is yours, because you have been so industrious," said Mother Hulda; and, besides that, she returned to her her spindle, the very same that she had dropped in the well. And then the door was shut again, and the girl found herself back again in the world, not far from her mother's house; and as she passed through the yard the cock stood on the top of the well and cried,

> *"Cock-a-doodle doo!*
> *Our golden girl has come home too!"*

Then she went in to her mother, and as she had returned covered with gold she was well received.

So the girl related all her history, and what had happened to her, and when the mother heard how she came to have such great riches she began to wish that her ugly and idle daughter might have the same good fortune. So she sent her to sit by the well and spin; and in order to make her spindle bloody she put her hand into the thorn hedge. Then she threw the spindle into the well, and jumped in herself. She found herself, like her sister, in the beautiful meadow, and followed the same path, and when she came to the baker's oven, the bread cried out, "Oh, take me out, take me out, or I shall burn; I am quite done already!" But the lazy-bones answered, "I have no desire to black my hands," and went on farther. Soon she came to the apple-tree, who called out, "Oh, shake me, shake me, we apples are all of us ripe!" But she answered, "That is all very fine; suppose one of you should fall on my head," and went on farther.

When she came to Mother Hulda's house she did not feel afraid, as she knew beforehand of her great teeth, and entered into her service at once. The first day she put her hand well to the work, and was industrious, and did everything Mother Hulda bade her, because of the gold she expected; but the second day she began to be idle, and the third day still more so, so that she would not get up in the morning. Neither did she make Mother Hulda's bed as it ought to have been made, and did not shake it for the feathers to fly about. So that Mother Hulda soon grew tired of her, and gave her warning, at which the lazy thing was well pleased, and thought that now the shower of gold was coming; so Mother Hulda led her to the door, and as she stood in the doorway, instead of the shower of gold a great kettle full of pitch was emptied over her. "That is the reward for your service," said Mother Hulda, and shut the door. So the lazy girl came home all covered with pitch, and the cock on the top of the well seeing her, cried,

> *"Cock-a-doodle doo!*
> *Our dirty girl has come home too!"*

And the pitch remained sticking to her fast, and never, as long as she lived, could it be got off.[23]

The industrious maid is really *monogenes*—an appellation used for Hekate[24]—meaning without siblings or relatives. She is an only child with no mother or sister on this earth. She has a substitute mother and sister who are each at least a "step" removed from her, leaving her quite lonely and therefore capable of finding solace, balance, and healing in another world. The beauty of the lower world compensates for the destructiveness of the upper world. The girl provides the counterbalance by going down to the good mother and bringing beauty and illumination up to the surface again, where she is recognized by the bird of the threshold, who announces her golden return. Then the story doubles back on itself or reverses—showing us the nonreflecting dark side (as of the moon). Now that beauty has been sent back up above, ugliness is below. The cock crows a second time—but this time it announces the coming of the dirty girl. Like Mary, the Black Virgin,[25] who was black in soul, the girl gets turned inside out —her true nature is revealed.

More than just a story of how the diligent and the idle get what they deserve, the tale of Mother Hulda delineates approaches to the unconscious. One daughter throws herself into the well in despair "the same way the spindle had gone" and the other jumps in willfully, intending to gain the same bounty and blessing. Part of what was lost to the golden girl—and found at the end—was her grasp of the tool that spun her own fate. The distaff side of the family did not exist in any organic way for her. There was no natural maternal inheritance. She was without any feminine model or reference point around which to spin the fantasies of her future. Not her will, but the pain of the situation, drove her to retrieve what she had lost. We are not told explicitly that her gesture was suicidal (like Psyche's wanting to throw herself into the river in utter resignation) but the combined despair at the loss of her spinning implement and misery of rejection compelled her to throw herself down into a watery darkness that seemed to be death. The process of individuation—of discovering who you are as unique person— often begins with confronting an insoluble problem: when there is no way out, no visible alternative, no apparent freedom to move. Finding yourself without a place of warmth or welcome, when all your work seems to come to nothing in the face of ingratitude and nonrecognition, opens a kind of trap door to depths of introversion never imagined and certainly not "chosen."

The second daughter who jumps into the well does it out of greed and "second-hand" knowledge. She has heard a description of this miraculous meadow and underground Mother and assumes that the experience can be imitated. No inner necessity compels her. She has seen that going into the unconscious (exploring dreams, active imagination) can yield certain treasures and wants to acquire them. Unfortunately, the unconscious has a certain will of its own represented in this case by its guardian, Mother Hulda.

Before proceeding further with the story I want to give you some background behind this particular unearthly Mother because she represents medial aspects of the feminine—not specifically mantic, having powers of prophecy and divination, but definitely otherworldly, related to the night-flying Hekate and spinning Fates. Hulda, Mother Holle, Hulle, Holl, Frau Holde is a kind, benignant, merciful goddess or lady. Her name means "hold" or "bend" or "bow."[26] The opposite notion of a malignant, diabolical being: unbending and unrestoring, informs another of her faces. She usually manifests a kindly disposition and is never cross except when she notices disorder in household affairs. Weather (the Earth Household) is her affair. When fog rests on the mountain Dame Holle has lit fire in her hill. When it snows she is making her bed. Herodotus said that the Scythians pronounced the northern regions inaccessible because they were filled with feathers. She makes the whirlwind follow the hunter and rides the air with snow-wives, witches, and a host of souls of unbaptized infants. At night she rides clothed in terror. At noon she bathes, disappearing in lake and fountain.

She is sometimes white and lovely but can assume the shape of a shrunken old crone with a long nose of iron, big teeth, and a mat of bristling hair. Children are frightened of her. A man whose hair sticks up in tangled disorder has "had a jaunt with Holle." A maid who does not have her spinning done by Sunday will have

Holle in her distaff to tangle it. She is a spinning wife. Cultivation of flax is assigned to her. She presents industrious maids with spindles, and spins their reels full for them overnight. When she enters the land at Christmastime all distaffs must be standing well stocked. No flax must be spun on her sacred holiday (the twelve days of Christmas), which ought to be a time of rest (Sabbath). She is queen of subterranean peoples—elves and fairies—and mistress of mountain sprites. In Swedish folk songs (this is important for our understanding of the story) one calls their *real* or archetypal mother "huldmoder, hulda moder." In Austria, where she is called Berchta she comes as a white ghost in the night to tread or stomp on children. Or she comes into nurseries in snow-white garments to rock babies while their mothers sleep. She acts as the old grandmother or ancestress of the family. Food left out for her resembles the food customarily offered to Hekate on the day of the moon's dark phase. Night hags and enchantresses follow in her train. Women and children leave dolls made out of rags on the windowsill for her. She brings presents, sometimes sending them via elves or dwarfs. When she chases through the woods she is accompanied by hounds. Cats were also sacred to her. Some accounts make her beautiful in front and ugly behind. Like the goddess Hel she is sometimes half "black."

Mother Hulda is not to be taken lightly. Her realm, for all its enchanting sunlit beauty, is fraught with hidden dangers. The only sign of this side that shows through when the golden girl approaches is the "toothiness" of the mother. The girl turns in terror, which is the appropriate thing to do in the face of such an encounter (just as the dreamer who had to approach her grandmother's casket balked in fear), but the old woman comes out to greet her, reassuring her that things will go well with her if she comes in. The sister's reaction at this point in the doubled story is inappropriate: thinking that she knows, she shows no fear of the unknown and strides blatantly into the maw. Everything about her approach is wrong. She is literally the good sister's shadow, wanting to assimilate the experience for selfish purposes. Her intention in approaching the unconscious (the realm of the

Mother heretofore unknown) is utilitarian. She wants only to make use of it—an attitude which always has destructive effects. For example, coming into analysis with specific ideas about what the process will give you—like the ability to stick to a creative task, or to sleep better or love better—usually does not work because the unconscious, once it is tapped, will go on giving. (In a variant of the story gold keeps coming out of the good sister's mouth whenever she speaks and snakes out of the bad sister's.) Forced introversion does not work. You cannot suddenly decide to withdraw from the surface of reality unless you have been pulled by an interior string. The fortune-seeking sister's timing is all off. She has no sympathy for the idea of organic ripening, for things happening "in their own time." She ignores the apples on the tree as well as the bread baking in the oven. Feminine mysteries of transformation are beyond her; she has no time for them. Instead, the fruit will stay attached to the mother tree and rot. And the loaves will remain too long in the mother oven and blacken. She is too much in the thrall of her greedy personal mother to obey the "laws" of Mother Nature, who is the archetypal and therefore the original or real Mother.

The sister who followed the way of her despairing heart found her "huldmoder," her spindle (feminine identity), and her way home. She knew when it was time to return to the upperworld. Her longing for home, even though it had been so disheartening a place, shows her willingness (psychologically) to integrate new-found contents into consciousness. Every hero brings the treasure (or else the curse of failure) back to the world. The Mother who sends her manifestations into the world knows that the threshold needs to be crossed again and says, "It pleases me well that you wish to return."

The old woman, who is regarded as the teacher of "song, story, and spindle," is Wisdom herself, spinning and weaving the thread of life. In Proverbs, where she is called "honey for the soul," her double nature as wise one and witch is described in the words of an old man talking to his son:

Say unto wisdom, Thou art my sister; and call understanding thy kinswoman: that they may keep thee from the strange woman, from the stranger which flattereth with her words.

The warning is that he be aware of the extremes to which his soul, the woman within, might pull. Seen from another perspective, it is a proverbial insight into the nature of the feminine at the medial pole. It is about the extremes to which a woman might herself be pulled (and about how close deception and truth are to each other) when perched on the brink of the unconscious. In fact, the golden girl and the dirty girl may be sisters in one psyche, or two faces of the same girl. One cannot draw near the nucleus—be it self or soul or spindle core—and the meaning of life, without also being on the edge of falling into greed, darkness, and the field of encircling shadows. Threshold gods and goddesses show human beings how to live on this particular edge without giving over completely to one side or the other. Hermes the *psychopomp*, leader of souls, who was at home in the shadows, and a companion of the medial Hekate, was credited with transmitting the enigmatic feminine art of soothsaying. When he was but a child in the cradle Apollo visited him with a gift:

There be certain Thriae, sisters born, three maidens rejoicing in swift wings. Their heads are sprinkled with white meal and they dwell under a ridge of Parnassus, teachers of soothsaying. This art I learned while yet a boy tending the herds, though my father paid no heed to it. From their home they flit continually hither and thither, feeding on honeycombs and bringing all things to fulfillment. They, when they are full of the spirit of inspiration, having eaten of the wan honey, delight to speak forth the truth. But if they be bereft of the sweet food divine, then lie they all confusedly. These then I give you; enquire of them strictly and delight your heart.[27]

These fabled bee sisters, whose ancient heads come up withered from pollen-filled flowers, are responsible for both poetic enthusiasm and madness. They swarm with enthusiasm when full but mingle words confusedly when empty. "Confusion of spirit" was a classical way of describing the state of psychic disorientation we call madness. The opposite state would be experienced as "clarity of spirit." Of the three sisters, one represents madness, another clarity, and the third the brink, the place or phenomenon of reversal. She is the one through whom things turn into their opposites. This sisterhood of clarity and confusion, truth telling and lying—which emanates from one and the same source—leads our exploration of the medial into one remaining field, that of a poet who was much taken with bees.

10
Reflection and Fabrication

In dark moments between sleep and waking, works of art and language take form in the minds of artists and dreamers now as with prehistoric cave painters forty thousand years ago. Hans Arp, the artist whose modern line drawings look primitive and surreal at once, used to work in a darkened room together with his wife. Their work at drawing is reminiscent of the Yeatses' work at fashioning a language of the soul out of waking dreams that began on their honeymoon train trip to a seaside cottage. The poet's wife began to receive messages from spirits that named themselves and spoke at length. Without knowing the origin of these voices, Yeats was impressed with their profundity and recorded the "otherworldly" data that eventually became a book.[1] The Arps, who "often drew their curved interpenetrating lines with half-closed eyes," had more of a sense of source for their work and compared it to the creation of prehistoric images:

Now, under lowered lids, the inner movement streams untainted to the hand. In a darkened room it is even easier to follow the guidance of the inner movement than in the open air. A conductor of inner music, the great designer of prehistoric images, worked with eyes turned inwards. So his drawings gain in transparency; open to interpenetration, to sudden inspiration, to recovery of the inner melody, to the circling approach; and the whole is transmuted into one great exhalation.[2]

The source for these unconscious collaborators is an inner one. They are shutting out the daylight in order to more carefully discern the shifting shapes (and sounds) that assail or delight those who look into the dark. Darkness and night share this capacity for making the world over as it were from the inside out. Our feelings assume the strange proportions of the dark: we are alarmed by the suddenly ominous robe hanging by the window or the magnified sound of an animal on the roof. In a context that is at first glance removed from the attempt to see how artists see, Walter Otto describes the shape-shifting qualities of night. He is leading up to a portrait of Hermes here, which, although more recent than the prehistoric period when artists transformed cave walls according to what imagination beheld, actually does tie the onlooker back into a similar space. Hermes, the comrade of night, was born in a cave and received his first cunning inspirations there in that gloom. When darkness falls:

Nighness vanishes, and with it distance; everything is equally far and near, close by us and yet mysteriously remote. Space loses its measures. There are whispers and sounds, and we do not know where or what they are. . . . There is a strangeness about what is intimate and dear, and a seductive charm about the frightening. There is no longer a distinction between the lifeless and the living, everything is animate and soulless, vigilant and asleep at once. What the day brings on and makes recognizable gradually, emerges out of the dark with no intermediary stages. The encounter suddenly confronts us, as if by a miracle: What is the thing we suddenly see—an enchanted bride, a monster, or merely a log? . . . Danger lurks everywhere. . . . Who can protect [the wanderer]? . . . The spirit of Night itself . . . its enchantment, its resourcefulness, and its profound wisdom. She is indeed the mother of all mystery. The weary she wraps in slumber, delivers from care, and she causes dreams to play about their souls. Her protection is enjoyed by the unhappy and persecuted as well as by the cunning, whom her ambivalent shadows offer a thousand devices and contrivances. . . . Music is the true language of her mystery—the enchanting voice which sounds for eyes that are closed. . . . The darkness of night which so sweetly invites (sleep) also bestows new vigilance and illumination upon the spirit. It makes it more perceptive, more acute, more enterprising. Knowledge flares up, or descends like a shooting star—rare, precious,

even magical knowledge. . . . So night, which can terrify the
solitary man and lead him astray, can also be his friend, his helper,
his counselor.[3]

And, we would add, his source of inspiration. Sometimes fears
inspired by the dark can be allayed by making something up—a
song, a pleasant fantasy, or an image. As a child once I had
darkness imposed on me for a week because of an eye injury that
required my wearing black patches. It was suggested that I try
drawing a series of pictures which I could examine once vision
was restored. The idea must have intrigued me because I can
remember looking later at the disconnected bodies of the numerous made-up animals that were strewn on papers about the bed-
room. At the moment of originally hurting myself all the children
were being taken to the Bronx Zoo to ride the camels—a treat
I had anticipated. But I had to miss it and instead carried my
perception of these animals into an enclosed space of my own
making. This, in a roundabout way, is how the prehistoric artist
must have worked. When the artists of the famous caves in Pech-
Merle drew horses, female figures, bison, mammoths, and birds
they did not have their models all gathered around on the cave
floor. Rather than imitating forms observed by the eye, they gave
form and expression to images of creatures carried within—carried by that faculty we call imagination or memory. Like the work
of contemporary artists who have to turn their eyes inward to
seize hold of picture-forming particles and strands of memory,
prehistoric artwork done in the close darkness of caverns il-
luminated only by flickering torches came into being as a direct
response to inner sight.

The connection I am making is between anterior and interior
perception. Anterior comes before in time. Interior comes from
within. If the two are drawn together they form a vast terrain
inviting exploration: it is as if your psyche were an unfathomably
deep, many-caverned lake. Beneath its mirror surface the water
extends infinitely downward. We would see ourselves in the sur-

face ripple, the history of all life in its dark depths. In one of the places where the poet Charles Olson talks about the data-giving depths of natural things he says that history *('istorin)* means "finding out for oneself."[4] Prehistory would then imply what you would have to know before being able to find out for yourself. It would be like going to the bottom of the lake in order to comprehend the surface from below. Our dreaming performs this feat for us: dreams are our own prehistory working itself up from the depths to the level of potential consciousness.[5] Once an image is up it is "open to interpenetration" like Hans Arp's drawings; something opaque has become transparent and is open "to sudden inspiration, to recovery of inner melody, to the circling approach." Jung called this circling approach to an image circumambulation. The best way to find out for oneself is to beat around the bush, to walk in circles, to see a thing from all sides without being distracted by associations that pull the vision in other directions.

Seeing through an image to its source can produce as much discord as melody. In a story called "The Lady in the Looking Glass," subtitled "A Reflection," Virginia Woolf induces a full prismatic range of emotion by gradually revealing the image of an approaching woman in the drawing-room mirror. She describes the quiet, beautiful, old country home with the bookcases and lacquer cabinets, plush couch, chimney pieces, billowing curtains: the estate of Isabella Tyson. As Isabella comes closer the elegant reverie is shattered by the realization that she is not what she seems. "The looking-glass began to pour over her a light that seemed to fix her; that seemed like some acid to bite off the unessential and superficial and to leave only the truth. It was an enthralling spectacle. Everything dropped from her—clouds, dress, basket, diamond. . . ."[6] It spared nothing. Isabella was empty, friendless, old, and dried. The reflection said she was unloved and cared for no one. The writer concludes that people should not leave looking glasses hanging in their rooms.

A client whom I saw only once had such a fear of seeing herself that she kept a very special looking glass hidden away in a closet. In her dream she was dressing for a party with great indecision—not knowing what to put on or how she wanted to look. While standing in front of the mirror she suddenly remembered a dusty box in the closet that contained a jewel given to her by her mother. The jewel was a small crystal ball, "the kind you look into to see the past and future." In a moment she decided to affix the beautiful jewel to her forehead. With this done she was ready for the party, but she had some doubt about whether or not it would stick.

This woman, who was not familiar with the mystical notion of a "third" or inward-looking eye, had chosen to oppose her loss of soul and sight by regaining a power to rule herself that could come only from gazing through an eye that sees more than the mirror can see. The decision made her beautiful, but she was not sure it would stick (or that she could stick to it)—and since she did not return to the inward-looking situation of therapy I have wondered whether the latter wasn't the case. There are cases where an insight of major importance can motivate the psyche to do its own work unaided by the *psychopomp* or *therapeutes*: often, especially in young people, short-term therapy is all that is needed to clear an obstruction to living. It is to be hoped that this was true for the indecisive woman in the dream; I am, however, doubtful because the work she was called to by the crystal ball would take her away from day-to-day life into the timeless realm of psyche, in which she had no sense of direction, having never explored its reaches. The gift from her mother (not her personal mother as much as her archetypal mother, her ancestral mother: Memory, the mother of musing) could have given her the imperative sense of direction. Like the innumerable fairy tale children who step through mirrors or wardrobes or trapdoors into fantasy worlds, or the initiates in ancient incubation rites who entered into the earth through cave entrances and clefts in the ground, she was being invited by the dream to a musing journey and "wide-eyed" return. In the language of the psyche that would have been making history.

Essential to the task of finding out for oneself is the willingness to engage in, or be engaged by, a process of reflection and fabrication—of seeing and making. In a poem where the poet is the mirror ("I am silver and exact") Sylvia Plath provides (*pro-vide*, foresees) a clear way to understanding such a necessary engagement:

> Now I am a lake. A woman bends over me,
> Searching my reaches for what she really is.
> Then she turns to those liars, the candles or the moon.
> I see her back, and reflect it faithfully.
> She rewards me with tears and an agitation of hands.
> I am important to her. She comes and goes.
> Each morning it is her face that replaces the darkness.
> In me she has drowned a young girl, and in me an old woman
> Rises toward her day after day, like a terrible fish.
>
> —*"Mirror"*

Reflection, "to reflect," means to bend back or to turn again. This is Sylvia Plath's reflection of herself and of Everywoman, who rises to the mirror each morning and turns to the moon each night. There is a difference in the light cast by each source: water-mirror, candle, and moon. They are more or less truthful. Gazing into the lake, the bending over herself, is the most dangerous. Like Persephone bending over the flower, the one-hundred-fold-blooming narcissus—she bends to admire herself and releases the pent-up forces of hell, Hades, underworld, or the unconscious, which carry her away on a long journey of losing and coming to herself again. "The danger is great," Mephistopheles says, "for these depths fascinate." Bending over to look for yourself means risking death. The death may be actual: people take their own lives out of desperation from what they see. Or it may be symbolic (no less real): it may be the death of the image of yourself in the world, a dying to what you have been.

This act of looking, then, of "searching the reaches," means stretching your imagination, stretching your capacity for seeing as far as the lake is deep. It means having the courage to plumb and read the "data giving depth of tissue" which is the all-inclusive body of personal and prehistorical experience. Myths of creation from cultures more in-going than our own stress this capacity for searching the imagination. The mode of cosmic becoming is marked by inner activity. (Perhaps these cultures are more feminine—inclusive rather than intrusive—a masculine mode of creation being one that seems to intrude upon matter.) Among the more introverted peoples like the Native Americans or Far Eastern Indians,

There is a tendency to describe creation as an inner process, an inner thought process in the Godhead. They try to search back into their own minds and come to insight and reflection, by bending their thoughts backwards towards the inside and towards the subjective factor, to watch and describe the process which precedes a creative idea or thought.

Wherever there is this tendency to describe the creative process in this form, you find introverted civilizations, with the tendency to mirror backwards into the mind. This is mostly worked out in the Far East where there is the idea of creation through *tapas* . . . originally meant to brood, to give warmth to the inner, to brood, so to speak, upon yourself; we would say to give libido to yourself.[7]

A Zuñi example:

In the beginning of things Awonawilona was alone. (He was the very first high God of the Zuñi Indians; he is a creator and the one who preserves everything.) There was nothing beside him in the whole space of time. Everywhere there was black darkness and void. Then Awonawilona conceived in himself the thought, and the thought took shape and got out into space and through this it stepped out into the void, into outer space, and from them came nebulae of growth and mist, full of power of growth. After the mist and nebulae came up, Awonawilona changed himself through his knowledge into another shape and became the sun, who is our father and who enlightens everything and fills everything with light, and the nebulae condensed and sank down and became water and thus the sea came into existence.[8]

Awonawilona conceived of something new and gave form to matter by turning in on himself. Even though it is a masculine father god, the mode of creation is feminine: to conceive, to incubate (brood or *tapas*), to carry a thing to term until it takes shape and steps into outer space, outside the body of the bearer. When the opposites turn toward each other something new is born. Such myths of creation tell the human story of the birth of creative thought from introversion. Introversion is the turning in of psychic energy, the sinking of libido "into its own depths," an abandonment of the upper world for the discovered place where memories and childhood are constellated.

It is easier for a naturally introverted person to engage in the process of being "sunk in thought." But the pull of inertia or fate in an outgoing person can sometimes be as great as the pull of an introverted nature. Jung writes that "when the libido leaves the bright upper world, whether from choice, or from inertia, or from fate, it sinks back into its own depths, into the source from which it originally flowed, and returns to the point of cleavage, the navel, where it first entered the body. This point of cleavage is called the Mother, because from her the current of life reached us."[9] And it is here that Jung says a person goes when there is a great work to be accomplished, an effort from which one recoils; when you doubt your strength or creativity or force of imagination, you move back to the source. (You may dive deep into the water in a dream or find yourself in the arms of your mother or sit sybil-like on a mound, the earth's navel, that leaks psychic messages from the underground.)

This is another potentially dangerous psychic moment: being back at the breast of the Mother, the (creative) matrix. It is possible to get stuck there and die. Or you can struggle loose again by pulling away from the inner world to forge or fabricate a way up, back to life. For the visitor to Delphi this meant directing the next step according to the interpretation of the oracle. For an artist this would mean starting the next work, bringing your creativity to bear on a piece of material, taking up the tool again. For the followers of Brahma, the Creator God, the rising to the surface meant the coming of wisdom represented by the books of the Vedas. It is said that Vishnu, the Everywhere-Active-One, sank into a profound trance. The outgoing godhead was drawn in a direction opposite to the world. In his slumber he brought forth a flower-enthroned, book-bearing god from his navel. This god was Brahma, who brought with him the Vedas, which he diligently read even as he was being born.

The emergence from the god's navel is the birth of creative thought from introversion or reflection. But then a mighty flood came because Vishnu sat in his deep sleep state for too long. Great confusion ensued, and a demon who took advantage of the watery chaos stole the Vedas and hid wisdom far down in the depths, where it remained until Brahma finally succeeded in waking Vishnu. Vishnu changed himself into a fish, plunged into the floodwaters, fought the demon, and recaptured the Vedas. Vishnu becomes a fish by being awakened, or being enlightened. The woman in Plath's poem becomes a fish by becoming old, haggard, and wise in the ways of water.

In *The Great Mother,* Neumann calls the medial woman "the lady of the wisdom-bringing water of the depths." Her murmuring, watery speech (the utterance of seerdom) is the expressed voice of her own unconscious, which rises up in her like the water of a geyser or, in time, as a terrible fish. The poem, like the lake, contains the history of a woman. This woman who became mirror to herself made a dwelling in the inner world. She gave her maidenhood over to that water-mirror ("In me she has drowned a young girl") and became identified with its depths. The identification is complete when the woman she recognizes as herself in the upper world turns her back on the lake, leaving the mirror woman in the lake alone with no face or external counterpart. The woman in the lake or the woman who is the lake is unable to free

herself from the source—the miracle of separation and emergence does not occur—so that she grows old in the unconscious
or in the inner world only. It is as if the wisdom-bringing flood
of libido or creative energy held her fast within its cycle of withdrawal and resurgence, never permitting her to step out of the
watery confines. I do not know if there is such a pattern in the
works and lives of poets, but twice in my experience a dream of
seeing up into the world from a fish's perspective has been followed by suicide or attempted suicide. Life's reflection rather
than life itself is lived out beneath a surface that cannot bear the
body's weight.

> *From the bottom of the pool, fixed stars*
> *Govern a life.*
> —SYLVIA PLATH, *"Words"*

And across the surface move phases of the moon: the young girl
of the new crescent is drawn into the full-moon pool. Out of that
round water mirror rises the old woman, the waning crescent, the
fishwife. But the cycle is not a natural monthly one any longer.
It has been accelerated to keep a mad pace with the poet's daily
coming and going. As if by the relentlessness of aging, she is
pursued by the Lamia, a decrepit goddess of death and the terrors
of night, who takes the form of a voracious fish. Her toothed
cavernous maw leads into a belly of darkness, a womb of black
water. (A terrible fish like the Terrible Mother would come to
take back what she had given.) A woman who is partially swallowed by the unconscious is a mermaid. A woman who grows old
in the belly of the inner world becomes the fishwife, the hag
whose only way of relating is devouring. Lamia, the nocturnal fish
specter, scares and destroys young children. Her revenge is on
Hera, the goddess who cursed her with stillborn children, or, in
terms of the life of the artist, with poems or pieces that never
come to life.

Plath's poems are not stillborn. This one has the effect of bearing something new each time it is read. It sheds the different kinds

of light that woman tries to see by: the true light of a lake's reflective surface and the deceptive lights of candle and moon. The poet carries the inquiry (begun in the preceding chapter) further, concerning the sameness of truth and deception on the edge of the self. Here the drawing power, the element that attracts, is the awareness of how lies turn heads—how readily a woman will turn from the faithful reflection. Rather than showing one's face as it is, candlelight and moonlight flicker and bathe a face in such a way that shadows form and dance, making familiar features strange and sometimes beautiful. Moonlight especially has been recognized as container of such magical powers.

Hag women of the old North knew how to "call down the moon from her appointed sphere." They "possessed a high reputation for magic, for prophetic powers, for creating illusions; and, if not capable of transformations of the human body, they were at least able to impose such fascination on the sight of their enemies, as to conceal for a period the objects of which they were in search."[10] When the object sought after is the self (the woman in the poem is searching the reaches for what she really is), the hag's intervention can prolong the search interminably. Sir Walter Scott, who describes the ways of the hag in his *Letters on Demonology and Witchcraft,* says that these women distinguished by intercourse with the spiritual world practiced a species of witchcraft called *deceptio visus*—they knew how to create deceptive visions.

The moon's split root (Chapter 1) clearly reveals the double-faced nature of the medial feminine: the poetry-sustaining root draws on words for blood flow, madness, heart-spirit, prophecy, possession, and lying or making up stories; the other root, which inspires quieter reveries, is related to measuring, remembering, wishing, dreaming, lingering. The woman searching the depths from the bank, the one who reflects, is in the second moon attitude: watching and waiting. And the one who turns her back to the faithful mirror is in the first moon attitude opposed to reflection, marked by tears and "an agitation of hands." Although agitation can be a useless hand-wringing expenditure of energy, it means "to set moving"—it is the unconscious urge to set a stuck process moving. The fact that her agitation is related to facing "those liars" may mean that the process of making up something is the one that is stuck. Making up something, or lying, is similar to making with the hands or fabricating. The moon oversees these double-edged creative states: fabrication and lying are inspired by the eruptive moon attitude.

Because deception and lying are so troublesome (especially to parents and lovers) I want to relate an old fairy legend that will tie together some loose ends of the medial fabric without losing the meaning of the poem. The tale concerns the fate of the poet Thomas of Erceldoune, called the Rhymer because of the romance he wrote on the subject of Tristan and Iseult. He lived during the reign of Alexander III of Scotland.

Like other men of talent of the period, Thomas was suspected of magic. He was said also to have the gift of prophecy, which was accounted for in the following peculiar manner, referring entirely to the Elfin superstition. As True Thomas (we give him the epithet by anticipation) lay on Huntly bank, a place on the descent of the Eildon hills, which raise their triple crest above the celebrated monastery of Melrose, he saw a lady so extremely beautiful that he imagined it must be the Virgin Mary herself. Her appointments, however, were those rather of an Amazon or goddess of the woods. Her steed was of the highest beauty and spirit, and at his mane hung thirty silver bells and nine, which made music to the wind as she paced along; her saddle was of royal bone (ivory), laid over with *orfeverie,* i.e. goldsmith's work: her stirrups, her dress, all corresponded with her extreme beauty and the magnificence of her array. The fair huntress had her bow in hand, and her arrows at her belt. She led three greyhounds in a leash, and three raches, or hounds of scent, followed her closely. She rejected and disclaimed the homage which Thomas desired to pay to her; so that, passing from one extremity to the other, Thomas became as bold as he had at first been humble. The lady warns him that he must become her slave, if he should prosecute his suit towards her in the manner he proposes. Before their interview terminates, the appearance of the beautiful lady is changed into that of the most hideous hag in existence; one side is blighted and wasted, as if by palsy; one eye drops from her head; her colour, as clear as the virgin silver, is now of a dun leaden hue. A witch from the spital or almshouse would have been a goddess in comparison to the late beautiful huntress. Hideous as she was, Thomas's irregular desires had placed him under the control of this hag, and when she bade him take leave of sun, and of the leaf that grew on tree, he felt himself under the necessity of obeying her. A cavern received them, in which, following his frightful guide, he for three days travelled in darkness, sometimes hearing the booming of a distant ocean, sometimes walking through rivers of blood, which crossed their subterranean path. At length, they emerged into daylight, in a most beautiful orchard.[11]

Thomas was near fainting for want of food at this point, but his conductress warned him not to eat since the trees bore the fatal apples of the garden of Paradise. She is then transformed back into her former spendor and dazzles him first with her affection and then with important instruction. Just as the sibyl who meets Aeneas at the gate of the underworld leads him on subterranean paths, this fairy queen takes him on a tour of another world, explaining the character of the country and the nature of specific paths as they go. Sibyls were borderland dwellers, not quite goddess and not quite human. The Celtic sibyl called Callileach or "roaring mouth" had seven periods of youth; she appears before a hero as a repulsive hag and suddenly transforms herself into a beautiful girl.[12] Another famous sibyl, a Greek one, was known as the daughter of Lamia. These women were of ambiguous longevity. Sometimes they were pictured as ancient creatures and sometimes as nymphs. It is said that the sibyl at Delphi was chosen from among young girls for many years but that later she appeared to be a woman over fifty.[13] Rare, precious, even magical knowledge belongs to the youngest and the eldest, the ugliest and the most beautiful. Continuing the story, Thomas's guide says she is taking him to Elfland:

"The lord of the castle is king of the country, and I am his queen. But, Thomas, I would rather be drawn with wild horses, than he should know what hath passed between you and me. Therefore, when we enter yonder castle, observe strict silence, and answer no question that is asked at you, and I will account for your silence by saying I took your speech when I brought you from middle earth."

Having thus instructed her lover, they journeyed on to the castle, and entering by the kitchen, found themselves in the midst of such a festive scene as might become the mansion of a great feudal lord or prince.

Thomas left his fatigue and joined the revelry, dancing, and drinking until his home in Eildon Hills was long forgotten. After a period of time that seemed quite short to him the queen asked how long he thought he had been there. "Not above seven days," answered Thomas.

"You are deceived," answered the queen, "you have been seven years in this castle; and it is full time you were gone. Know, Thomas, that the fiend of hell will come to this castle to-morrow to demand his tribute, and so handsome a man as you will attract his eye. For all the world would I not suffer you to be betrayed to such a fate; therefore up, and let us be going." This terrible news reconciled Thomas to his departure from Elfin land, and the queen was not long in placing him upon Huntly bank, where the birds were singing. She took a tender leave of him, and to ensure his reputation, bestowed on him the *tongue which could not lie.* Thomas in vain objected to this inconvenient and involuntary adhesion to veracity, which would make him, as he thought, unfit for church or for market, for king's court or for lady's bower. But all his remonstrances were disregarded by the lady, and Thomas the Rhymer, whenever the discourse turned on the future, gained the credit of a prophet whether he would or not; for he could say nothing but what was sure to come to pass.

The mistress of *deceptio visus* grants the poet the skill of fabricating without lying. He can speak of invisible things, foretell the future, and acknowledge the existence of a dreamlike world where years pass as days and strict silence passes over into prophecy. Below "middle earth" there is a world more real and beloved to him than Eildon Hills. If others spoke of it their fantastic tale telling would be called lies but what is deceiving to them is truth to Thomas the Rhymer. Experience makes it so: "I wake to sleep, and take my waking slow. I learn by going where I have to go" (Roethke). All of us are probably dreaming all the time —not just during certain periods of night sleep. What seems a lie or an intentionally woven web of deception may be a dream speaking.

If we ordinarily see according to set horizons or try to talk in straight lines then a lie might be what is spoken between lines. The fabric of fabrication is woven by strands that move in opposite directions. Yarns of distinct color take on different shades (of meaning) when woven together. The product no longer resembles the familiar parts: a transformation has occurred such as the one suggested by the superstition that women boiling yarn should tell lies over it in order to turn it white. Purity and invention intertwine. Yarn spinners and tale tellers who "make things up" are making up for something that is missing. Poets, artists, and pregnant women are alike in their capacity for fabricating. Even God enacts this miracle of creation, as the Psalmist says, "I was woven together in my mother's womb"; the ever-present Creator is here the great fabricator, making something out of nothing.

Mirrors don't make things up, but the moon does. The woman who can bend enough to go from reflecting to fabricating will be the one who can make up for something that is missing in the world. She is the one who can give shape to things lying beneath the surface, things overlooked by people who are afraid of mirrors or who can't work like Hans Arp or the cave painter or Sylvia Plath: with eyes turned inward toward the dark. When light was not artificially prolonged in the course of a day by house lights and streetlamps, the "deceptive" lights of candle and moon still worked their magic. These lights of lesser intensity permitted fantasy; they were more fitted to wishes and inspired those tellers of tales who were ready to respond to and make articulate the rhythm of the night. Activity of astonishing pattern and intention unfolds busily in the dark, as in a beehive or the bee box of Plath that is, like the mind at nightfall:

> *locked, it is dangerous.*
> *I have to live with it overnight*
> *And I can't keep away from it.*
> *There are no windows, so I can't see what is in there.*
> *There is only a little grid, no exit.*
>
> *I put my eye to the grid.*
> *It is dark, dark. . . .*
> —*"The Arrival of the Bee Box"*

She lays her ear to the "furious Latin," she has "ordered a box of maniacs." Like the ancient incubant or hive-dweller (Figure 6) she puts herself in position for messages from an unseen world. It is worth the risk of madness to bend and look and listen, for

> *I*
> *Have a self to recover, a queen.*
> —*"Stings"*

Turning the eyes inward is a way of following the fairy queen. Her land is usually underground—sometimes beneath the dwellings of human beings, sometimes deep within earthen hills. Entrance is gained through caverns, clefts, mounds, and wells, or by going through water: diving or jumping into wells, rivers, lakes, or sea. That this fairyland is a region of spirit, psyche, or personality interpenetrating our daily consciousness was known long before psychology developed the tools of depth perception. A saying from New Britain puts it this way: "If our eyes were turned so that what is inside were now outside, we would see that *mantana nion* [the land of the blessed] was very near to us and not far away at all."[14] Elfland is behind our eyes. Elves are within us

and around us. Denise Levertov describes the graceful, mercurial
creatures who walk among us looking for love:

> *Their beauty sets them aside*
> *from other men and from women*
> *unless a woman has that cold fire in her*
> *called poet: with that*
>
> *she may see them and by its light*
> *they know her and are not afraid*
> *and silver tongues of love*
> *flicker between them.*
>
> —*"The Elves"*

Speaking in tongues is poetry—not to be interpreted by priests
but rather by those who are knowledgeable in fairy ways. A
"tongue that cannot lie" can tell fantastic tales, mouth myths,
narrate invisible realities, open the "eyes at the back of our
heads." This same tongue that is true to an inner reality can cloud
the familiar daylight world over with a haze of misunderstanding
because the material drawn on for its fabrication is not congruous,
it doesn't always fit with how others see it. Then, instead of silver
tongues of love it may be a blackened tongue that flickers and
darts with the venom of deceit. The tarnished truth is another side
of the poets' mirror, silver and exact.

Poets, artists, muse(r)s, gossips, bees, elves, fairies, and children move between worlds of dream and waking reality as if
there were no boundaries. Not recognizing fixed boundaries
makes them susceptible to being caught in that confusion-of-spirit
called madness by the ancients. The so-called real world becomes
disenchanting in contrast and may cease to recall the dreamer
whose dwelling is in the unconscious. Rather than arousing admiration then, the enchanted ones arouse suspicion. Being suspect
means to be looked at from an opposing angle. The *suspicious* are
"under-lookers" (from *sub spicere*); they look askance at the object
or being in question. Because of its connections to the under-

world and the unconscious the medial personality rouses suspicion. Medial women make spectacles (specters, spy glasses, spaewives) of themselves. Cognates of *specere*, the root of spectacle, are *speha*, which means close attention; *spahen*, to spy out; *spahi*, wise or shrewd; and *spa*, prophecy. To *speculate* is to mediate. A *specula* is a lookout tower. A *speculum* is a mirror and also an instrument for rendering a hidden part accessible to observation: it is a peculiarly feminine mirror, a literal reflection of woman's hidden parts.

The ability to switch with grace from *mantana nion* to the present requires a conscious act of recollection. All your many facets, the many faces of your nature, hidden and familiar, need to be remembered. Those who dwell in the realm of the blessed (who live only the life of the spirit) cease to cast a shadow (Peter Pan) or reflection in a mirror (vampires). Keeping a mirror in your pocket is a precautionary measure to be taken whenever there might be fear of losing yourself to the other side:

> *Woman fears for man, he goes*
> *out alone to his labors. No mirror*
> *rests in his pocket.*
>
> *. . . When she goes out*
> *she looks in the glass, she remembers*
> *herself.*
> *Stones, coal,*
> *the hiss of water upon the kindled*
> *branches—her being*
> *is a cave, there are bones at the hearth.*
> —DENISE LEVERTOV, *"Abel's Bride"*

At the points of remembering, the woman is forging an ethic for herself. *Ethos* is the cave of inner being that contains the elements of our prehistory. Out of it we evolve a sense of self that includes many selves, multiple reflections. "Forging," apart from the fire and pressure it implies, has the same double meaning as "fabricate" (i.e., forge a tool, forge a signature). Like other two-faced words, "lie" and even "myth," "forging" requires that more than one meaning be present for the heating and moving of elements into new forms. The medial aspect of the feminine is the principle that makes possible such fabrication as the forging of an ethic or the forging of an image because it is flexible and visionary and accustomed to mirrors. Bending back far enough to get a sense of one's own prehistory is the first step in the process of conscious evolution. It not only "furthers one to have somewhere to go," as it says in the *I Ching,* it furthers one to know the place and patterns of origin.

For the Bushman of Africa the place of origin and ending is literally one. Old people always seek the familiar terrain of their homeland when they are dying—even if they lived far from home most of their lives. When the end is near they leave their families and possessions and go off singly to trace their way back. It is said that no harm can come to these seekers. They can be seen feeling their way slowly along difficult paths cutting through enemy territory and no alien hand is ever raised against them. No one will block the path to your cave of birth, being, and death—except perhaps your own refusal to take the necessary steps to discovery.

That mirrors have always been necessary for this soul journey is attested to by the fact of their burial with the dead in cave sites all over the world. Mirrors, like lake surfaces, glass, and the eye of another person, are thought of as reflecting, abstracting, and containing the soul of the onlooker. Consequently, it is dangerous to break a mirror or to throw a stone into the image of a person gazing into the water. At the sanctuary of the goddess Demeter at Petrae a combination of mirror and water was used to ascertain the fate of the sick. Suppliants tied a mirror to a fine cord and let it down into the sacred well, judging the distance carefully so that it would not sink deep into the spring, yet would go far enough to skim the surface. "Then they prayed to the goddess and burned incense, after which they would look into the mirror to discern the image of the patient either alive or dead."[15]

Because they provided entrance to the spiritual world mirrors were a widespread tool of initiation ceremonies. If mirrors were left hanging on the wall in the house of one who had died, it was customary either to turn the image-holding surface to the wall or to drape it with black cloth. Similarly, in a European custom called "the telling of the bees," the bee hives were informed of their owner's death and draped with black cloth:

> *Went drearily singing the chore-girl small,*
> *Draping each hive with a shred of black.*
> —JOHN GREENLEAF WHITTIER, *"Telling the Bees"*

Chore girl and choir girl are the same. They grow up to be charwomen, woodwomen blackened by fire and time (kindled branches, coal at the hearth). These women return: *char* is turn, return, a turn of work, a day's labor. "All in a day's work" includes the labors of a lifetime, the eternal labors of Nature, moving in concert with an ancient hum. The humming response of the bees tells the chore girl that they will stay and not follow the dead person's soul to another world. Being borderland workers they could swarm after the soul of the departed or stay to give honey to the descendants.

> *Will the hive survive, will the gladiolas*
> *Succeed in banking their fires*
> *To enter another year?*
> *What will they taste of, the Christmas roses?*
> *The bees are flying. They taste the spring.*
> —SYLVIA PLATH, *"Wintering"*

Periodically the medial feminine gets buried by the debris of cultures less interested in the energy-conserving structure of hives and flower bulbs, the spiritual hunger fed by Christmas, and the miracle of springtime quickening. When this happens we might say that the bees have swarmed (and been shot down or flown away). Our access to the otherworldly is shut off. The mirror has been turned against the wall; some part of ourselves has died and our fear of the dark and unknown is magnified beyond bearing.

Our collective chore then becomes the "upsinging" of the medial woman into being. (Sound is the creative power. Giving voice to desire—"saying makes it so." To the imagination of the past the world was "upsung into being," says the mystic Celtic poet, A. E.) Singing in the dark shapes the space to be moved in. Special songs are customarily sung at turning points in a person's life: at a child's birthday, on marriage days, at ceremonies of burial. Music is magical. It is medial also, because it mediates the unknown.

Hans Arp attributes the recovery of a certain inner rhythmic strain to a person's ability to enter the "cave-dark," the place behind lowered eyelids or the place where Hekate, the dark of the moon, dwells. Women have traditionally sung phase-specific songs at the rising of the moon out of the dark or raised great shouts at its "full" and its "fall." This use of sound may be related to the din created during certain women's festivals in Greece, especially at the Thesmophoria, when the descent and ascent, the uprising or *anados* of the goddess was enacted.[16] The designated "drawers up" would go into earthen chasms accompanied by a rattling din made by attendants. The purpose of the loud sound making may have been twofold as it was in the crossroads ceremonies of Hekate: to scare away the overwhelming powers of darkness and to invoke the goddess by making a space in the air for her entry. This sound sense and the reasons for making it can be extended further to a physiological understanding of the inhalation and exhalation, the raising and lowering of the diaphragm, the transformation of interior body space that occurs when singing or shouting. It is as if the noise maker (making a joyful noise unto the Lord . . .) is making room for interior expansion, establishing a reverberating beat and bond with other celebrants in order to effect a change in both the psychic and physical environment.

The "drawers up" at the Thesmophoria were assistants at the birth of the underworld goddess. They acted as midwives to an aspect of feminine nature not-yet-arrived. As shown on the an-

FIGURE 28

cient frieze (Figure 28), the goddess is half evolved—her feet are still measuring the underworld. Her uprising signals the coming of spring, the new rising of the virgin moon, the return of the repressed, the acceptance of the psyche, and the triumph of the medial. "Triumph" itself means a great shout: *triumphus,* a noise made at a Roman fertility festival. A triumph is a hymn sung in Greek processions of the god Dionysos. But even more appropriate for the conclusion of our study of the medial feminine, a triumph, *thriambos,* is the honey-intoxicated bee song of the Thriae, the old Delphic prophetesses, teachers of fabrication, who spun golden webs of truth or madness.[17] Jane Ellen Harrison likens these ancient bee maidens to the maenads who nursed the young things of the woodland. The mad song, the hymn they raised, was in honor of the flowering, pollen-producing rod, the magical wand of the god that reunified the torn-apart realms of nature and spirit.

> *And all the mountain felt*
> *And worshipped with them; and the wild things knelt,*
> *And romped and gloried, and the wilderness*
> *was filled with moving voices and dim stress.*[18]

Long after the din has died out and the sun has risen high over
their city homes and ordered lives, the women who have left their
medial selves in the ancient moonlit hills sing the sober song of
remembrance, the first in the slow cycle leading to eventual "triumph":

> *Will they ever come to me, ever again,*
>   *The long, long dances,*
> *On through the dark till the dim stars wane?*
> *Shall I feel the dew on my throat and the stream*
> *Of wind in my hair?*[19]

Conclusion

I sometimes think I see that civilizations originate
in the disclosure of some mystery,
*   some secret,*
and expand with the progressive publication
*   of that secret*
and end in exhaustion
when there is no longer any secret,
when the mystery has been divulged
*   that is to say,*
*   profaned.*
There comes a time
when civilization has to be renewed
by the discovery of new mysteries,
by the undemocratic but sovereign power
*   of the imagination.*
            —NORMAN O. BROWN, *"Apocalypse"*

Having come full circle: the revaluation of the feminine attempted here (prompted by the original moon missive) has
brought the manifold goddess to mind. She who is "of one name
and many forms" has crossed the threshold of our imaginations,
where those daughters of ancient Greek citizens still run mad and
unattended, for having held the image of the great goddess
cheap. Hera, the Queen of Olympus, manifested herself to mor-

tals in Child form, as Fulfilled or Full Grown Woman and as Woman Alone or Woman of Sorrows.[1] She is ancestor and descendant, bud, flower, and seed. (When love is ripe beyond bearing it goes to seed.) Her middle name is Teleia: the raging after loss of self comes upon women in midlife when they are *os eteleiothesan,* full grown, but still refusing the rites of maturity and the inevitability of the often lonely passage that stretches one between "an initiation and a terminus I cannot name" (Robert Duncan). It was perilous then, as it is now, to grow up without these rites which stretch the self forward and backward to include a sense of origins and of potential.

> *I am the first or the last*
> *of a flock or a swarm; . . .*
>
> *I have gone forward,*
> *I have gone backward.*
>
> *I have gone onward from bronze and iron.*
> —H. D., *"The Flowering of the Rod"*

In the ages of bronze and iron, hard-hearted human beings dwelt on this earth. Hesiod describes the men generated by the gods in the Bronze Age as springing from ash trees terrible and strong. They loved warfare and deeds of violence, ate no bread, and were hard of heart like stubborn men who are afraid. Their armor was of bronze, their houses of bronze, their implements of bronze. These brazen ones destroyed themselves and passed into the dark house of Hades, leaving no name and only the bright light of the sun behind. Long after the earth had covered the traces of the Bronze Age, Zeus made yet another generation of mortals, among whom the poet counts himself:

For now truly is a race of iron, and men never rest from labour and sorrow by day and from perishing by night; and the gods shall lay sore trouble upon them. But, notwithstanding, even these shall have some good mingled with their troubles.[2]

He does not proceed to describe any of the good things coming out of the Iron Age, but rather goes on to say that people age quickly, children turn against their parents, comrades against comrades, guest against host. The elders are dishonored, no one keeps promises, and everyone praises the wrong doer, honoring the foul-mouthed and speaking against the reverent.

And then Aidos and Nemesis, with their sweet forms wrapped in white robes, will go from the wide-pathed earth and forsake mankind to join the company of the deathless gods: and bitter sorrows will be left for mortal men and there will be no help against evil.

These sisters, who abandon human beings at the end of the Iron Age, are shame and righteous anger. Without them wickedness knows no restraint and mortal life is rung round with shadows.

It takes either a collective effort or an act of recollection to face the shadows of evil. Between the second and third centuries B.C. there were women in a town called Amphissa who held hands against the darkness of the Iron Age. It happened that a band of Thyiades, priestesses of Dionysos who leapt and danced on Mount Parnassus in a midwinter rite, lost their way and stumbled into Amphissa during the night.[3] Still bewildered and exhausted by their ritual, half entranced, they fell asleep in the market place, unaware that they had come into a town at war with their own. The women of Amphissa found them there and called upon one another to form a protective circle around the sleeping strangers. No harm came to the Thyiades that night and in the morning the women of Amphissa fed them and obtained permission to accompany them to safety at the edge of town, where the road rejoined a footpath leading up to the holy mountain.

A circle of awareness (the townswomen did not sleep that night) and concern held back the wolflike shadows. *Eisengrimm,* a northern name for the wolf, means iron rage or cold ferocity. It is a characteristic animal or under-running instinct of the Iron

Age. Evil and darkness of soul are not aspects of human existence that can be banished or outgrown, but they can perhaps be mediated by the feminine principle wherever there is a willingness to call the sisters Aidos and Nemesis back down from the snowy peaks. Nemesis pits her awareness and righteous anger against the cold, unconscious rage of the wolf—like the women of Amphissa, who stood their ground against the war instinct; and Aidos instills the quality of reverence essential for the recognition of redemptive mysteries in our midst. As her name suggests (modesty, the demurrer—see page 52 above), there is something godlike or transcendent about maturity—something rather more mysterious than mundane wrapped up in Aidos's white robe.

An immature generation, such as the one Hesiod describes as preceding the Bronze Age, stays too long at the mother's knee: "one hundred years playing childishly at home." When these Silver Age beings were full grown, having come lately to the measure of their prime, they lived only a short while because they were ill prepared for birth into the outer world. To be mature means not only to be ripe like the full red sun at dawn and ready to cross the world horizon, but to recognize your spiritual ancestry, and to move accordingly. Maturity is rooted in knowing the favorable moment (*maturus*), morning (*māne*), goodness (*mānis*), and the family's ancestral spirits worshiped as gods (*mānēs*). In Rome these roots grew up into Mater Matuta, goddess of dawn, of growth, of midwifery and matrons. Like Hera, she was the essence of the stretched-out, all-encompassing life of woman.

Plutarch, who said that "the race of mortals, like the realm of plants, always moves in a circle,"[4] stretched his life out to make contact with its organic roots by writing letters to his spiritual ancestors—Hesiod among them. In this way we can choose our ancestors: fantasy works in the service of identity and longevity by extending "familial" connections as far as the imagination can reach. No one need remain an orphan—like the dreamer here who was given an unexpected, living link with her past.

I am standing on a cliff that looks down upon a golden sandy beach and a placid blue ocean. Sunshine everywhere. Then my self-consciousness divides: I am observing from the cliff and walking on the beach below simultaneously. There is a group of people adjacent to me on the cliff watching the "me" on the shore. They run down the embankment towards the second self. My consciousness then unifies in this second self. They ask me: "Do you know who your ancestors were?" "No," I reply, "I'm an orphan." (This is not true in waking life, I grew up in a family situation.) I am very comfortable with this "lie." They continue speaking with one voice—the anonymity of a Greek chorus. "We are here to tell you about your female ancestors. Your people came from Holland." (This is not a true fact.) They show me a picture. "This is a picture of your great-grandmother. She died in childbirth during a voyage to America." It was an antique group picture of the passengers posing before their voyage. I felt a real sense of empathy for this woman, my foremother, too young and too full of expectations to die. "Now," said the voices, "we will take you to see the wise old man." I was then transported to a room filled with the golden aura of wood and candlelight. A bearded old man moved about the room but did not speak: he seemed busy and impersonal. I felt peaceful and awkward at the same time. Finally the old man said that either the mother or the grandmother of the woman who had died aboard ship had been located in Holland. She was being brought to the United States to see me. I was so happy to know I had a living relative. A link with my past. Again I was transported to the beach, amid the chorus figures who reiterated the old woman's discovery. The old woman and I were suddenly back in the room of the wise old man. She wore a bonnet, a shawl, and a long skirt and carried a carpet bag. Her countenance was stern (industrious, purposeful and hearth-minded like the Amish). The old man was dressed for bed and carried a candle. "Finally," he said, "I can go to sleep." He then blew out the candle, leaving the old woman and me standing there.

A rite of passage is enacted here on many levels. There is the passage from above to below, the passage from orphanage to adoption, the deep-sea journey, and the "transportation" between the beach and the golden room. There is a death—of the dreamer to her actual family in the world to whom she admits no psychic link—and a death of the expectant young woman on her way to a new world. The death of the "old" self prepares the way for the inheritance of the new. By declaring herself an orphan (a fabrication in the double sense) she prepares herself to learn about her female ancestors—to heal a certain split in consciousness, to be made whole again. Perhaps this is why she chose Holland. Hōl-land, the land that (by phonetic association) "makes whole," is also the Motherland or Grandmotherland, the land of the goddess Holl, who acts as the ancestress of families and is the "real," or archetypal, mother of lost women.

An orphan is one who is deprived of parents, inheritance, and soul. ("Orphan" is related to "robot" by the common root *orbus,* meaning bereft, and *arbi,* meaning toil and trouble. A robot "works" but is soulless.) All the great mystery religions of the world find their source in the striving of human beings for soul or immortality, the hoped-for inheritance from the ancestral spirits or gods. In order to make the request, an initiate into the mysteries of Orpheus has first to disclaim his or her earthly parentage: "I am a child of Earth and Starry Heaven, but my race is of Heaven alone."[5] In other words, I was born of mortal parentage, but belong truly to the blessed immortals. Born into grievous, ceaseless toil, I will be reborn, or "risen free," into sweet mirth and the land of plenty. An important part of this ceremonial passage was the stepping into and out of a sacred circle: the initiate says first, "I have passed with eager feet to the Circle desired," and then, "I have passed with eager feet from the Circle desired."

Jane Ellen Harrison describes the circle ceremony as a way of taking a stand. Stepping onto or into the sacred circle, ring, or enclosure—possibly an enclosure of flowers—means "to enter into" or "embark upon" a new course of action. One who has "gone through the hoops" has enacted the hopeful rite of mimetic rebirth and adoption. The new births are often accompanied by the giving of a new name.

Victory will be above all
To see truly into the distance
To see everything
Up close
So that everything can have a new name.[6]

The circle stepped into and out of in the course of this book was drawn to include myriad faces of the soul, only a few of which have been brought up close enough to name. Mother, Amazon, Hetaira, and Medium are pivotal points, way stations, or resting places like the ones Psyche came to in the roundabout search for her scattered self. Some people see these named facets of the feminine in an evolutionary sense, thinking that we move away from the Mother to the Amazon stage in adolescence, on to the capabilities of the Hetaira in midlife, eventually to discover Medial possibilities late in life. Others have seen the circle as a schematic globe or map that shows their place of birth (not necessarily the "mother pole") and the places they want to get to know before they die. I prefer to see it the way a Hindu might, as a circle like the moon at full, containing seeds of the souls of psychic ancestors. This way it stands as a circle of hope for all who have been orphaned by a civilization whose mystery is exhausted.

I bit on a seed and it spoke on my tongue
of day that shone already among stars
in the water-mirror of low ground . . .

In her poem to "The Goddess," Denise Levertov greets the dawn from the mud-splattered place on the ground where the angry goddess has thrown her. Lying outside the sacred enclosure, she is in a position to see the distant day approaching. When Jane Ellen Harrison wrote that our hearts are sore for the outrage done to the order of ancient goddesses,[7] she was looking at the diminished vitality and freedom of movement with which the late goddesses were depicted in stone. Their beauty and strength were forced into the recesses of the rock the way the Mysteries were forced back into the natural *megara,* the rock clefts, at Eleusis by the raising of a Christian Church and the construction of a grave-yard on the sacred dancing ground. But, as the poet knows, and as Harrison would no doubt have seen, the goddess can reassert herself powerfully in the imagination. Her rites are enacted on an interior dancing ground that has gone to seed. Precisely this "seediness" and the corrupt overlay of time (the compost and fruitful decay) make possible the drawing up of a new harvest, a new mystery out of the remnants of the old order.

Bachofen thought it "no free invention or accident" that the spiritual embellishments of life (such as reverence and peace) were known by feminine names and that *Telete,* "initiation" (as in Hera, Teleia), is personified by a woman.[8] The Matriarchs served as conscientious guardians of the mystery, just as the stra-tum of matriarchal consciousness coming alive at present contains a treasure—a trove of well-guarded secrets, a welter of psychic seeds: a quiver, a bow, a cauldron, a spindle, a spoon, masks, mirrors, wreaths of string, and "forgotten signs all bringing the soul's travels to a place of origin" (Denise Levertov). It may be that the origin-seeking dreamer above dreamed a dream of the end of an age. If the feminine link with the past is recovered, the old wise man, the worn Patriarch, can retire, leaving us face to face with the future.

"Finally," he said, "I can go to sleep." He then blew out the candle, leaving me and the old woman standing there.

Notes

PREFACE

1. As C. G. Jung explains in his essay on *Four Archetypes*, excerpted from the *Collected Works*, Vol. 9, part 1, trans. by R. F. C. Hull, in a footnote to paragraph 167: " 'Types' are not individual cases, neither are they freely invented schemata into which all individual cases have to be fitted. 'Types' are ideal instances . . . with which no single individual can be identified." The arrival at a concept of types, in his case and in Toni Wolff's, is based on therapeutic experience with numerous individuals and countless dreams.

2. Eric Partridge, *Origins: A Short Etymological Dictionary of Modern English*. Unless otherwise noted, word derivations in the text are from this source, *Webster's Third New International Dictionary*, or the *Oxford English Dictionary*.

3. Marie-Louise von Franz speaking in Notre Dame, Indiana, in April of 1975, at C. G. Jung: A Centennial Conference.

4. Sigmund Freud quoted in John Layard, "The Incest Taboo and the Virgin Archetype," *The Virgin Archetype*, p. 282. Layard attributes the conception of analytical psychology and "true religion of a properly balanced kind" to this admission of Freud's.

5. *Prolegomena to the Study of Greek Religions*, p. 164. (Italics mine.)

6. J. J. Bachofen, *Myth, Religion, and Mother Right, Selected Writings*, trans. by Ralph Manheim with introduction by Joseph Campbell, pp. 11–12 and xxvii.

CHAPTER 1. THE MOON AND THE VIRGIN

1. In her chapter on "The Man in the Moon" in *Woman's Mysteries, Ancient and Modern*, M. Esther Harding explains the changing aegis of the moon. At a very early stage the moon was masculine because it was seen as the fertilizing influence on women. See especially Chapter 7 (p. 95) for a brief summary of the stages of the moon's sexual evolution.

2. Bachofen, p. 148.

3. Dr. Edmond Dewan's experiments with light and ovulation were conducted at the Boston Rock Reproductive Clinic. Gay Gaer Luce

reports on his work in *Body Time, Physiological Rhythms and Social Stress*, pp. 279–282.

4. *Listen to Me* (a play, 1936), Act III, Scene II, "The Moon." Dialogue presented as a running piece in *Technicians of the Sacred: A Range of Poetries from Africa, America, Asia and Oceania*, ed. by Jerome Rothenberg, p. 414.

5. Ian I. Mitroff, "Science's Apollonic Moon," in *Spring, An Annual of Archetypal Psychology and Jungian Thought*, 1974, p. 109.

6. *Paracelsus, Selected Writings*, ed. with an introduction by Jolande Jacobi, pp. liii, liv.

7. *Zeus, A Study in Ancient Religions*, Vol. II, p. 501.

8. *Zeus*, p. 629.

9. Erich Neumann, "On the Moon and Matriarchal Consciousness," trans. by Hildegard Nagel, in *Fathers and Mothers*, a collection of papers on the archetypal background of family psychology, ed. by Pat Berry, p. 42.

10. Quoted by Harding, p. 48.

11. M. Esther Harding's work on women's mysteries includes the most thorough understanding of virginity as "a recreative submission to the demands of instinct." See also John Layard's essay "The Incest Taboo and the Virgin Archetype" in *The Virgin Archetype*, especially p. 288 on virginity as spiritual pregnancy.

12. "Descent of Ishtar to the Netherworld," lines 77–80, trans. by E. A. Speiser in *Ancient Near Eastern Texts*, ed. by James B. Pritchard.

13. "Descent of Ishtar to the Netherworld," lines 4–6. See also N. K. Sandars, *Poems of Heaven and Hell from Ancient Mesopotamia*, for the Sumerian version called "Inanna's Journey to Hell." The Sumerian Inanna and Akkadian Ishtar are the same goddess.

14. Quoted in Harding, p. 163.

15. Charles Olson, "For Sappho, Back," in *Archaeologist of Morning*. These excerpted phrases are from his poem of woman's search and self-containment.

16. A description of the dark enchantress from the *Papyri Graecae Magical*, quoted by Marie-Louise von Franz in an article on "The Problem of Evil in Fairy Tales" in *Evil*, a collection of essays ed. by the Curatorium of the C. G. Jung Institute, Zürich, p. 112.

17. *New Introductory Lectures on Psychoanalysis*, trans. by James Strachey, p. 135. Freud concluded his Lecture XXXIII, "Femininity," by saying: "That is all I had to say to you about femininity. It is certainly incomplete and fragmentary and does not always sound friendly. But do

not forget that I have only been describing women in so far as their nature is determined by their sexual function. It is true that that influence extends very far; but we do not overlook the fact that an individual woman may be a human being in other respects as well. If you want to know more about femininty, enquire from your own experiences of life, or turn to the poets, or wait until science can give you deeper and more coherent information." For an extraordinary picture of Freud from a woman's point of view, see H. D.'s *Tribute to Freud,* an account (more or less) of her experience of psychoanalysis with him.

18. Ibn ᶜArabī, "Book of Theophanies" quoted in Henry Corbin, *Creative Imagination in the Sufism of Ibn ᶜArabī,* p. 174.

19. Jalāluddīn Rūmī, quoted in Corbin, p.171.

CHAPTER 2. PSYCHE'S SEARCH

1. The tale of Amor, or Eros, and Psyche as told originally by Apuleius has been translated many times. I have relied on Robert Graves's, Jack Lindsay's, and H. E. Butler's translations. Butler's is included in Erich Neumann's commentary, *Amor and Psyche, The Psychic Development of the Feminine.* See also Marie-Louise von Franz, *Apuleius' Golden Ass.* For a less comprehensive but intriguing perspective, see Robert Johnson's *She.* Ann Ulanov, in *The Feminine in Jungian Psychology and Christian Theology* (Chapter 11), interprets the tale as the development of a man's anima.

2. *The Archetypes of the Collective Unconscious,* Collected Works, Vol. 9, part 1, p. 26.

3. Gary Snyder's book of poetry, *Regarding Wave,* written for his wife and first-born son, reflects "a half-buried series of word origins dating back through the Indo-European language: intersections of energy, woman, song and 'Gone Beyond Wisdom.' " Regarding the "welter" he writes:

> *wave   wife.*
> *woman-wyfman-*
> *"veiled; vibrating; vague". . .*
>
> *great dunes rolling*
> *Each inch rippld, every grain a wave.*

4. The Hellenistic mysteries of Isis, like the mysteries of Demeter discussed in Chapter 4, were matriarchal mysteries enacted to procure rebirth or immortality for the initiate's soul. Isis (in Egypt, where these

later mysteries had their origin) was a great moon goddess, whose companion, Osiris, was destroyed by the enemy Typhon (also called Set). The ritual drama is based on the long search of Isis for the scattered parts of her brother-lover. She wanders the earth to gather together his dismembered body and finds all the parts save the phallus. This missing piece she fashions herself. As a consequence, castration, or the overcoming of instinctual sexuality, in favor of a redeemed, or spirit-informed sexuality, figures in her mysteries. Typhon, the original destroyer, was an ass.

5. Norman O. Brown in a taped lecture, "Georgics: A Palinode in Praise of Work, or Homage to the Working Class," included in unpublished series *To Greet the Return of the Gods,* University of California at Santa Cruz, 1971. See also footnote 15 below.

6. See C. A. Meier, *Ancient Incubation and Modern Psychotherapy;* Joseph L. Henderson, *Thresholds of Initiation;* Henderson and Maud Oakes, *The Wisdom of the Serpent,* especially Chapters V, VI.

7. *The Archetypes of the Collective Unconscious,* p. 58. See Aniela Jaffé, *The Myth of Meaning,* trans. by R. F. C. Hull, Chapter 2, "The Unconscious and the Archetype," for a clear summary of the development and definition of archetype as used by Jung.

8. *Description of Greece,* 9.39.

9. C. A. Meier, pp. 99–100: "Amnesia is an essential condition if the patient is to give himself up completely to the experience of incubation. This is in direct contrast to the high valuation of anamnesis which prevails elsewhere in medicine. Here, anamnesis applies exclusively to the unconscious experiences which are visualized during incubation, and its purpose is to make them accessible to consciousness and reality and also to make it possible to utilize them."

10. Norman O. Brown, *Love's Body,* pp. 46–47. This chapter, "Nature," about mothers, caves, copulation, and eternal life leads beyond a restricted sense of analysis: "Here is the point where we have to jump, beyond psychoanalysis: They know not of Regeneration, but only of Generation. Therapy must be rebirth, but psychoanalysis does not believe that man can be born again; and so it does not believe that man is ever born at all; for the real birth is the second birth," p. 54.

11. C. Kerényi, *Dionysos, Archetypal Image of Indestructible Life,* Part One, Chapter II, "Light and Honey," p. 34.

12. Pausanias, *Description,* 9.39.

13. See C. A. Meier, and Carl Kerényi, *Asklepios: Archetypal Image of the Physician's Existence,* trans. by Ralph Manheim, for detailed accounts of cures recorded in stone and in *paeans,* hymns to the healer, Apollo. Apollo and Asclepius are related in their patronage of healing and the

arts—one may be the father of the other. Meier, p. 66, writes of the cured patient: "Apparently the patient had no further obligation after recording the dream, apart from certain thank offerings and the payment of the fee. People gave what they could, in proportion to their wealth. Asclepius often required a literary production of some kind as a thank offering—a paean, for example. Thus he became the patron of cultured and learned men and of artists."

14. Written in a commentary to the author by Kenneth Criqui.

15. Gaston Bachelard understands this feminine element in language; see especially p. 30, *The Poetics of Reverie: Childhood, Language and the Cosmos.* A poetic, phenomenological interpreter of archetypal psychology, Bachelard is a genius of words. What he describes as the language of the *anima* is like the language of soul making called for by James Hillman in *The Myth of Analysis,* p. 206: "So Psyche requests the psychologist to remember his calling. Psychological remembrance is given by the kind of speech that carries remembrance within it. This language is both of culture and uncultured, is both of art and artless. It is a mythic, metaphoric language, a speech of ambiguities that is evocative and detailed, yet not definitive, not productive of dictionaries, textbooks, or even abstract descriptions. Rather, it is a speech that leads to participation, in the Platonic sense, in and with the thing spoken of, a speech of stories and insights which evoke, in the other who listens, new stories and new insights, the way one poem and one tune ignite another verse and another song. It is conversation, letters, tales, in which we reveal our dreams and fantasies—and our psychopathology. It evokes, calls forth, and creates psyche as it speaks."

16. Harding, pp. 41, 90, 163.

17. Layard, drawing on the work of Gershom Scholem in his essay "On Psychic Consciousness," in *The Virgin Archetype,* p. 283.

18. *A Room of One's Own,* p. 102.

19. Nicholas Berdyaev quoted in June Singer, *Androgyny, Toward a New Theory of Sexuality,* p. 328.

20. "Structural Forms of the Feminine Psyche," trans. by Paul Watzlawik (privately printed for the C. G. Jung Institute, Zürich, July, 1956). See also Ann Ulanov, Chapter 10, for a description of Wolff's structure. ́

CHAPTER 3. A MOTHER ESSAY IN IMAGES

1. Brown, *Love's Body,* p. 50.

2. *The Gate of Horn: A Study of the Religious Conceptions of the Stone Age, and Their Influence upon European Thought,* p. 57. In this chapter on the

Mother Goddess Levy sees caves as Stone Age wombs of the Mother, places of rebirth.

3. Excerpted from the "Hymn to Phanes with Proem from the *Orphic Argonautica*" (700 B.C.) in *Origins, Creation Texts from the Ancient Mediterranean*, ed. and trans. with an introduction and notes by Charles Doria and Harris Lenowitz, p. 311.

4. Erich Neumann, *The Great Mother*, p. 114, fig. 11.

5. Continuation of "Hymn" cited above from *Origins*, p. 311.

6. Toni Wolff, "A Few Thoughts on the Process of Individuation in Women" (privately translated and printed for the students of the C. G. Jung Institute, Zürich, May, 1934), p. 86.

7. Bachofen thought of the matriarchal period of culture as comprised of various "orders." The Aphroditic-hetairist order was, like the goddess Aphrodite, full of the spontaneity of natural life (see Chapter 7 following). The Demetrian order was calm, well tended, and dignified in comparison. Demeter was the mother of grain (see Chapter 4 following). Aphrodite was the mother of teeming swamp life. In the Roman myth system Aphrodite was Venus, principle of abandoned lovemaking, and Demeter was called Ceres, corn goddess and guardian of family life.

8. From Bachofen's introduction to "Mother Right, An Investigation of the Religions and Juridical Character of Matriarchy in the Ancient World" in *Myth, Religion, and Mother Right*, p. 91.

9. Mircea Eliade, *The Forge and the Crucible*, pp. 42–43.

10. Anton Unternährer, "Geheimes Reskript" (1821), quoted in C. G. Jung, *Symbols of Transformation*, Collected Works, Vol. 5, p. 377.

11. *Woman and Labor*, pp. 130–131.

12. Carl Kerényi, *Eleusis, Archetypal Image of Mother and Daughter*, p. 40. See also Chapter 4 below.

13. Richard L. Farnell, *Cults of the Greek States*, Vol. II, p. 628.

14. Neumann, *The Great Mother*, p. 140, fig. 25. Neumann calls her Isis here. He discusses the "ritual baring" of other related goddesses on pp. 139–140.

15. Quoted in George E. Mylonas, *Eleusis and the Eleusinian Mysteries*, p. 294.

16. *Steatopygous*, fat or "tallow-full" buttocks, especially characteristic of certain South African peoples. Sometimes Aphrodite is called "Kallipygos" or "she of the beautiful buttocks," who lifts her dress high about her. See Carl Kerényi, *Gods of the Greeks*, p. 80. In an ancient figurine she comes flying on the back of a great bird. See Neumann, *The Great Mother*, pl. 137.

17. Marie-Louise von Franz, *Patterns of Creativity Mirrored in Creation Myths*, p. 144.

18. Neumann, *The Great Mother*, p. 137.

19. Bachofen, "An Essay on Ancient Mortuary Symbolism" in *Myth, Religion, and Mother Right*, p. 29.

20. Von Franz, *Patterns of Creativity*, p. 148.

21. Brown, *Love's Body*, p. 185.

22. "The Elves" in *Household Stories*, trans. by Lucy Crane, p. 174.

23. Von Franz, *Patterns of Creativity*, p. 136. Speech is similarly born through the splitting of a mouth like an egg. Jung, *Symbols of Transformation*, p. 161.

24. Levy, *The Gate of Horn*, p. 97.

25. Neumann, *The Great Mother*, p. 123.

26. Marina Warner, *Alone of All Her Sex*, p. 203.

27. Ovid, *Metamorphoses*, trans. by Rolfe Humphries, Book I, "Apollo and Daphne," l. 549.

28. A. B. Cook, *Zeus, A Study in Ancient Religion*, Vol. II, p. 403.

29. Levy, Chapter II on the milk-yielding tree, figures 59, 60, 61.

30. Jane Ellen Harrison, *Myths of Greece and Rome*, p. 37.

31. Neumann, *The Great Mother*, pp. 31–32.

32. Jung, *Symbols of Transformation*, p. 375.

33. Curt Sachs, *The World History of Dance*, p. 128.

34. Kerényi tells the story of the flower named Trittai sent up through Earth's well in *Gods of the Greeks*, p. 100. It is reminiscent of the "flowering" of Kore, Persephone the Maiden, who was awaited by her mother at the well: "It was a mythological well, known by different names in the different versions of the holy story. It was called Parthenion, 'virgin's well,' no doubt because it was connected with the destiny of a virgin, and Anthion, 'well of flowers,' presumably because a flowering from the depths was thought to take place here. . . . They [the south Italian cult of Persephone] represent the event in the form of sprouting flowers, plants or ears of grain." Kerényi, *Eleusis*, pp. 36–37.

35. The first stanza of Rilke's poem, translated by Robert Bly in *Sleepers Joining Hands*, p. 44, goes back to an Egyptian saying of Ptahhotep repeated here in the first line:

> *"We must die because we have known them." Die*
> *of the unbelievable flower of their smile. Die*
> *of their delicate hands. Die*
> *of women.*

36. Hekate's vision encompasses the stages of psychological development that do not necessarily occur in sequence. In *Origins and History of Consciousness* Erich Neumann describes the images and functions of "stadial" development in the mythologies of various cultures and in individual psychology. The essential archetypal motif in "Everywoman . . ." is simply getting stuck—turning to stone, falling asleep, being given impossible tasks to perform. This extreme stage of development generally occurs—but not always—prior to enantiodromia, to the creative freeing of bound-up psychic energy. See also M. Esther Harding, *Psychic Energy: Its Source and Its Transformation.*

CHAPTER 4. MOTHERS AND DAUGHTERS

1. *Letters to a Young Poet,* trans. by M. D. Herter Norton, p. 58. For full quote see Chapter 8 below.

2. *Hesiod, The Homeric Hymns and Homerica,* trans. by H. G. Evelyn-White, "Hymn To Demeter" II, l. 289–293. All further citations are from this source, lines 297, 303, 309, 311, 315.

3. The mixed drink called the *kykeion* here described became an essential communion act of the Eleusinian mysteries. It was made with grain and commemorated the sorrows of the goddess. For more information about the drink and possible use of intoxicants in the rites, see Kerényi, *Eleusis,* Appendix I.

4. C. G. Jung and Carl Kerényi, *Essays on a Science of Mythology, The Myth of the Divine Child and the Mysteries of Eleusis,* pp. 132–134.

5. *My Mother's House and Sido,* trans. by Una Vicenzo Troubridge and Enid McLeod, p. 172.

6. James Hillman discusses the archetypal themes of mothering and nursing in an article, "Abandoning the Child," from *Loose Ends: A Collection of Primary Papers in Archetypal Psychology.*

7. *The Feminine in Fairy Tales,* p. 23. Whether the period of sterility will result in new integration or a psychotic break depends upon the attitude of the person. Mary's forbearance after the annunciation, when "she held these things in her heart," is an instance of the kind of meditative attitude that yields to a birth rather than a break.

8. Quoted in Kerényi, *Eleusis,* "Testimonies to the Beatitude of the Initiates," pp. 13–16.

9. Quoted in Kerényi, *Eleusis,* p. 15.

10. C. G. Jung, "Psychological Aspects of the Kore," in Jung and Kerényi, *Essays,* p. 162.

11. Extraction is a new suction method by which the accumulation of menstrual blood can be drawn out of the uterus at the beginning of a woman's period, thus eliminating the normal days of flow.

12. *The Three Marias: New Portuguese Letters* by Maria Isabel Barreno, Maria Teresa Horta, Maria Velho de Costa, p. 47.

CHAPTER 5. SPIRITUAL PREGNANCY

1. "On the Significance of the Indian Tantric Yoga" in *Spiritual Disciplines,* Eranos Yearbook 4, pp. 4–5.

2. *Themis, A Study of the Social Origins of Greek Religion,* p. 495. Relief from the Capitoline altar, p. 493, fig. 143.

3. *Love's Body,* p. 192.

4. Heinrich Zimmer, p. 23.

5. Robert Bly, *Sleepers Joining Hands,* "I Came Out of the Mother Naked," p. 29.

6. R. D. Laing, *The Facts of Life, An Essay in Feelings, Facts, and Fantasy,* p. 57.

7. Brown, *Love's Body,* p. 210.

8. "On the Moon and Matriarchal Consciousness" in *Fathers and Mothers,* p. 58.

9. Charles Olson, *Proprioception,* p. 2. Olson knows that the body's data is psyche or soul:

"ACTION"—OR, AGAIN, "MOVEMENT"
> *This "demonstration" then leads to the same*
> *third, or corpus, thing or "place," the*

> proprious-*ception*
> *"one's own"-ception*

> *the "body" itself as, by movement of its own*
> *tissues, giving the data of, depth. Here, then,*
> *the soul is   wld be what is left out? (by the old psychology)*
> *proprioceptive*

10. "On the Moon and Matriarchal Consciousness," p. 46.

11. Quoted by Kerényi in "Kore," Jung and Kerényi, *Essays,* p. 101.

12. Herodotus, *The Persian Wars,* Book I.199.

13. From a poem by Ellen Kennedy, "Admissions of a Conspicuous Romantic," given to the author. Perhaps the "wreaths of string" and "lines of cord" were signs of humility and bondage. H. R. Ellis Davidson, in *Gods and Myths of Northern Europe,* p. 59, describes the religious custom of a Germanic people who gathered yearly in a woodland temple grove to observe a literal human sacrifice: "Whoever entered the wood

had to be bound with a cord as a sign of humility before the god."
. . . She goes on to suggest that this custom might represent the power
of the god to bind his followers.

14. Sir James George Frazer, *The Golden Bough, A Study in Magic and Religion,* abridged edition, vol. I, pp. 278–279.

15. *A General Introduction to Psychoanalysis,* pp. 21–22.

16. Jane Ellen Harrison, *Themis,* p. 139.

17. *In the Trail of the Wind, American Indian Poems and Ritual Orations,* ed. John Bierhorst, p. 112.

18. *The Alaskan Eskimos, As Described in the Posthumous Notes of Dr. Knud Rasmussen,* ed. by H. Ostermann, pp. 38–42. This myth, related by Sagdluaq of Colville River, requires more attention than can possibly be given in the chapter on spiritual poverty and spiritual pregnancy. It contains the potential for world community made conceivable by the resonating vibrations of the Great Mother's heart. The mountain is also the Mother. Men climb her to attain a higher consciousness, a more inclusive perspective on human being. Her rites, given to mankind as Demeter gave hers, become the way of transforming animal nature into human spirit. The tale takes place on the edge of the unknown (the sea) where the old ones live. The third son (the third one makes community necessary: "Two's company, three's a community"—N. O. Brown) hunts in the interior. He goes into the psyche seeking an answer the first two brothers could not find because of their fatal pride and arrogance that kept them from facing the Great Eagle Mother.

CHAPTER 6. ARTEMIS

1. Pp. 117–118. A walk-about is a period of time spent alone wandering in the bush or the outback (Africa, Australia) in initiatory rites for young men. It represents a break in time, a life transition or passage.

2. Stories about the Lone Woman are gathered in a reprint from the "Reports of the University of California Archaeological Survey, No. 55," *Original Accounts of the Lone Woman of San Nicolas Island,* ed. by Robert F. Heizer and Albert B. Elasser.

3. Emma Hardacre (1880), "Document 2A: Eighteen Years Alone; A Tale of the Pacific," in *Original Accounts of the Lone Woman of San Nicolas Island,* p. 24.

4. *Hesiod, The Homeric Hymns and Homerica,* "Hymn to Artemis," XXVII.

5. Quoted in Robert Eisler, *Man into Wolf, An Anthropological Interpretation of Sadism, Masochism and Lycanthropy,* p. 158.

6. Quoted in Eisler, p. 221.

7. Robert Graves, *The Greek Myths,* Vol. I, p. 83.

8. Ingmar Bergman describes this strange time in his film *The Hour of the Wolf.*

9. *Technicians of the Sacred,* ed. by Jerome Rothenberg, p. 338.

10. Davidson, *Gods and Myths of Northern Europe,* p. 68.

11. Eisler, p. 159.

12. Curt Sachs, *The World History of Dance,* p. 285.

13. Marie-Louise von Franz, *Individuation in Fairytales,* p. 88. Von Franz discusses the relationship between magic and ego will power in the context of a Persian fairy tale.

14. Von Franz, *Shadow and Evil in Fairy Tales,* p. 44.

15. C. G. Jung, "Problems of Modern Psychotherapy," *Modern Man in Search of a Soul,* p. 30. Healing begins with the end of psychic concealment. Confession is the first stage of treatment, followed by education and transformation.

16. *Technicians of the Sacred,* p. 338.

17. *Hesiod, The Homeric Hymns and Homerica,* "Hymn to Apollo," III.

18. Kerényi, *Gods of the Greeks,* p. 105.

19. From Tertullian's "Address to the Soul," quoted in Hillman, *The Myth of Analysis,* pp. 166, 206.

20. James Hillman, *Pan and the Nightmare,* p. xxxi.

21. This lonely song is sung by Iphigenia, daughter of Agamemnon, who was to be sacrificed to Artemis because one of the goddess's favorite stags had been killed. Artemis intervened at the last moment and whisked the maiden away to serve as her priestess at Taurica. Euripides, *Iphigenia in Tauris,* l. 1095.

22. Cook, "Apollon and Artemis" in *Zeus,* Vol. II, p. 471.

23. Kerényi, *Gods of the Greeks,* p. 173. On hymns and hymens, weaving and unweaving: Norman O. Brown, "The Robe," in taped lecture series: "To Greet the Return of the Gods," University of California at Santa Cruz, 1971.

24. "The Rape of Demeter/Persephone and Neurosis," *Spring* 1975, p. 186.

25. *The World History of Dance,* p. 101. See also p. 92.

26. *Intermediate Types Among Primitive Folk.* The quote is from an earlier work by Edward Carpenter, *Love's Coming of Age,* "The Intermediate Sex," pp. 120–124.

CHAPTER 7. HETAIRA

1. Erich Neumann in "The Psychological Stages of Feminine Development," an essay privately translated by Rebecca Jacobson from Neu-

mann's *Zur Psychologie Des Weiblichen* (Zürich, 1953), describes the development of the feminine proceeding from the stage of original psychic containment through the experiences of surrender and realization leading to the full individuation of woman. He is consciously considering this unfolding in the context of the "psychological patriarchy" we live in; consequently there is a significant stage of confrontation and separation that comes after the third circle as I have drawn it.

2. Stephens, *Deirdre*, p. 55.

3. Smith, *Daughters of the Promised Land, Women in American History*, p. 35.

4. John Layard explores the problem of incest archetypally and anthropologically in his paper on the incest taboo in *The Virgin Archetype*. Vera von der Heydt brings the problem to a more personal level in her article "On the Father in Psychotherapy," published in *Fathers and Mothers*. Here, in the context of discussing the arousal of a girl's sexuality with regard to man, she writes (p. 136): "The incestuous desires are deeply repressed by the child; but quite as often the father is as unconscious of his desires and of the strength of his feelings for, and jealousy of, his daughter. It depends on his attitude to his feminine side, to his relationship with his wife, and to the relationship he had with his mother as to how he will react to his daughter's desires and fears. His reaction then will influence the girl in her attitude to her emotional life and in her relationship to man. When her feelings are ignored or laughed at, she will have feelings of shame and inferiority which go very deep and are difficult to overcome. When father reacts too strongly, a girl may become frightened of physical contact: father becomes disgusting. She will fear both father's reaction and her own feelings." There are of course many psychological factors that determine whether or not actual incestual relations occur between father and daughter—not the least of which is fantasy and the awareness on the father's part of how it affects his actions.

5. Pp. 70–74. In Chapters V and VI of this book, *The Feminine in Fairy Tales*, von Franz interprets the tale of "The Handless Maiden." Although she does not see the maiden specifically as "hetaira," I owe my understanding of the maiden's fate to von Franz's clear and illuminating amplification.

6. Von Franz, p. 85.

7. "Psychological Aspects of the Mother Archetype" in *Four Archetypes*, p. 33.

8. *The Greek Myths*, Vol. I, p. 39.

9. Introduction to *Mother Right*, p. 109.

10. Olive Schreiner, *Dreams* (1890).

11. Amy Allenby, "The Father Archetype in Feminine Psychology," *The Journal of Analytical Psychology,* Vol. 1, No. 1, p. 82.

12. Allenby, p. 87.

13. Allenby, pp. 90–91.

14. From a letter to Norman Holmes Pearson quoted in his forward to H. D.'s *Tribute to Freud,* p. ix.

15. Joyce, p. 628.

CHAPTER 8. MEDIAL FEMININE: SIBYL

1. *Letters to a Young Poet,* p. 58.

2. In Arnold van Gennep's classic work, *The Rites of Passage,* written in 1908, the system of ritual classification is laid out as follows, pp. 10–11: "I have tried to assemble here all the ceremonial patterns which accompany a passage from one situation to another or from one cosmic or social world to another. Because of the importance of these transitions, I think it legitimate to single out *rites of passage* as a special category, which under further analysis may be subdivided into *rites of separation, transition rites,* and *rites of incorporation.* . . . Rites of separation are prominent in funeral ceremonies, rites of incorporation at marriages. Transition rites may play an important part for instance, in pregnancy, betrothal, and initiation."

3. Robert Duncan, "Rites of Participation," *Caterpillar,* No. 1. See also Gary Snyder's essay "Re-Inhabitation," *The Old Ways,* p. 63.

4. Aniela Jaffé, *The Myth of Meaning,* pp. 28–29. Natural sciences and psychology have framed corresponding hypotheses of a hidden reality underlying the phenomenal world. Jaffé quotes Jung: "The archetype in itself is empty and purely formal, nothing but a *facultas praeformandi . . .* our comparison with the crystal is illuminating inasmuch as the axial system determines only the stereometric structure but not the concrete form of the individual crystal. This may be either large or small, and it may vary endlessly by reason of the different size of its planes or by the growing together of two crystals. The only thing that remains constant is the axial system, or rather, the invariable geometric proportions underlying it. The same is true of the archetype. In principle, it can be named and has an invariable nucleus of meaning—but always only in principle, never as regards its concrete manifestation."

5. Harding, *Woman's Mysteries, Ancient and Modern,* p. 61.

6. Harding, pp. 62–63.

7. Related in Neumann, *The Great Mother,* pp. 288–289.

8. Pär Lagerkvist, *The Sibyl,* pp. 46–50.

9. Lemprière, *Classical Dictionary,* revised edition by F. A. Wright, entry for "Delphi," p. 198.

10. Rilke, from *The Notebooks of Malte Laurids Brigge* (1908), quoted by Denise Levertov, *The Poet in the World,* pp. 109–110: ". . . verses are not, as people imagine, simply feelings (we have those soon enough); they are experiences. In order to write a single poem, one must see many cities, and people, and things; one must get to know animals and the flight of birds, and the gestures that flowers make when they open to the morning. One must be able to return to roads in unknown regions. . . . And still it is not yet enough, to have memories. One must be able to forget them when they are many and one must have the immense patience to wait till they are come again. For the memories themselves are still nothing. Not till they have turned to blood within us, to glance and gesture, nameless and no longer to be distinguished from ourselves —not till then can it happen that in a most rare hour the first word of a poem arises in their midst and goes forth from them."

11. *The Alaskan Eskimos,* p. 102.

12. Brown, *Love's Body,* chapter on "Food," especially p. 171.

13. John Layard, "The Malekulan Journey of the Dead" in *Spiritual Disciplines,* Eranos Yearbook 4, p. 138.

14. Plutarch, *Moralia* VII, "The Divine Vengeance," 566 B.C., (p. 287 in the Loeb Classic edition).

15. W. F. Jackson Knight, *Vergil: Epic and Anthropology,* "Cumaean Gates," p. 140, *Aeneid* VI, 42.

CHAPTER 9. MEDIAL FEMININE: OLD WISE WOMAN

1. Meridel Le Sueur at a workshop, winter, 1974.

2. Jacob Grimm, *Teutonic Mythology,* Vol. III, trans. by James Steven Stallybrass, p. 1031.

3. Grimm, pp. 1038–1039.

4. Translated by N. K. Sandars in *Poems of Heaven and Hell from Ancient Mesopotamia.* See also Bachofen for the relationship between the origin of writing and women's "convenient leisure" or "confinement." He cites as example Atossa, the mother of Xerxes: "Elsewhere the political matriarchy was protected by its very weakness, or bolstered by artificial forms, such as are indicated by imputing the origin of letter writing to Asiatic queens confined to the interior of their palaces," introduction to *Mother Right,* p. 108.

5. "The String Game," *Technicians of the Sacred,* p. 100.

6. Describing the way an artist works, Erich Neumann writes: "The seemingly inexplicable arbitrariness with which new motifs suddenly

appear only to be set aside for a while and then later taken up once again and developed further, proves to be an inner necessity in the life of creative individuals." *The Archetypal World of Henry Moore*, p. 83. Rather than proceeding straight forward to a preconceived goal the creative individual follows a "drop-stitch" pattern of engagement and disengagement with the threads of ideas and images that make up the fabric of his work.

7. "The Song of Helgi" from *The Poetic Edda*, trans. by H. A. Bellows, quoted in Neumann, *The Great Mother*, p. 229.

8. Neumann, *The Great Mother*, p. 250.

9. The Eddic "Lay of Darts" (or spears) is discussed and translated in both Neumann, *The Great Mother*, p. 232, and Davidson, *Gods and Myths of Northern Europe*, p. 64.

10. Neumann, *The Great Mother*, p. 298. This root *(us-gais jan)* is one that James Joyce picks up in *Finnegans Wake* and transforms into *us-quabe*, whiskey or spirits.

11. "Psychological Aspects of the Mother Archetype" in *Four Archetypes*, pp. 23–24.

12. The *vagina dentata* or toothed vagina is a common motif in folklore, mythology, and modern dreams. Many heroes have died a gruesome death attempting intercourse with a "tooth mother." Variations on the theme are caves with spike-like rocks at the entrance and giant, carnivorous, open-mouthed fishes. Funk and Wagnalls, *Standard Dictionary of Folklore*, Vol. II, p. 1152, cites examples from North American Indian cultures.

13. *The Feminine in Fairy Tales*, p. 45.

14. Quoted in Davidson, *Gods and Myths of Northern Europe*, p. 121.

15. Quoted in Davidson, p. 121.

16. Jung, *Symbols of Transformation*, p. 369.

17. *Symbols of Transformation*, p. 249.

18. Davidson, p. 122.

19. Davidson, p. 122. Queens and housewives are alike in their confinement. In *The Bacchae* (Euripides), we hear about housewives at the loom and queens in their palaces being similarly "crazed."

20. Grimm, *Teutonic Mythology*, Appendix I, "Superstitions," No. 125.

21. "Superstitions," No. 878.

22. Davidson, p. 119.

23. Brothers Grimm, "Mother Hulda," *Household Stories*.

24. Farnell, *Cults of the Greek States*, Vol. II, p. 502. This appellation will be confusing in light of the sisterhood or cousin relationship with

Artemis stressed in Chapter 6 above. Hekate-Monogenes is probably the earliest form of the goddess that emphasizes her virginity (untouched, unrelated, distant) and her greatness.

25. Harding, *Woman's Mysteries,* pp. 112–113. There are as many forms of the Dark Virgin as there are of the pure, white virgin. Among them, "Mary the Harlot was black in character; Mary the Egyptian was black in face. In a Roman Catholic book of the saints is recorded a legend of this Egyptian Mary·to the effect that, wishing to go to the Holy Land on a pilgrimage, her only way of obtaining passage was to offer herself as a prostitute to the sailors on a vessel bound for that shore. Thus she earned her way to the Holy Land, where she lived for years as an anchorite in the desert."

26. The citations that follow, regarding the character of Mother Hulda, are from Grimm, *Teutonic Mythology,* Vol. I, pp. 266–282, 312, and Vol. IV, pp. 1367–1369.

27. Composite translation of the "Hymn to Hermes" IV, l. 553, *Hesiod, Homeric Hymns and Homerica,* and Andrew Lang's translation (1899), quoted in Carl Kerényi, *Hermes, Guide of Souls,* p. 41.

CHAPTER 10. REFLECTION AND FABRICATION

1. W. B. Yeats, *A Vision.* The author tells the story of the evolution of his (his wife's) vision in the introduction.

2. S. Giedion, *The Eternal Present: The Beginnings of Art,* Vol. I, p. 55. In a similar remark, Picasso said once that, if you want to paint, "close your eyes and sing."

3. Walter Otto, *The Homeric Gods,* pp. 118–120, quoted in Kerényi, *Hermes, Guide of Souls,* pp. 48–50.

4. Charles Olson, *A Special View of History,* p. 20.

5. Dream research has shown that the sequence of dreams in a single night may be evolutionary, evolving historically through the life of the dreamer. Some think dreamers work backward into "prehistory" so that the first dreams in the night represent the most recent life situation, and the later dreams, the earliest. See *Sleep and Dreaming,* edited by E. Hartmann, for related theories and findings.

6. Woolf, "The Lady in the Looking Glass," *A Haunted House and Other Short Stories,* p. 93.

7. Von Franz, *Patterns of Creativity,* p. 129.

8. *Patterns of Creativity,* p. 128.

9. *Symbols of Transformation,* p. 292.

10. Sir Walter Scott, *Letters on Demonology and Witchcraft,* p. 93.

11. The full tale of Sir Thomas of Erceldoune is told by Sir Walter

Scott in *Letters*, pp. 119–123, from which these excerpts are taken.

12. Knight, *Vergil: Epic and Anthropology*, "Cumaean Gates," p. 168.

13. *Funk and Wagnalls, Standard Dictionary of Folklore*, Vol. II, entry for "Delphic Oracle," p. 305.

14. J. A. MacCulloch, "Fairy," J. Hastings's *Encyclopedia of Religion and Ethics*, V, p. 688.

15. *Pausanias, Description of Greece*, trans. with commentary by J. G. Frazer, Vol. IV, commentary on Book VII, Chapter XXI, 12.

16. Jane Ellen Harrison, *Prolegomena to the Study of Greek Religion*, p. 122.

17. Harrison, *Prolegomena*, pp. 441–445.

18. Euripides, *The Bacchae*, trans. by Gilbert Murray, l. 723.

19. *The Bacchae*, l. 862.

CONCLUSION

1. Kerényi, "Kore," *Essays on a Science of Mythology*, p. 121. See also Jane Ellen Harrison's article on "initiation" (Greek) in Hastings's *Encyclopedia of Religion and Ethics*, VII, p. 322. The relationship between the words for initiation *(telete)* and maturity (Hera, Teleia) is made clear.

2. Hesiod, "Works and Days" in *Hesiod, The Homeric Hymns and Homerica*. All further citations are from this source, ll. 176–179, ll. 196–199.

3. Plutarch, "On the Bravery of Woman," *Mul Virt* (249 EF), quoted and commented on by J. E. Harrison in *Prolegomena*, p. 393.

4. Quoted in Bachofen, *Mother Right*, p. 125.

5. See Harrison, *Prolegomena*, Chapter XI for discussion of Orphic ritual formularies.

6. Guillaume Apollinaire's praise poem quoted in *Technicians of the Sacred*, p. 393.

7. *Prolegomena*, p. 320.

8. Bachofen, introduction to *Mother Right*, p. 91.

Bibliography

A. E. *Candle of Vision.* Wheaton: University Books, 1965.

Allenby, Amy I. "The Father Archetype in Feminine Psychology," *The Journal of Analytical Psychology,* Vol. I, No. 1. 1955.

Apuleius. *The Golden Ass.* Robert Graves, trans. New York: Farrar, Straus & Giroux, 1970.

Bachelard, Gaston. *The Poetics of Reverie, Childhood, Language, and the Cosmos.* Daniel Russell, trans. Boston: Beacon Press, 1969.

Bachofen, J. J. *Myth, Religion, and Mother Right.* Ralph Manheim, trans. Princeton: Princeton University Press, Bollingen Series LXXXIV, 1967.

Barreno, Maria Isabel, Maria Teresa Horta and Maria Velho de Costa. *The Three Marias: New Portuguese Letters by Maria Isabel Barreno, Maria Teresa Horta, Maria Velho de Costa.* Helen R. Lane, trans. New York: Doubleday & Company, 1975.

Bergman, Ingmar. *Scenes from a Marriage.* Alan Blair, trans. New York: Bantam Books, 1975.

Bierhorst, John, ed. *In the Trail of the Wind, American Indian Poems and Ritual Orations.* New York: Farrar, Straus & Giroux, 1971.

Bly, Robert. "I Came Out of the Mother Naked," *Sleepers Joining Hands.* New York: Harper & Row, 1973.

Briffault, Robert. *The Mothers.* New York: Macmillan Company, 1927. 3 vols.

Brown, Norman O. "Apocalypse: The Place of Mystery in the Life of the Mind", Harper's Magazine, 1961.

———.*Closing Time.* New York: Random House, 1973.

———. *Love's Body.* New York: Vintage Books, 1968.

———. "To Greet the Return of the Gods," unpublished lecture series, University of California at Santa Cruz, 1971.

Carpenter, Edward. *Intermediate Types Among Primitive Folk, A Study in Social Evolution.* New York: Arno Press, 1975.

———. *Love's Coming of Age.* New York: Boni and Liveright, 1911.

————. *Pagan and Christian Creeds: Their Origin and Meaning.* New York: Harcourt, Brace and Howe, 1920.

Carroll, Paul, ed. *The Young American Poets.* Chicago: Follett Publishing Company, 1968.

Charbonneaux, J., R. Martin, and F. Villard. *Classical Greek Art, 480–330 B.C..* London: Thames and Hudson, 1972.

Colette. *My Mother's House and Sido.* New York: Farrar, Straus, 1953.

Cook, Arthur Bernard. *Zeus, A Study in Ancient Religion,* Vols. I and II. New York, Biblo and Tannen, 1964.

Corbin, Henry. *Creative Imagination in the Sūfism of Ibn 'Arabī.* Ralph Manheim, trans. Princeton: Princeton University Press, Bollingen Series XCI, 1969.

Davidson, H. R. Ellis. *Gods and Myths of Northern Europe.* Middlesex: Penguin Books, 1964.

De Castillejo, Irene Claremont. *Knowing Woman, A Feminine Psychology.* New York: G. P. Putnam's Sons, 1973.

Dinesen, Isak. *Out of Africa.* New York: Random House, 1937.

————. *Shadows on the Grass.* New York: Vintage Books, 1974.

Di Prima, Diane. *Loba, Part 1.* Santa Barbara: Capra Press, 1973.

Doria, Charles, and Harris Lenowitz, ed. and trans. *Origins, Creation Texts from the Ancient Mediterranean.* New York: Anchor Books, 1976.

Duncan, Robert. *Bending the Bow.* New York: New Directions, 1968.

————. *The Opening of the Field.* New York: Grove Press, 1960.

————. "Rites of Participation," *Caterpillar, No. 1* New York: AMS Press, 1967.

————. *The Truth and Life of Myth: An Essay in Essential Autobiography.* Fremont, Michigan: Sumac Press, 1968.

Eisler, Robert. *Man into Wolf, An Anthropological Interpretation of Sadism, Masochism, and Lycanthropy.* New York: Greenwood Press, 1951.

Eliade, Mircea. *The Force and the Crucible.* New York: Harper & Row, 1971.

————. *Rites and Symbols of Initiation, the Mysteries of Birth and Rebirth.* New York: Harper & Row, 1958.

Euripides. *The Bacchae, Iphigenia in Tauris, Medea,* in *The Complete Greek Drama.* Whitney J. Oates and Eugene O'Neill, Jr., eds. New York: Random House, 1938. 2 vols.

Farnell, Richard L. *The Cults of the Greek States.* New Rochelle, New York: Caratzas Brothers, 1977. 5 vols.

Frazer, Sir James George. *The Golden Bough.* New York: Macmillan Company, 1922.

Freud, Sigmund. *A General Introduction to Psychoanalysis.* New York: Boni and Liveright, 1924.

———. *The Interpretation of Dreams.* James Strachey, ed. and trans. New York: Avon Books, 1967.

———. *New Introductory Lectures on Psychoanalysis.* James Strachey, ed. and trans. New York: W. W. Norton, 1964.

Giedion, S. *The Eternal Present: The Beginnings of Art.* New York: Pantheon Books, Bollingen Series XXXV, 1962. 2 vols.

Gimbutas, M. *The Gods and Goddesses of Old Europe, 7000 to 3500 B.C. Myth, Legends and Cult Images.* Berkeley: University of California Press, 1974.

Graves, Robert. *The Greek Myths.* Baltimore: Penguin Books, 1968. 2 vols.

———. *The White Goddess, A Historical Grammar of Poetic Myth.* New York: Noonday Press, 1966.

Grimm Brothers. *The Complete Grimm's Fairy Tales.* New York: Pantheon Books, 1972.

———. *Household Stories, from the Collection of the Bros. Grimm.* Lucy Crane, trans. New York: Dover Publications, 1963.

Grimm, Jacob. *Teutonic Mythology.* James Steven Stallybrass, trans. New York: Dover Publications, 1966. 4 vols.

Hamsun, Knut. *Growth of the Soil.* W. W. Worster, trans. New York: Alfred A. Knopf, 1968.

Harding, M. Esther. *The "I" and the "Not-I," A Study in the Development of Consciousness.* Princeton: Princeton University Press, Bollingen Series LXXIX, 1970.

———. *Psychic Energy, Its Source and Transformation.* New York: Pantheon Books, Bollingen Series X, 1947.

———. *Woman's Mysteries, Ancient and Modern.* New York: G. P. Putnam's Sons, 1971.

Harrison, Jane Ellen. *Ancient Art and Ritual.* Cambridge: The University Press, 1913.

———. *Myths of Greece and Rome.* London: Ernest Benn, 1928.

———. *Prolegomena to the Study of Greek Religion.* New York: Arno Press, 1975.

———. *Themis, A Study of the Social Origins of Greek Religion.* Cleveland: Meridian Books, 1962.

Hartmann, Ernest, ed. *Sleep and Dreaming.* International Psychiatry Clinics, Vol. 7, no. 2. Boston: Little, Brown and Company, 1970.

Hastings, James, ed. *Encyclopedia of Religion and Ethics.* New York: Charles Scribner's Sons, 1912. 12 vols.

H. D. (Hilda Doolittle Aldington). *The Flowering of the Rod.* London: Oxford University Press, 1946.

———. *Hermetic Definition.* New York: New Directions, 1972.

———. *Tribute to the Angels.* London: Oxford University Press, 1945.

———. *Tribute to Freud.* New York: McGraw-Hill Book Co., 1974.

———. *The Walls Do Not Fall.* London: Oxford University Press, 1944.

Heidegger, Martin. *Poetry, Language and Thought.* Albert Hofstadter, trans. New York: Harper & Row, 1971.

Heizer, Robert F. and Albert B. Elasser, eds. *Original Accounts of the Lone Woman of San Nicolas Island.* Ramona, California: Ballena Press, 1976.

Henderson, Jeffrey. *The Maculate Muse, Obscene Language in Attic Comedy.* New Haven: Yale University Press, 1975.

Henderson, Joseph L. and Maud Oakes. *The Wisdom of the Serpent.* New York: George Braziller, 1963.

———. *Thresholds of Initiation.* Middletown: Wesleyan University Press, 1967.

Herodotus. *The Persian Wars.* George Rawlinson, trans. New York: Modern Library, 1942. 9 books. (Book I.)

Hesiod, The Homeric Hymns and Homerica. Hugh G. Evelyn-White, trans. London: William Heinemann, 1967.

Hillman, James. *Loose Ends.* Zürich: Spring Publications, 1975.

———. *Pan and the Nightmare.* Zürich: Spring Publications, 1972.

———. *The Myth of Analysis.* Evanston, Illinois: Northwestern University Press, 1972.

I Ching or *The Book of Changes.* Richard Wilhelm translated and Cary F. Baynes rendered into English. Princeton: Princeton University Press, Bollingen Series XIX, 1967.

Jaffé, Aniela. *The Myth of Meaning.* R. F. C. Hull, trans. New York: G. P. Putnam's Sons, 1971.

Joyce, James. *Finnegans Wake.* New York: Viking Press, 1968.

Jung, C. G. *Analytical Psychology, Its Theory and Practice.* New York: Pantheon Books, 1968.

———. *The Archetypes of the Collective Unconscious. Collected Works of C. G. Jung,* Vol. 9, part 1. R. F. C. Hull, trans. Princeton: Princeton University Press, Bollingen Series XX, 1971.

——— and Carl Kerényi. *Essays on a Science of Mythology, the Myth of the Divine Child and the Mysteries of Eleusis.* R. F. C. Hull, trans. Princeton: Princeton University Press, Bollingen Series XXII, 1971.

———. *Four Archetypes.* R. F. C. Hull, trans. Princeton: Princeton University Press, Bollingen Series XX, 1959.

———. *Modern Man in Search of a Soul.* Cary F. Baynes and W. S. Dell, trans. New York: Harcourt, Brace, 1933.

———. *Psychology and Religion, West and East.* Collected Works, Vol. 11. R. F. C. Hull, trans. Princeton: Princeton University Press, 1969.

———. *Symbols of Transformation.* Collected Works, Vol. 5. R. F. C. Hull, trans. Princeton: Princeton University Press, Bollingen Series XX, 1956.

Jung, Emma. *Animus and Anima.* Cary F. Baynes and Hildegard Nagel, trans. Zürich: Spring Publications, 1972.

Keats, John. *Selected Poems and Letters.* Douglas Bush, ed., Cambridge: Riverside Press, 1959.

Kerényi, Carl. *Asklepios, Archetypal Image of the Physician's Existence.* Ralph Manheim, trans. New York: Pantheon Books, Bollingen Series LXV, 3, 1959.

———. *Dionysos, Archetypal Image of Indestructible Life.* Ralph Manheim, trans. Princeton: Princeton University Press, Bollingen Series XLV,2, 1976.

———. *Eleusis, Archetypal Image of Mother and Daughter.* Ralph Manheim, trans. New York: Schocken Books, 1977.

———. *The Gods of the Greeks.* Norman Cameron, trans. London: Thames and Hudson, 1974.

———. *Hermes, Guide of Souls: The Mythologem of the Masculine Source of Life.* Murray Stein, trans. Zürich: Spring Publications, 1976.

Knight, W. F. Jackson. *Vergil: Epic and Anthropology.* John D. Christie, ed. New York: Barnes & Noble, Inc., 1967.

Lagerkvist, Pär. *The Sibyl.* Naomi Walford, trans. New York: Vintage Books, 1958.

Laing, R. D. *The Facts of Life, An Essay in Feelings, Facts, and Fantasy.* New York: Pantheon Books, 1976.

Lang, Andrew. *Custom and Myth.* London: Longmans, Green, 1884.

———. Homeric Hymns. New York: Longmans, Green, 1899.

Lantero, Erminie Huntress. *Feminine Aspects of Divinity.* Wallingford, Pennsylvania: Pendle Hill Publications, 1973.

Lao Tsu. *Tao Te Ching.* Gia-Fu Feng and Jane English, trans. New York: Vintage Books, 1972.

Lavard, John. "The Malekulan Journey of the Dead," *Spiritual Disciplines.* Joseph Campbell, ed. Princeton: Princeton University Press, Bollingen Series XXX, 1970.

———. *The Virgin Archetype.* New York: Spring Publications, 1972.

Leach, Maria, ed. *Funk and Wagnalls Standard Dictionary of Folklore, My-*

thology and Legend. New York: Funk & Wagnalls, 1949. 2 vols.

Lederer, Wolfgang. *The Fear of Women.* New York: Grune & Stratton, 1968.

Lemprière, J. *Classical Dictionary of Proper Names Mentioned in Ancient Authors.* F. A. Wright, ed. London: Routledge & Kegan Paul, 1963.

Le Sueur, Meridel. *Rites of Ancient Ripening.* Minneapolis: Vanilla Press, 1975.

Levertov, Denise. "Poems," *Anglican Theological Review,* Vol. L, no. 3. Evanston, Illinois, July, 1968.

_____. *The Freeing of the Dust.* New York: New Directions, 1975.

_____. *The Jacob's Ladder.* New York: New Directions, 1961.

_____. *The Poet in the World.* New York: New Directions, 1973.

_____. *Relearning the Alphabet.* New York: New Directions, 1970.

_____. *The Sorrow Dance.* New York: New Directions, 1966.

_____. *O Taste and See.* New York: New Directions, 1964.

Levy, Gertrude Rachel. *The Gate of Horn: A Study of the Religious Conceptions of the Stone Age, and Their Influence upon European Thought.* London: Faber and Faber, 1948.

Lewis, Richard. *Miracles, Poems by Children of the English-Speaking World.* New York: Simon & Schuster, 1966.

Luce, Gay Gaer. *Body Time, Physiological Rhythms and Social Stress.* New York: Pantheon Books, 1971.

Lullies, Reinhard, and Max Hirmer. *Greek Sculpture.* Michael Bullock, trans. New York: Abrams, 1957.

McGrath, Thomas. *Letter to an Imaginary Friend.* Chicago: Swallow Press, 1970.

Meier, C. A. *Ancient Incubation and Modern Psychotherapy.* Monica Curtis, trans. Evanston, Illinois: Northwestern University Press, 1967.

Mitroff, Ian I. "Science's Apollonic Moon: A Study in the Psychodynamics of Modern Science," *Spring, An Annual of Archetypal Psychology and Jungian Thought.* New York: Spring Publications, 1974.

Moffat, Mary Jane, and Charlotte Painter, eds. *Revelations: Diaries of Women.* New York: Vintage Books, 1974.

Mylonas, George E. *Eleusis and the Eleusinian Mysteries.* Princeton: Princeton University Press, 1974.

Neumann, Erich. *Amor and Psyche, The Psychic Development of the Feminine. A Commentary on the Tale by Apuleius.* Ralph Manheim, trans. Princeton: Princeton University Press, Bollingen Series LIV, 1971.

_____. *The Archetypal World of Henry Moore.* R. F. C. Hull, trans. New York: Pantheon Books, Bollingen Series LXVIII, 1959.

──────. *The Child: Structure and Dynamics of the Nascent Personality.* New York: G. P. Putnam, 1973.

──────. "On the Moon and Matriarchal Consciousness," *Fathers and Mothers.* Pat Berry, ed. Hildegard Nagel, trans. Zürich: Spring Publications, 1973.

──────. *The Great Mother, an Analysis of the Archetype.* Ralph Manheim, trans. New York: Pantheon Books, 1963.

──────. *The Origins and History of Consciousness.* R. F. C. Hull, trans. Princeton: Princeton University Press, Bollingen Series XLII, 1971.

──────. "The Psychological Stages of Feminine Development," *Zur Psychologie Des Weiblichen.* Rebecca Jacobson, trans. Zürich: Rascher Verlag, 1953.

Olson, Charles. *Archaeologist of Morning.* London and New York: Cape Goliard Press in association with Grossman Publishers, 1970.

──────. *Human Universe and Other Essays.* Donald Allen, ed. New York: Grove Press, 1967.

──────. *Proprioception.* San Francisco: Four Seasons Foundation, 1965.

──────. *Selected Writings of Charles Olson.* Robert Creeley, ed. New York: New Directions, 1966.

──────. *The Special View of History.* Ann Charters, ed. Berkeley: Oyez, 1970.

Ostermann, H., ed. *The Alaskan Eskimos, As Described in the Posthumous Notes of Dr. Knud Rasmussen.* Copenhagen: Gyldendalske Boghandel, Nordisk Forlag, 1952.

Ovid. *Metamorphoses.* Rolfe Humphries, trans. Bloomington: Indiana University Press, 1955.

Paracelsus. *Selected Writings.* Jolande Jacobi, ed. Princeton: Princeton University Press, Bollingen Series XXVIII, 1969.

Partridge, Eric. *Origins: A Short Etymological Dictionary of Modern English.* New York: Macmillan Company, 1966.

Pausanias. *Description of Greece.* J. G. Frazer, trans. New York: Biblo and Tannen, 1965. 6 vols.

Plath, Sylvia. *Ariel.* New York: Harper & Row, 1965.

──────. *Crossing the Water.* New York: Harper & Row, 1971.

Plutarch. *Plutarch's Moralia III.* F. C. Babbitt, trans. Cambridge: Harvard University Press, 1968. 15 vols.

──────. *Plutarch's Moralia VII.* Phillip H. De Lacy and Benedict Einarson, trans. Cambridge: Harvard University Press, 1968. 15 vols.

Pritchard, James B., ed. *Ancient Near Eastern Texts Relating to the Old Testament.* Princeton: Princeton University Press, 1969.

Rilke, Rainer Maria. *Letters to a Young Poet.* M. D. Herter Norton, trans. New York: W. W. Norton, 1962.

———. *The Life of the Virgin Mary.* C. F. MacIntyre, trans. Berkeley and Los Angeles: University of California Press, 1947.

———. *Selected Poems.* C. F. MacIntyre, trans. Berkeley: University of California Press, 1968.

———. *Sonnets to Orpheus.* M. D. Herter Norton, trans. New York: W. W. Norton, 1942.

Roethke, Theodore. *Roethke: Collected Poems.* Garden City, New York: Doubleday & Company, 1937.

Rose, H. J. *A Handbook of Greek Mythology, Including Its Extension to Rome.* New York: E. P. Dutton, 1959.

Rothenberg, Jerome, ed. *Technicians of the Sacred: A Range of Poetries from Africa, America, Asia and Oceania.* Garden City, New York: Doubleday & Company, 1969.

Sachs, Curt. *The World History of Dance.* Bessie Schönberg, trans. New York: W. W. Norton, 1963.

Sandars, N. K., trans. *Poems of Heaven and Hell from Ancient Mesopotamia.* Middlesex, England: Penguin Books, 1971.

Sappho. *Sappho.* Mary Barnard, trans. Berkeley and Los Angeles: University of California Press, 1966.

Schreiner, Olive. *Olive Schreiner: A Selection.* Uys Krige, ed. London and New York: Oxford University Press, 1968.

———. *Woman and Labor.* New York: Frederick A. Stokes, 1911.

Scott, Sir Walter. *Letters on Demonology and Witchcraft.* New York: A. L. Fowle, 1900.

Singer, June. *Androgyny, Toward a New Theory of Sexuality.* Garden City, New York: Anchor Press, 1976.

Smith, Page. *Daughters of the Promised Land, Women in American History.* Boston and Toronto: Little, Brown, 1970.

Snyder, Gary. *Earth Household.* New York: New Directions, 1969.

———. *Myths and Texts.* New York: Totem Press in association with Corinth Books, 1960.

———. *The Old Ways.* San Francisco: City Lights Books, 1977.

———. *Regarding Wave.* New York: New Directions, 1970.

Stephens, James. *Deirdre.* New York: New American Library, 1951.

Ulanov, Ann Belford. *The Feminine in Jungian Psychology and in Christian Theology.* Evanston, Illinois: Northwestern University Press, 1971.

van der Post, Laurens. *A Mantis Carol.* New York: William Morrow & Co., 1976.

van Gennep, Arnold. *The Rites of Passage.* Monika B. Vizedom and Ga-

brielle L. Caffee, trans. Chicago: University of Chicago Press, 1975.
von Franz, Marie-Louise. "The Problem of Evil in Fairy Tales," *Evil.* Edited by the Curatorium of the C. G. Jung Institute, Zürich. Evanston, Illinois: Northwestern University Press, 1967.

————. *Individuation in Fairytales.* Zürich: Spring Publications, 1976.

————. *Patterns of Creativity Mirrored in Creation Myths.* Zürich: Spring Publications, 1972.

————. *Problems of the Feminine in Fairytales.* New York: Spring Publications, 1972.

————. *Shadow and Evil in Fairy Tales.* Zürich: Spring Publications, 1974.

Warner, Maria. *Alone of All Her Sex, The Myth and Cult of the Virgin Mary.* New York: Alfred A. Knopf, 1976.

Wheelwright, Philip. *Heraclitus.* New York: Atheneum, 1968.

Williams, William Carlos. *Paterson.* New York: New Directions, 1963.

————. *Pictures from Brueghel, and Other Poems.* New York: New Directions, 1962.

Wolff, Toni. "A Few Thoughts on the Process of Individuation in Women," unpublished lecture printed for the students of the C. G. Jung Institute, Zürich, May, 1934.

————. "Structural Forms of the Feminine Psyche." Paul Watzlawik, trans. Privately printed for students of the C. G. Jung Institute, Zürich, July, 1956.

Woolf, Virginia. *A Haunted House and Other Short Stories.* New York: Harcourt, Brace, 1944.

————. *Orlando.* New York: Harvest Books, 1956.

————. *A Room of One's Own.* New York: Harcourt, Brace, 1957.

Yeats, W. B. *A Vision.* New York: Collier Books, 1967.

Zimmer, Heinrich. "On the Significance of the Indian Tantric Yoga," *Spiritual Disciplines.* Joseph Campbell, ed. Princeton: Princeton University Press, Bollingen Series XXX, 1970.

Index

Page entries in italics refer to illustrations.